HISTORY
of
PERRY COUNTY
KENTUCKY

Written and Published

By

HAZARD CHAPTER
DAUGHTERS OF THE
AMERICAN REVOLUTION

Compiled By Eunice Tolbert Johnson

This volume was reproduced from
An 1953 edition located in the
Publisher's private Library

All rights reserved. No part of this publication may be reproduced,
stored in a retrieval system, transmitted in any form, posted
on to the web in any form or by any means without
the prior written permission of the publisher.

Please direct all correspondence and orders to:

www.southernhistoricalpress.com
or
SOUTHERN HISTORICAL PRESS, Inc.
PO BOX 1267
375 West Broad Street
Greenville, SC   29601
southernhistoricalpress@gmail.com

Originally published: Hazard, KY. 1953
Copyright 1953 by Hazard, KY Chpt. D.A.R.
ISBN #0-89308-919-2
All rights Reserved.
Printed in the United States of America

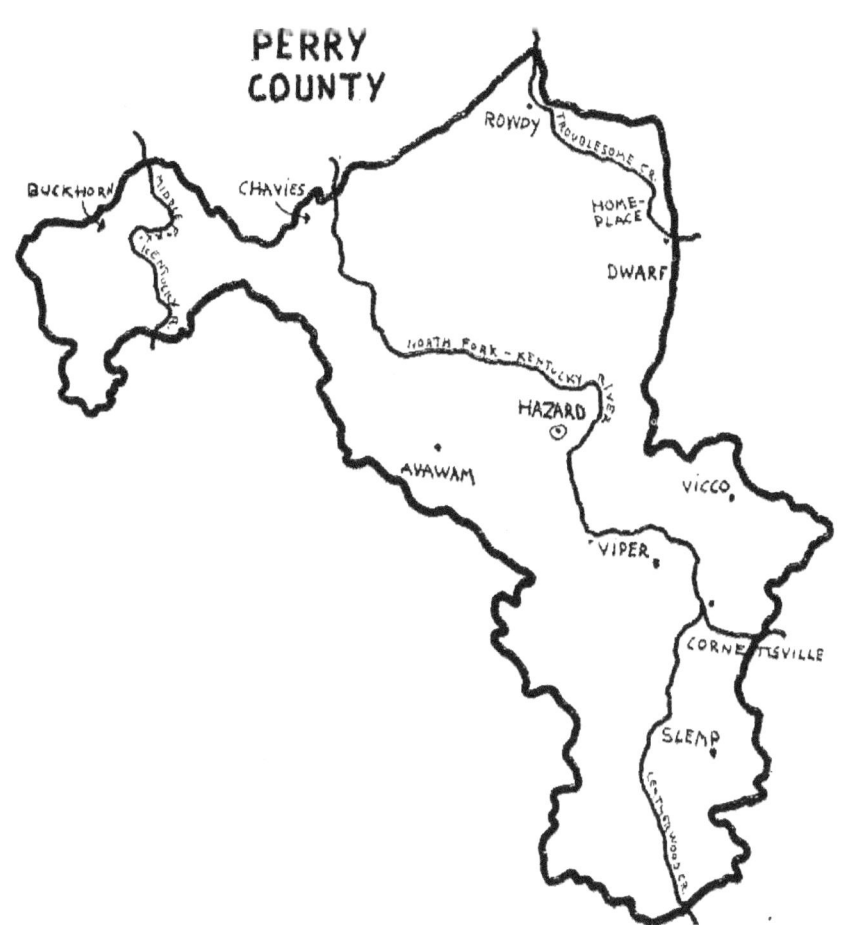

PREFACE

This history was undertaken as a project of the Hazard Chapter of the D.A.R. to preserve old records and from its sales to provide money for a scholarship fund for Perry County students.

The need for this first history was realized and an attempt has been made to bring to light early facts concerning the people, schools, churches, customs and laws that have been mis-represented in the past.

The names for the biographies were selected from the first tax list of Perry County, and the sketches appearing in this book are of those families on this list who are living in the county today.

The research and the contacts made during the past three years have been pleasant and interesting and it is hoped that the people of Perry County enjoy reading this book.

ACKNOWLEDGEMENTS

To the long list of persons who supplied information and help in the preparation of this history, we wish to express our appreciation. Among those from Perry County are Mr. J. B. Allen, Mr. Prentiss Baker and personnel of the County Court Clerk's office, Mr. C. A. Noble, Mr. C. D. Carpenter, Mr. A. B. Combs, Aunt Mary Combs, Mr. Douglas Combs, Mr. John Combs, Mr. Thee Combs, Mr. Elhanon Crawford, Mrs. Kendrick Combs, Mr. W. E. Davis, Mr. Lee Daniel, Mr. Robert Dickson, Mr. Logan Duff, Mr. Scott Duff, Mr. J. C. Eversole, Mr. John B. Eversole, Mr. R. C. Eckert, Mrs. Jack Francis, Mr. John Hensley, the Hazard Coal Operators Association, Mr. Green Holliday, Mr. Farmer Johnson, Mr. F. M. Medaris, Mr. and Mrs. T. E. Moore, Jr., Mr. J. W. Speaks, Mrs. J. S. Trosper, Mr. E. C. Wooten, Mrs. C. A. Zoellars, Mr. M. C. Napier, Mr. Carl Walker, Mr. and Mrs. L. O. Davis, Mrs. Victor Brashear, Mr. John Fitzpatrick, Mrs. Bailey P. Wootton, Mr. I. A. Bowles, Mr. R. O. Davis, Mr. J. D. Smith, Mr. Walter Campbell, Mr. Walter Green, Dr. E. E. Gabbard, Mr. Ed Johnson, Mr. R. F. Johnson, Mr. Frank Smith, Judge J. A. Smith, Mr. Dewey Daniel, Mr. Clyde Baumgardner, Mr. T. H. Hines, Mr. Henry Spaulding, Judge Fred Combs, Sheriff John Gross, Mr. Calloway Colwell, Mr. Mark Stanifer, Mrs. Boyd Combs, Mrs. J. V. Hines, Jr., who assisted in typing and proof-reading, and Miss Margaret Johns for typing; those who contributed articles for this history, the Hazard Herald for the By-Pass cut, the Hazard Fire Department for the use of several cuts of early Hazard, and Hal Cooner Studio for copying old pictures of Hazard.

Those from Lexington who rendered valuable assistance in securing data for this book are University of Kentucky Library personnel, University of Kentucky Department of Geology, Prof. C. S. Carter, University of Kentucky, Dr. W. R. Jillson, Transylvania University, Mr. W. H. Roll, Miss Betty Sue Scott, Mrs. T. H. Corbett and Mrs. W. E. Bach.

Especially are we grateful to Dr. Thomas D. Clark, University of Kentucky, who gave generously of his time to help plan the detail work of both the writing and the printing of this book, and who read the manuscript in its entirety, making suggestions and corrections.

Those from Louisville who gave valuable assistance to our history and to whom we are indebted are Mr. T. E. Owens, editor of the L&N Magazine, Mr. J. C Nickerson, Mr J. K. Dent, vice-president of the L&N Railroad, Mr. F. A. Goering, Miss Ludie Kincaid, curator of the Filson Club, and Mr. Joseph Barker of the Courier-Journal Lithographing Co.

Others who assisted with this book are Dr. Josiah H. Combs, Mary Washington College, University of Virginia, Fredricksburg, Va., Mr. Alexander Bonnyman, Knoxville, Tenn., Mr. Calvin Holmes, also of Knoxville, Mr. E. C. Perkins, Cincinnati, O., Mrs. S. A. D. Jones, Paterson, N. J., Mr. Boswell Hodgkins, Frankfort, Ky., Mr. Jim Mattingly, Hyden, Ky., Mrs. Beulah Howard Jankowski, Harwood, Md., and Mr. Bayless Hardin, Kentucky Historical Society, Frankfort, Ky.

THE PIONEERS OF PERRY
Josiah H. Combs

All hail to those brave pioneers of old
Who crossed the lofty mountains to behold
The land of fair Kentucky, their new State,
To settle down in Perry—happy fate !
From old Virginia, Motherland, they came,
From Carolina and Tennessee the same.
No map to guide them on their winding way,
No shining compass through the night and day.
From Yadkin and the Holston to the Gap
Across Clinch Mountain, and into the lap
Of River Clinch, then Powell Valley fair,
Then on up Indian Creek, with courage rare;
They reach Pound Gap with cautious step and slow,
And stop to gaze up on the scene below.
Each family with pack horses, cow, and hog,
A sheep, a rifle, seed corn and a dog;
An axe, a weeding hoe, a frow and glut,
All needed later with a mountain hut.
No inn or tavern greets them in the wild,
They eat wild game, each father, mother, child;
No music greets their weary ears by night,
Except the lonely screech owl in its fright.
They braved the weather, tempest and the cry
Of savage Indian whom they durst defy,
And traveled ever onward in their quest
Of land and forest, and of happiness.

This is the stature of the hardy men
That breached the wilderness, and came by **Pound**,
To reach the land of Perry, where they stopped
To labor, toil, and build a better life.
'Twas old, 'tis new, and Perry marches on,
To meet full tilt the challenge of our time.

CONTENTS

Map of Perry iii
Preface ix
Acknowledgements x
Pioneers of Perry xi
Map—Perry County 1772-1951 xiv

Chapters
- I   Formation 1
- II   Settlement 9
- III Social Growth 14
- IV Folkways and Customs 35
- V   Industries
  - 1. Salt 41
  - 2. Lumber 43
  - 3. Coal 50
- VI Communities and Their Growth
  - 1. Buckhorn 68
  - 3. Dwarf 78
  - 4. Hazard 79
  - 5. Homeplace 94
  - 6. Leatherwood 98
  - 7. Rowdy 100
  - 8. Slemp 101
  - 9. Viper 101
- VII Education Growth 105
- VIII Religious Growth 119
- IX Courts 158
- X   Transportation
  - 1. Highways 172
  - 2. Aviation 185
  - 3. River 186
  - 4. Railroad 190
- XI Early Perry County Families 207

List of Illustrations 234

Appendixes:
- Footnotes 255
- Bibliography 257
- Census—1830-1950 259
- Census, District, 1950 259
- List of Donors 260
- County Officers, 1821-1952 261
- Postmasters, 1820-1952 263
- Tax List—1822 266
- Hazard Chapter of Daughters of the American Revolution, 1951-52 270
- Index 271

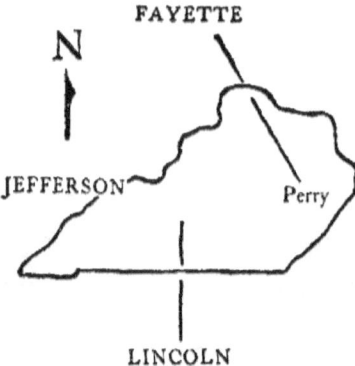

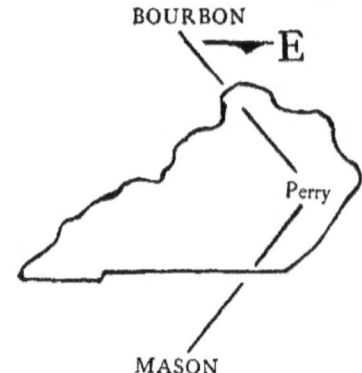

The Kentucky territory was first established in 1772 as Fincastle County, Virginia. In 1776 it became Kentucky County and from 1783 to 1792 was known as the Kentucky District. This was divided in 1780 into three counties: Fayette, Jefferson, and Lincoln.

In 1785, while Kentucky still belonged to Virginia, a portion of Fayette County which included the Perry section became Bourbon County. Mason County was formed in 1788 from that part of Bourbon County which had contained the Perry land.

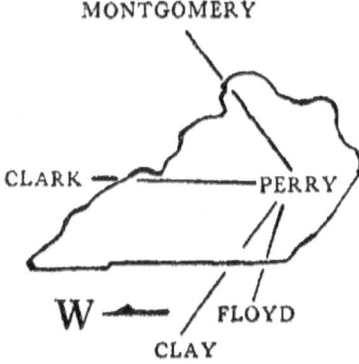

Kentucky became a state in 1792, and from this date the Perry section was successively a part of Clark (1793), Montgomery (1796), Floyd (1799), and Clay (1806) counties. In 1820 the boundaries of Perry as an independent county were defined.

Between the years 1820-1884, the county of Perry was divided and five other counties were created from the original 1820 territory. They were: Breathitt (1839), Letcher (1842), Owsley (1843), Leslie (1870), and the last, Knott (1884).

PERRY COUNTY, 1772-1951

CHAPTER I

FORMATION

Eunice Tolbert Johnson

Perry County had its origin when citizens from Clay and Floyd, praying for the erection of a new County seat out of parts of each county, presented a petition to the State Senate on Wednesday, December 8, 1819, at the regular session of that year. The sponsor of the petition was Senator Joseph Eve, then representing the counties of Clay, Harlan, Knox and Whitley. The bill was read, laid aside, then read again at a later date by Samuel McKee.[1]

Thus, Perry County, 68th in formation, was created from Clay and Floyd counties, the necessary legislation having been enacted at the session of 1820-21 and signed by Governor John Adair on November 2, 1820.

The new county was first given the name "Perry"[2] on January 19, 1820, in honor of Oliver Hazard Perry,[3] a hero of the naval battle of Put-in-Bay on Lake Erie in which a number of Kentuckians had fought as volunteers and had helped win the War of 1812.

The pedigree of Perry as it exists today may be traced back to 1772 when all of what is now the State of Kentucky was in the frontier county of Fincastle County, Virginia. In 1776, Fincastle was divided and this section became Kentucky County, Virginia.

Then, in 1780, Virginia set aside all land in Kentucky County for soldiers who had served in the Revolutionary War[4] and the rush to take up the land in Kentucky County started. Kentucky County was divided into three counties, Jefferson, Fayette and Lincoln. This section (Perry) became Fayette County, Virginia, and comprised more than one-third of the entire area of Kentucky County east and north of the Kentucky River and its Middle Fork. Fayette, in turn, was divided in 1785 and this part (Perry) became Bourbon County, Virginia. In 1788 Bourbon was divided, and all the territory in Eastern and Northern Kentucky to the mouth of the Licking River was called Mason County, Virginia. By this time there were nine counties in the Kentucky District. In 1792, shortly after Kentucky was made a State, this section became Clark County, Ky., the new county having been formed from Bourbon and Fayette. In 1796 this part (Perry) became Montgomery County.[5] Then in 1799 the part that is now Perry County on the East side of the Kentucky River became Floyd County since the Floyd County line started at the Virginia State line and extended to the headwaters of the Kentucky River, then down the same to the mouth of Quicksand Creek. Where Hazard stands and up Lotts Creek to its head was called Clay in 1806, this territory having been taken from Floyd, Mason and Knox. Most of what is Perry County was taken from Floyd, first to help form Clay, then Perry. In 1820, Perry County was formed from Clay and Floyd counties.

The subdivision of the counties was generally to increase the nearness of the county seats, as the citizens labored under great inconvenience in attending courts, due to the distance and the bad roads they had to travel.

When first formed in 1820, Perry was a very large county, its boundaries beginning on the Middle Fork of the Kentucky River where the Estille line crossed, up Laurel to War Gap on Pine Mountain, along the mountain to the dividing ridge between the waters of the Kentucky River and the Big Sandy and then along the ridge to the head of the North Fork of Quicksand Creek, then pursuing the ridge to the Estille County line.[6]

Since Perry County was created in 1820, the boundaries, as shown by the Kentucky ACTS, have been changed thirteen times between 1820 and 1890, sometimes to take parts to form new counties, and other times to define and change the boundary line until it has been reduced to its present size of 343 square miles.

Five counties have been formed from the territory originally belonging to Perry; Breathitt in 1839, Letcher in 1842, Owsley in 1843 (from Breathitt), Leslie in 1870 and Knott in 1884. Perry County today is smaller in area than any of the counties it adjoins except Owsley County.

Perry County lies in the southeastern part of the state,

bordered on the north by Breathitt, east by Knott and Letcher, south by Letcher and Harlan and west by Leslie, Clay and Owsley.

The North Fork of the Kentucky River drains the central part of the county. Troublesome Creek drains the northeastern section and the Middle Fork of the Kentucky River crosses and drains the western end of the county. Among their tributaries are Leatherwood Creek, Macy's Creek, Williams, Big Creek, Lotts Creek, Laurel, Squabble, Grapevine, Buffalo and Carrs Fork.

The topography of the county is hilly and mountainous and a large portion is unsuitable for farming. Coal is the principal industry.

In section 7 of the Kentucky ACT of November 2, 1820, creating the county of Perry, it was enacted that Hugh White and Daniel Garrard of Clay County, Henry B. Mayo and Harry Stratton of Floyd County and Hezekiah Branson of Harlan County be appointed Commissioners to ascertain and fix on the most convenient and suitable place for the permanent seat of justice of Perry County. They met at the home of Elijah Combs on the fourth Monday in April for that purpose and after a majority agreed on any place, they reported to the next court. And says the ACT, "it shall be the duty of the county court as soon as practicable thereafter to cause the necessary public buildings to be erected, and in every other respect, lay off and do that which may be necessary or which may be required by law in the establishment of towns." The section then concludes with this provision: "The courts for the county of Perry shall continue to be held at the home of Elijah Combs, until the necessary buildings are erected." For some reason, the foregoing provisions appear not to have been carried out by the Commissioners named in the ACT of November 2, 1820, so that the Legislature, by an ACT approved November 23, 1821, enacted that Elijah W. Smith of Rockcastle, Burton Litton of Whitley, Claiborne White of Clay, Thomas Johns and Peter Amyx of Floyd were appointed Commissioners to fix on a place for the seat of Justice for the County of Perry. They were to meet at the house of Elijah Combs on the first day of Spring Circuit Court for Perry County or as soon thereafter as might be practicable and to select a place for the permanent seat of justice of said county, having due regard for the convenience of the inhabitants. The Commissioners, having selected the place for the permanent seat of justice, certified the same to the court, who at their first session after the report of the Commissioners had been lodged with their clerk, proceeded to appoint five trustees whose duty it was to lay off the town at the place fixed on by the Commissioners for the permanent seat of justice for Perry County. Having set apart such portions of ground as they thought necessary for the erection of public buildings for that court, the trustees laid off the residue of the land so appropriated into convenient town lots, streets and alleys, and proceeded to sell the lots at public auction for the best price that could be had, on such terms of payment, and in such proportion as they deemed most advantageous, giving public notice of the time and terms of sale.

This ACT further provided that the Commissioners, before they fixed the place for the seat of justice, obtain from the owners a declaration in writing, containing the terms of the agreement with the Commissioners together with an application in writing to the justices of the county court that the owner conveyed to the said trustees or their successors in office, the legal title to at least ten acres of land to be laid off by the trustees into a town and sold as directed by this act. To this was added that the county, from time to time, have full power to fill vacancies in the Board of Trustees.

In 1821, when the county was actually organized, there was in force a number of laws regulating towns. These laws provided that the County Court should have the power by order, to "fix the name" by which the towns within the bounds of the newly found county may be called and to "fix the number of trustees" for the town, which number until otherwise directed shall remain five, "any three of whom shall be a sufficient number to do business." Also it was provided that the holders of lots in any town, when their number amounted to fifteen might elect their own trustees. The election was to be held annually by the clerk on the first Monday in August, and each free male person of the age of eighteen years being an actual resident of the town, or holding title to real estate therein, was entitled to vote. If no election was held, the County Court, at their next session, would appoint trustees and fill vacancies when necessary.

The trustees were directed to have the plans of their towns recorded in the County Courts, and were given power to make rules for the regulation and good order of the place as they deemed necessary, providing it was not contradictory to the law of the land. They were to pass ordinances for suppressing tippling houses, and for restraining and punishing slaves found rambling about the town without lawful passes. The trustees were authorized to make regulations respecting any public springs within the town, as they might think proper for keeping it in good order, and they were empowered to "cause streets to be cleaned and repaired by the inhabitants" but the "inhabitants of the town shall not be bound to work on the roads more than one-half mile from the town."

In the matter of revenue and taxation it was provided that the "trustees shall, for the benefit of the town, have power to tax the inhabitants and free-holders of the town, providing such tax shall not amount to more than six shillings annually on any one person."

It was under this law that the first trustees, five in number,[7] were appointed by the County Court of Perry and that the first town and county seat took the name of Hazard, although for many years it was referred to as Perry Court House, both locally and in legislative phraseology.[8]

The community of Hazard was referred to in legislative acts as Perry Court House because, until 1854, the local Post Office bore that name. The first Minute Book of Perry County Court shows that court was held at the house of Elijah Combs in Hazard on June 22, 1822, so actually the town was given the name Hazard from the very beginning of the county's formation.

What appears to be the first legislative mention of

Hazard by name was an act passed by the Kentucky General Assembly in 1831. That act provided that the Registrar of the Land Office be instructed to issue to Elijah Combs, William Begley and Colonel Felix Gilbert of Perry and Clay counties $200.00 worth of land warrants, free of charge for improvements of the road leading from the salt furnace of James White in Clay County to "Hazzard" in Perry County, the warrants to be appropriated upon vacant lands in Perry and Clay counties.

The town known as Hazard from the time Perry County was formed in 1821 was not deeded as such until July 18, 1826, by Elijah Combs as is shown below . . .

ELIJAH COMBS AND SARAH COMBS
TO/DEED

Trustees of Town of Hazard:

This Indenture of Bargain and sale made this 16th day of July, 1826, entered into between Elijah Combs and Sally his wife of the County of Perry and the State of Kentucky of the one part and the trustees of the Town of Hazard of the other part. Wittnesseth that in consideration of a bond the said Combs gave on the location of said Town aforesaid the said Combs and wife doth here by alien and convey to the trustees of the Town of Hazard and their successors in office forever the following boundary of land in the County of Perry on the North Fork of the Kentucky River and including the town aforesaid containing ten acres bounded as — followeth — Beginning at the bounded stake 5 poles below the said Combs' chicken house, thence running N 27 W40 poles to a stake, thence S 63 W 40 poles to the stake, on the banks of said North Fork, thence running up said Fork as aforesaid; S 27 E 40 poles to a stake; thence N63 E 40 poles to the beginning containing ten acres, to be the same, more or less.

Together with all and singular the appurtenances there unto belonging or in any wise appertaining.

To have and to hold the land hereby conveyed with the appurtenance unto the said Trustees and their successors in office; and the said Elijah Combs, for himself, his heirs, executors and administrators, the aforesaid tract of land and appurtenances unto the said trustees and their successors in office, against the claims of all and every person or persons whatsoever, doth and will forever warrant and defend by these present.

In witness thereof, the said Elijah Combs, together with Sary Combs, his wife, who hereby relinquishes right of dower in ad to the land conveyed in this deed, hath hereunto set their hand and seal the day and date first written above.

Signed, sealed and delivered / Elijah Combs (S)
/ Sary Combs (S)

In the presence of:
Jesse Combs
State of Kentucky.

Perry County Sct. I, Jesse Combs, clerk of the County Court for the county aforesaid do hereby certify that Elijah Combs and Sally Combs his wife, parties of the deed within personally appeared before me in open court this day, subscribed and acknowledged this same to be their act and deed. She the same Sally Combs being examined by me separately, privily and apart from her husband and the said deed was there and then shown and fully explained to her and upon such privy examination she declared that she did freely and willingly seal and deliver the said writing and wishes not to retract it and did acknowledge the said writing again, shown and fully explained to her to be her act and consented that it might be recorded, which is done accordingly given under my hand as a clerk aforesaid this tenth day of July, 1826.

Jesse Combs, C.P.C.C. [9]

The first survey of the town of Hazard was made and signed by John A. Duff, county surveyor, and by Jesse Combs and Austin Godsey, the Sworn Chain Carriers. The certificate and plat of the town was received by the court December 10, 1836, and ordered to be inserted into the court records by the clerk. It was approved and entered in the first Minute Book of Perry County Court, however it was not recorded until 1891, when R. G. Cornett was clerk. [10]

This survey shows ten acres on the north side of the Kentucky River. It is laid off in 29 quarter acre lots, 82 feet in front and 141 feet in back. Three of the sections were reserved for the public square and the only street was Main Street. This ten acre square began where the Grand Hotel now stands and ran down Main Street as far as the site now occupied by the First Baptist Church, including all the land back to the river. Then the square extended across Main Street up to the old County road, now High Street. The original plat is reproduced herewith:[11]

North Fork of the Kentucky River

22	23	24	25	26	27	28	29
14	15	16	17	18	19	20	21
6	7	8	9	10	11	12	13

MAIN STREET

1	2	3	PUBLIC SQUARE	4	5

Hazard was not incorporated until 1884.[12] By this time it had grown larger than the ten acres until it extended three-quarters of a mile in every direction from the Court House. The municipal affairs were controlled by the five trustees, who at this time were J. E. Campbell, J. C. Eversole, J. H. Combs, Bud Morgan and B. F. French, their term of office being for one year. The police judge and town marshal were commissioned by the Governor and their term was two years. W. W. Baker was the appointed police judge and A. G. Duff was the town marshal.

By 1890, Hazard had begun to develop into a county town with board walks and dirt streets. Its boundaries and main streets were outlined. Perry County itself was pretty well defined as it was to exist, and subsequent improvement of transportation facilities broke the barriers of isolation.

CHAPTER II

SETTLEMENT

Eunice Tolbert Johnson

Christopher Gist is believed to have been the first man to have traveled through Perry County. In 1751 on his return trip to Virginia as explorer for the Ohio Land Company, his trail led up Red River, by way of the Kentucky-Red River Divide, to the North Fork of the Kentucky River and upstream to Pound Gap.[1]

The next to travel in this vicinity were the McAfee brothers. On their return trip to Virginia in 1773 they started at Harrodsburg, came past Richmond through a gap in Big Hill to Irvine and up the Kentucky River as far as Leatherwood Creek in Perry County. Here they left the main trail which continued on through Pound Gap and went by another trail which led them over Black Mountain to the Clinch Valley Trail.[2]

There is a tradition in Eastern Kentucky that Daniel Boone visited this section in 1776. He had first come to Kentucky in 1769 with Finley and Stuart to hunt and explore. In 1773, with other families he came to Kentucky to make his home. Being the explorer that he was, he undoubtedly went to the head of the Kentucky River, as he and a companion were often absent for days at a time, exploring the wilderness. It is said that he camped near Storm King, 3½ miles north of Hazard, on the old William Cornett land, and that he carved "D. Boone, 1776" on a rock there. It is now covered with sand.

These early explorers followed the narrow Indian trails along the streams. These trails are believed to have been hunting or war trails, as no Indians are known to have lived in this section. R. H. Collins writes in his HISTORY OF KENTUCKY, 1847, that the Indians had passed high in Perry in 1794. Mounds and burial grounds were found along the trail and at one time Hiram Cornett had a collection of tomahawk and arrowheads that he had found in the vicinity of Hazard.[3] In 1824, C. F. Rafinesque, Professor of Natural History at Transylvania reported that he had found a long Indian dromus near Hazard. He did not mark the location of this mound and the older people in the county do not remember it. Anne Guerrant, in a letter to her sister, Grace, in 1894, mentions visiting Indian graves on a mountain on Big Creek.

The settlers were the next to penetrate this section. The early pension lists of the United States indicate that they came chiefly from Virginia and North Carolina, possibly because they were nearest to this section. Most of them were of English and Scotch-Irish descent, although a few German and French names are found. By 1790, the level lands in Kentucky had been taken, so the overflow came into the mountains. While it was Kentucky District, of Virginia, all the land had been reserved for Revolutionary War veterans, but after Kentucky became a state in 1792, land was open for settlement to any house-keeper over 21 years old, and having a family. (4)

It is not known just who the first settlers were, but from family histories, tradition, early birth records and land grants, it is known that several families came during the 1790's. Jacob Eversole settled at the mouth of Lick Branch around 1790, while this was still Kentucky District. The log house he built there in 1802 is the oldest log house still standing in Perry County today.

Birth records show that Robert Bustard Cornett, son of William Cornett, Revolutionary soldier, was born on Leatherwood in 1798. Richard Smith was living on Lotts Creek around 1795, and his sons William and Samuel were born there before 1799. Samuel Lusk settled on Line Fork, Abel Pennington and William Begley on the Middle Fork around 1800, William Stamper was an early settler on Rockhouse and Gideon Ison settled on Big Branch in 1804.

Benjamin Webb, one of the first Justices of Perry County, settled on Boone Fork, 1797, later Perry County now Letcher. He was Sheriff of Perry in 1831-32 and a December term of Court that year thought he should be fined for not attending court since he was High Sheriff of Perry County. Distances and bad roads did not seem to be any excuse to the courts for his absence.

John and Nicholas Combs and their sons came here

and settled in the 1790's in different parts of the county (see biographies). John's son, Elijah, was the first to settle on the present site of Hazard. His children, Jesse, born in 1798 when this was Montgomery County, and Polly, born in 1802 when this was Floyd, were the first children to be born in what was later Hazard. When Jesse became Clerk of Perry County in 1822, he recorded the births and deaths of his family in the back of the first marriage license book of Perry County.

Elijah Combs built the first two houses where Hazard now stands. His first house was built to the rear of the Court House. Soon after building this house, he returned to Virginia and married Sarah (Sally) Roark then returned to Perry with his bride and two slaves. After his return, he built a second and more pretentious house. It was a two-story log structure near the end of the bridge, about where Goad Hardward now stands. Court was held in this house for several years and one room was used as a tavern.

As is shown by the First Minute Book of Perry County, Elijah Combs was a progressive man and may well be called the Founder of Hazard. He was instrumental in getting the new county formed; he held practically all the offices in Perry County at one time or another; he was one of the first Justices, a legislator, a Sheriff and a Justice of the Peace. He had the first salt wells in Hazard, he helped with the road building, he operated the first ferry, and helped secure the first public buildings. He was called "Gineral Lige" possibly because he had served with the State Militia. He was one of the first settlers to receive land grants in what is now Perry County; he received a land grant patent number 10,881 on June 5, 1810, for 250 acres of land then lying and being in Clay County on the North Fork of the Kentucky River.[5] This patent included land up Messers Branch and all of Big Bottom, or the east section of Hazard.

The graveyard where Elijah, his wife, Jesse, and several of their children are buried can be seen today on Broadway behind the Boggs Building.

The Combs family controlled the politics of early Perry County because they had intermarried and were related.

Most of the offices in Court were held by relatives. They were the largest land owners in the County, with Nicholas Combs, Sr., holding the largest tracts. He had settled on the Kentucky River near Combs Bend. The log house built by his son, "Bird-eye" Combs, is the next to the oldest log house standing in Perry County today.

Others receiving these early grants of 1810 that cover any of what is Perry today were: Jeremiah Combs, Nicholas Combs, Sr., George Combs, Henry Combs, Mason Combs, Roderick McIntosh and John Fields. These grants were from 75 to 250 acres, being in Clay County on the North Fork of the Kentucky River. Most of the early patents were for the level land only, as no one wanted to pay taxes on the mountainsides. The next earliest grants issued were to Woolery Eversole and Shadrack Combs in 1815, and to Jesse Bowling, Silas Davidson, John Combs, Henry Combs, Sr., John Campbell and William Campbell from 1815 to 1821. All were on the North Fork of the Kentucky River.[6]

The only Virginia land grant still active in Perry County is a part of the Marshall-Pickett grant issued by that state on May 5, 1792. Parts of it were sold several times and on September 17, 1821, John Spencer of Perry bought 150 acres of it around Grapevine and Campbell's Bend. In 1896 Jesse Combs' heirs bought 75 acres of it which they still own. Prior to receiving these grants many families are known to have lived on these lands and claimed them for their own several years before. Some of the earliest settlers did not apply for patents until after the county was formed in 1820. One of the last grants patented in Perry County was a small grant to D. Y. Combs in 1923.

Most of these grants were overlapping and are still contested in court; however, if one could keep his claim fifteen years without its being contested, he had a clear title to it.

By 1821 when the county was formed, patents were issued to nearly all the families living in Perry County, and the population had increased to several hundred, as shown by the Perry County Tax List of 1820-21. (see appendix.) In 1820-21, when the county was formed, there was already a settlement on Troublesome Creek,[7] possibly because of the salt works there.

From 1821 through 1837 Justices who served in the Perry County Courts were: James Turner, Abel Pennington, William Begley, Jesse Spurlock, Joseph Cockrel, John Haddix, Thomas Francis, George Ison, John Campbell, William Campbell, Hiram Hogg, Ezekiel Brashear, Robert Cornett, James Collins, Joseph Hammons, Moses Ison, Isom Stamper, Benjamin Webb, Benjamin Hall, Henry Duff, Spencer Adams, John Adams, Charles Smith, Wiley Cope, Robert Hicks, Jesse Boling, Samuel Hurley, William Stamper, Stephen Hogg, Elijah Combs, Jeremiah Combs, William Williams, Robert S. Brashear, Alexander Patrick, Daniel Duff, John Boling, William Lewis and Nicholas Combs. These men had to travel from the far corners of the county to serve in Court. They may well be called the "Fathers of Perry County" for it is their records we have searched to find the material for this History.

CHAPTER III
SOCIAL GROWTH
Eunice Tolbert Johnson

The growth of Perry County from 1820 to 1890 was slow. During this seventy year period, the population barely doubled. The mountains were natural barriers to road building and it was not until the coal mines were developed and the railroad was built that the isolation was broken. From 1900 to 1920, a period of twenty years, the county had its largest growth; the population trebled, or increased 315%. From 1920 until the present time (1950) the population has almost doubled, or increased 178%. (For Census, see appendix.)

The early families were almost entirely self-sustaining. They built their own homes, first from logs; later with the use of a whipsaw, from rough boards. It was not until about 1897 that a planing mill was brought into Perry County and planed lumber was available for home building.

The first farmers raised hemp, flax and cotton, fibers of which they spun and wove into coverlets, clothes and linens. They also tanned the leather for their own shoes. Aunt Mary Combs, of Lotts Creek, and Aunt Nancy Francis, of Ary, both remember wearing such shoes. The tops were made from the soft leather and the soles from the tough. To remove the hairs, they tanned beef hides by soaking them in a trough with chestnut or oak tan-bark; then they beat them until pliant. Shoes were put together with pegs. All kinds of herbs were used for medicines and dyes; salt licks were nearby and game was plentiful.

The early settlers got along with little help from the outside. They grew their own food and there were many orchards. Perry County, then, as well as today, was well adapted to fruit growing, apples being the leading fruit crop. The first commercial orchard was started by Captain A. C. Rhinehart, below Dwarf, about 1912. Today there are six, of four or five acres each, owned by Jim Esteppe and John Hall, of Viper, Harlan Smith of Dwarf, Green Campbell of Yerkes, William Allen of Sixteen-Mile, Homeplace and numbered 14 and had sales of $5,986,000. There were 13 service firms which collected $103,000.

Employment in the county also rose during the period between 1939 and 1948 for the above trades.

Various aspects of the development of Perry County in its early stages and its part in more recent enterprises are described in the following sub-topics.

First History Written About Perry County

The first history of Perry County was written by Lewis Collins in 1847. It is less than a printed page, and in it he states that Perry County lies at the headwaters of the Kentucky River, defines its boundaries, which were different then (in 1847), in that Floyd was a boundary and the counties of Owsley, Leslie and Knott had not been formed. He also says the county is drained by the North and Middle Forks of the Kentucky River, which are navigable for descending boats the greater part of the year. He says the valleys are fertile and productive with a sandstone foundation; also, that the surface is hilly and mountainous and a large portion is unsuitable for cultivation, but well suited for wool-growing. The principle articles of export are horses, cattle, hogs, salt, coal, ginseng and wool. All he has to say of Hazard is that Hazard, the county seat, is a small village situated on the North Fork of the Kentucky River. He mentions a party of Indians crossing through Perry County high upon the Kentucky River in 1794.

In 1874, Richard H. Collins revised his father's work, bringing the history of the counties up-to-date. His description of Perry County was about the same as his father's, except that he mentioned salt wells on Leatherwood, firestone on Macy's Creek, and coal seams in the North Fork of the Kentucky River. He also gave the slave and white census and the early legislative members of Perry County. There were no resident Senators, but the county was represented by the following members of the House; Henry Duff, 1833; John Haddix, 1835; Elijah Combs, 1840; Joseph Eversole, 1848; Zachariah Morgan, 1867-69; and Josiah

Buckhorn School.[1] In 1924, Perry County was among the outstanding apple-growing counties in Kentucky, with a harvest of 117,029 bushels[.2] Perry County has an ideal home market for everything produced here, and there is not enough grown locally to supply the demand. In 1949, eighteen 4-H Club members raised over 2,000 gallons of strawberries, and farmers produced 4,000 gallons. The County Agent, Mr. Paul Keen, says that there is definite indication that Perry County could develop into a good strawberry region. Strawberries provide a high cash income per acre and require only a small acreage of fertile land. He says that the main agricultural program is the "live at home" program which encourages production on home farms of all necessary foods for home use and the selling of the surplus within the community. Perry Countians produce some of the finest gardens in the state and with the increase in production of dairy and animal products the diet of the average family in the county has been greatly improved. Corn is the leading farm crop produced in the County. In early times, livestock was driven across the mountains to Georgia, Alabama and Virginia. Later sheep were driven to the Bluegrass region. In cash income for Perry County, farm products and livestock rank third, coal being first and lumber second.

According to the 1948 Census of Business, released by the Bureau of Census, U. S. Department of Commerce, business in Perry County has tripled in the last ten years. Retail sales in the county were $23.2 million, an increase of 218% over the $7.3 million in 1939. Wholesale sales in the county reached $11.0 million in 1949 as compared with $2.5 million in 1939.

In Hazard, there were 146 retail establishments grossing $13,725,000 and employing 128 persons. Wholesale firms totaled 15 in 1948 and grossed $5,058,000. There were 30 service trade firms with sales and receipts amounting to $595.00.

In the county there were 352 retail stores which grossed $9,490,000 and employed 273 persons. County wholesalers

Combs, 1871-73. There were also the following representatives from Perry and Clay counties: Alexander Patrick, 1827-28-30-31; E. W. Murphy, 1829; Robert S. Brashear, 1837; and John C. Wilson, 1839.

Collins had this to say of the towns: "Hazard, the county seat, is a small village on the North Fork of the Kentucky River, about 150 miles S. E. of Frankfort, 71 miles W. of Grayson, 36 miles N. W. of Whitesburg, 53 miles S. of Manchester. Brashearsville, 14 miles away, and Saltcreek, 12 miles from Hazard are post offices and stores." (1874).

The next history written about Hazard was a small book called **Pearl of the Mountain** by Louis Pilcher, dealing mostly with the people living in Hazard in 1913. Kerr's **History of Kentucky,** published in 1922, contains the biographies of several men living in Hazard, and is probably the first biography written about citizens of Perry County. The only other history containing biographies of Perry County men is the **Sesqui-Centennial History of Kentucky** by Hambleton Tapp, published in 1945.

Floods

Collins' **History of Kentucky** cites many floods on the Kentucky River since the earliest settlements. One he mentioned was "April 9, 1872, the greatest flood on the Upper Kentucky River since 1817; river rose fifteen feet in six hours; over 20,000 saw logs, the property of the poor people, floated off and were lost, above Irvine, Estill County, most of those residing on the river bottoms were driven from their homes by the rising floods; many houses, coal, iron boats and corn boats were washed away and stock drowned."

Aunt Mary Combs, of Lotts Creek, who is ninety years old, remembers this flood. She says that their home at the mouth of Messer's Branch, by the sulphur spring, (Colt Duff's store) was washed away. She was a small child, but she can remember that the water reached over all the level land of Hazard. She said that the men used boats made by scooping out the inside of poplar logs.

The present generation has seen the river high and over its banks many times, but the worst flood that ever hit Perry, and the one never to be forgotten, came May 30, 1927. Two Hazard bridges washed out, every Hazard business suffered losses, and some were six or seven feet under water. Most residents of the Big Bottom section of Hazard had water in their houses ranging from two feet to second story depth. The **Hazard Herald** of June 3 reported the losses to be five million dollars, and deaths in the section to number 62. Hundreds were made homeless; water flowed down Main Street in Big Bottom as swiftly as it did in the river bed. The same conditions existed throughout the county and all who lived near the river suffered from the effects of this flood.

Military History

It is not likely that any men from this section fought in the War of 1812, as most of the volunteers from Kentucky who defended Lake Erie with Admiral Perry were included in the 100 volunteers sent by General Harrison from his army to reinforce Admiral Perry's crew. They were dressed in fringed shirts and leggings and had long rifles which they knew how to use. "For sniping work, they cannot be surpassed" wrote General Harrison, as he sent them to Perry.[3]

If men from Perry County served in the Mexican War, their names are not known. Most of the men who fought in this war of 1846 were volunteers from Central Kentucky, due to the fact that the mountain counties were late receiving their call.

The Pension List, Enrollment under the Act passed June 7, 1832, shows twenty-six Revolutionary War veterans living in Perry County before 1840, namely: Anthony Hall, Simeon Justice, Edward Polly, John Combs, Charles Ellis, Drury Bush, Stephen Caudill, James Caudill, Achilles Craft, Peter Hammond, William Cornett, William Hagan, Henry Hurst, James Howard, Thomas Howard, Andrew Harwell, Samuel Stidham, Roger Turner, Thomas Watkins, David

May, Leonard Pigman, Jesse Boling, Andrew Burns, John Kelly, George McDaniel, and Joshua Mullins.

The Military History of Kentucky states that each county in Kentucky had locally organized Militia which was necessary to the pioneer for preservation of the community, and that all able-bodied men were connected with some command. Musters and parades were as much of a social function as a military event. While belonging to one of these Militia Companies in Perry County, Elijah Combs won his nickname "Gineral Lige."

John Fitzpatrick, of Hazard, has the original "Annual Return" of the 98th Regiment of the Kentucky Militia for 1849. His great-grandfather, Captain Jacob Fitzpatrick, led the Regiment of 73 enlisted men and three commissioned officers. Lt. David W. Allen, Ensign Henry Brown, Capt. J. F. Patrick and three Sergeants, Joseph Hackworth, Alexander Hamilton and William Haywood. The report shows the number of rifles, shot pouches, powder horns, loose balls and pounds of powder given to each man. They were ordered to hold a three day drill parade in October, 1849, and were notified of a Battalion muster to be held in Paintsville in May, 1849. At that time, Captain Fitzpatrick was living in what is now Whitesburg.

In the Civil War, many families were divided in sentiment and found themselves on opposite sides. However, in the mountains of Eastern Kentucky, there were fewer men on the Confederate side.

A report dated July 28, 1862, was made by the Adjutant General showing the number of men Kentucky had furnished to the United States service from Perry to be 296. There were no battles in Perry County but shortly after the Civil War, Rebels came through and fired on the old Eversole home at Krypton. Ef Sizemore and Major John C. Eversole were killed. It is said that Black Jim Campbell, a Union soldier, went back as long as he lived on Decoration Day and put flowers on the Rebels' graves.

J. D. Cornett, in his Cornett Genealogy, says that there was a Confederate Camp on Big Leatherwood, with a Major

Chineworth in command. He tells of Gib Creech being captured and shot because he was caught ambushing some of the Confederate soldiers. He mentions the following men as serving in the Civil War: Ezekial Brashear, a Confederate soldier killed in action at Cynthiana, Ky.; Anderson Eversole, a sergeant in the Union Army; 1st Lt. Thomas Johnson; Capt. Anderson Hayes; and Kendrick Combs, who died in Jackson as he was walking home at the end of the war. William Eversole was a Captain in the 14th Kentucky Cavalry and Abner Eversole was a Lieutenant in the same regiment.

In the book **Begley-Allen-Mays** by Jackson Allen Begley, he states that Hiram Begley, who took the first Census of Perry County, was a veteran of the 39th Kentucky Mounted Infantry and that he helped chase John Morgan's Raiders out of Kentucky.

A great many Perry County men joined in the Spanish-American War (1898). These men mostly belonged to the Fourth Kentucky Infantry Regiment. Some went into the regular army and participated in the Battle of San Juan Hill. Some from Perry County, still living, who served in this war are Press Plummer, Henry Caudill, Pete Standifer, Mark Standifer, John McIntosh and Jackson Allen Begley. Some of these men were in a Company commanded by Capt. William Dixon of Hyden, Ky. Samp Brashear, of Company M, was killed in the Philippines.

In World War I, Hazard was made the Headquarters of a Company of the 1st and 2nd Infantry under Capt. Isaac Wilder, who established out-posts in Perry County at the bridge over the North Fork of the Kentucky River and at the Hazard Tunnel.[4] The most seriously wounded man in World War I is said to have been Sgt. Samuel Joseph, of Hazard, who received 102 injuries.[5]

In order that World War I history would be recorded accurately, the Kentucky Council of Defense inaugurated a state-wide movement in 1918, while the war was still raging, to preserve the military records and activities of civilians in all branches of war work; a local historian was appointed in every county. The historian completed this work, had the volume bound in book form and placed in the office of the County Court Clerk. W. W. Peavyhouse was the historian in Perry County. This survey contains a complete statement of the service of every solider, sailor or marine and the work done by civilians. It shows 377 men inducted from Perry County 1917-1919 and 26 deaths.[6]

According to the records of the State Headquarters for Selective Service (ending April 1, 1947), there were 4,712 men from Perry County inducted and enlisted into the Armed Forces during World War II. The Honor Roll of Dead indicated that there were 144 Army casualties in that period. The exact number of dead from the other branches of the service is not known, but it is believed to be around 50, making the total number of Perry County casualties approximately 200.

Not much can be said statistically of the present conflict in Korea, but the first Kentucky casualty was Pfc. Hubert Stacey, of Perry County.

Post Offices

The United States Post Office records show that the first post office established in Perry County was at Patrick's Salt Works, on May 9, 1821, with Alexander Patrick as postmaster. According to mail route 1757, it was located 23 miles from Perry Court House, and 20 miles from Crawfords, Estille County.

The second county post office was established at Brashearsville on February 21, 1829, with Robert S. Brashear as postmaster. The third to be established was at Grapevine on September 10, 1834, with Henry Duff as Postmaster. By 1874, there were post offices at Cutshin and Hazard and post offices and stores were combined at Brashearsville and Salt Creek.[7] Mrs. Hannah W. B. Seaber was appointed the first woman postmistress in Perry County on January 15, 1879, at Gay's Creek. By 1893, there were 16 post offices in this county.[8] These were popular stopping places for mail carriers and other travelers en route from Manchester and Prestonsburg.

As early as 1828 the county had some system of getting

mail in parts of the county where there were no post offices. The First Minute Book of Perry County Courts of October, 1828, defined the boundaries of an election precinct as being a straight line from the **mail box** at the forks of Caney to the Estille County line. By 1830, a number of rural routes, crossing Perry from several directions had been established. (See Appendix for rural routes.)

Until the railroad came in 1912, the mail was brought from the nearest railroad station on horseback. Even now, the horse is still being used in some parts of Perry County to carry mail, but it is gradually being replaced by the jeep.

The post office where Hazard now stands was established on April 22, 1824, and called Perry, Perry County, Kentucky (often referred to as Perry Court-House). Elijah Combs, Jr., was appointed the first postmaster. The name was changed to Hazard on June 20, 1854, with John C. Lacy as postmaster at that time. It was discontinued August 17, 1865, re-established March 6, 1866, discontinued again on October 12, 1868, and re-established finally on November 12, 1868. These interruptions were possibly caused by the Civil War.

Some of the last carriers before the railroad came were W. O. Davis, who had the route from Hazelgreen to Whitesburg around 1873. It was while carrying mail on this route that he met and married Celia (Aunt Bink) Cornett, daughter of Elijah Cornett. Another was George (Bear) Combs, who started carrying mail when he was fifteen years old. His route was from Hazard to Hindman, a trip which was full of hardships. In 1883, Lee Daniel's route went to Whitesburg once a week; he would pay 25 cents each for his horse and himself for the night. His pay was $5.00 a month, plus room and board.

In 1885, old settlers say that the Hazard post office was located in Robin Baker's log house near where the Peoples Bank now stands. Later it was in Col. Salyer's house, located near the present Johnson Dept. Store.

After the railroad was built to Jackson, the mail came to Hazard from there. By 1910, Hazard had a population of 537 and the mail had become so heavy that it was impractical to carry the bulk on a horse, so a hack was used to make the trip, as often as it could get through. The mail was often robbed, and it was reported in the **Hazard Herald** of 1911 that on one trip to Hindman both the postal rider and his horse were killed.

On The Grapevine . . .

The following letters from Grace Guerrant were written on a trip to the mountains with her father, Rev. E. O. Guerrant, in 1896 and best describe the prevailing conditions.
"Dear Anne,

You don't get many letters from the mountains, so I thought I would write you one. Papa promised to take me with him the next time he went up into the mountains to preach, so we started on the 10th of July, and at Lexington took the Kentucky Union Railroad for the mountains. We went one hundred miles to Jackson, in Breathitt County. The road went up the Red River, where the big cliffs stand up on both sides of the road, hundreds of feet high. Many of the mountains have rocks on top like domes, bigger than a church. They are grand. The river was lined with beautiful flowers of ivy and laurel.

I saw some men cutting oats with a big scythe, with fingers on it; Papa told me they were cradling. That was curious to me. One big tree was growing on top of a big rock. About six in the evening, we reached Jackson, on the North Fork of the Kentucky River. It is a very nice town, and we have a church and a college there, where a few years ago we had none.

On Wednesday morning we started for the mountains in Perry County. Mr. Charles Little, Papa's friend, went along with us, and took his niece, Miss Kate Patrick, to sing. He had two buggies; we rode in one, and they in the other. Papa brought a little Estey organ and we tied it on behind our buggy.

We went up the Kentucky River ten miles to the mouth of Troublesome Creek. Here we got into trouble enough. We had to get out and help the buggy down the rocky stairsteps in the road. We went up Troublesome a mile, then up Lost Creek ten miles, then the man there said there were ten thousand big saw logs in the creek. I never saw the like. The little houses all had martin boxes, but no yard or shade.

Down on Troublesome, we saw some ladies bare-footed, and one old lady had on shoes, but no stockings, and one had on a dress shorter than mine. I guess she must have been an old maid.

The mountains were very steep, but had corn growing on their sides nearly to the top. They can't plow them up and down, but crossways. We saw coal mines all along the road, just sticking out of the mountains. Sometimes we rode over solid coal beds, and the biggest trees I ever saw grow along the creeks and rivers. They are awfully big. We saw a big boy, who had only a shirt on, and most of the men were barefooted, but they were very clever.

When we went ten miles up Lost Creek, we turned up a creek called 'Ten-Mile' Creek. Well, it was awful. I thought we had passed bad roads, but we were just beginning them. Three men went along to cut trees and roll rocks out of the road. And such a road! Over big rocks and logs and steep banks and deep holes and around splash-dams. I thought our buggy would be smashed all to pieces. The horse pulled our trace in two, and a big rock broke a spoke out of the buggy. Sometimes we had to walk and climb. When we rode over the rocks, we couldn't keep our hats on. Sometime I bumped Papa, and sometimes he bumped me. It was too funny. Papa got a man to lead the horse around a big tree on the mountain while he and and another man held the buggy. The horse got strangled and the man cried out, 'Here's a dead horse,' and scared me nearly to death. But they got the horses up and we went over a mountain to the Grapevine Creek. Here we had a time getting down the mountain, the path was so steep and sidelong. Mr. Little's horse went over the mountainside and he jerked him back and he fell down, with the buggy on him. Papa and some men helped to take him out, then the buggy got away and ran down the mountain and broke the shaft. Then they all took our horse out and got the buggy down to the foot of the mountain by the hardest work.

Papa said that this was my vacation trip. I think it was. I never saw as much in my life. The day seemed a week long. The road down the Grapevine was no road at all. Mr. Little and Papa had to walk and lead and roll logs out of the way. It took us five hours to go seven miles. We came to the mouth of Grapevine about dark, twenty-seven miles by the road we came and forty by the river, above Jackson. Papa had a friend there named Dr. Wilson, but we could not get our buggies to his house, so we crossed the river and stayed at Mr. Tom Johnson's. They are very clever people indeed. Papa and Mr. Little crossed the river and stayed at Dr. Wilson's.

Mr. Sawyers, our missionary, was there. Papa is preaching in the little school-house, on the bank of the river, and it is crowded at 10:00 a. m. and 4:00 p. m. Miss Kate Patrick and I play the little organ, the first one ever played in this county for worship. Emma Johnson has the only one in the county. The people are very clever and attentive, and most of them walk to church. About twenty-five have joined, and Mr. Johnson was the first one, and an old man nearly seventy, and a real pretty girl named Dora Duff. Mr. Johnson is the leading man in the county, and lives in the only brick house.

We went swimming in the river one evening; it was about a foot deep, and we had lots of fun. It is cool and quiet in these mountains. Sunday we are going to take dinner to church and have an all-day meeting. Next week we are going to Hazard, the only town in Perry County. They say the road up Campbell Creek is worse than 'Ten-Mile' and Grapevine. If it is, I pity it. But I guess we will go it. Papa is going to preach on Big Creek next week. When you get tired and want a vacation, come to Grapevine. The people will be glad to see you. They are as clever as can be. Goodbye,

Your sister,
Grace."

To Big Creek ...

"Dear Anne,

My last letter brought you to the mouth of Grapevine Creek. Well, we had a big meeting there Sunday from 10.00 a. m. til 5:00 p. m., two hours for dinner. There was a crowd —the schoolhouse was packed—and it was so hot I could hardly get my breath. Papa preached morning and evening; thirty-five joined, and he had to baptize most of them, as they had never been baptized. Some people had to stand out in the rain. Monday morning we bade all goodbye, and started to Big Creek. The roads were worse and worse. One clever man went along to hold the buggy. We went up the Kentucky River then up Campbell's Creek, then across an awful mountain to Forked Mouth Creek. Oh, me! A bad boy would say it was 'forked lightening.' We got down it alive, by walking and climbing and leading and holding the buggies. The mountains and rocks just covered up the road entirely. We passed a little school-house and all the children ran out to see the buggies. They were curiosities to them. One little boy said he lived up a creek, but didn't know its name. He saw big rattle snakes up there too. One funny man was riding an ox, and he had a bed quilt for a saddle and bark for a girth. Another man had an ox geared up like a horse and it was plowing for him. An old lady was carrying her baby and a little pig was following her like a dog. When she stopped, it lay down at her feet. One little house had a pole put up in the front yard, and three bottles hung up on top for ornaments. There were no trees in the yard. One lady had a naked tree in her yard, covered with egg shells, like a snowball bush. It was funny to me.

Well, after a hard journey over mountains and more creeks we reached Big Creek. Papa had been there before, and the good people came walking up the road to meet us. I never saw cleverer people, though they are not rich or proud. Kate and I stayed at Mr. Field's up on Big Creek, and Papa and Mr. Little had to stay down at Mr. Wiley Couch's, as there was not room for all of us at one house. Papa preached in the school house for four days, and twenty-seven joined the church. We met some nice girls at Big Creek. One of them told us she could sing twice as loud as we could, and I believe it. We went fishing and caught some nice fish and ate them. The people were so clever, we enjoyed our visit there. The little deaf boy who joined the church before was there; he is a smart boy, and can talk a little. He is going to the institute at Danville. His name is Willie Fugate.

On Friday evening we crossed the mountain, and went to Hazard, the county seat. It is a little town of about one-hundred people. It used to have a bad name, because so many people were killed there. It is better now. The Methodist Church is not quite done, and ours is just begun. The river runs between the town and the mountains. They never had a church here before. Papa preached in the Court House. Many people came, and twenty-three joined. He preached in the jail one day, and three poor prisoners joined. It was an awful place, and I felt sorry for them. The doors were iron bars, with big locks and bolts to hold them safe. A mountain preacher came to church, and he had been shot in the ear by some bad men. They said he killed their hogs. A big freshet came down the river and carried away hundreds of saw logs. They said a water spout broke on a creek called "Kingdom Come."

We walked up the river one day and met two men carrying a hundred fish, called red horses. They were very pretty. We climbed to the very top of a big mountain with Mr. Sawyers, and he said we could see the Cumberland Mountains away off. There were some Indian graves up there. The mountains were covered with trees broken down by the snow in May. On Tuesday morning Papa preached in Hazard the last time, and we started after dinner, to Jackson, forty miles away, over the mountains. They have no regular hotel in Hazard. Somebody burned up the hotel about a year ago.

We drove twenty miles Tuesday evening down the river, up Lotts Creek, down Lost Creek, to Mr. Watts', which we reached about dark. The road was pretty bad. We were almost turned over in Lost Creek once, in a hole full of big rocks. Mr. Little's harness kept breaking, until he tied it with wire. One clever old lady said I looked the 'naturalest'; I don't know what she meant. Maybe she thought I favored Papa. When we played the organ, they wondered why we used our feet. They couldn't understand, but they are as clever as can be, and one of them told Papa that they were poor, but their souls were worth as much as a rich man's soul. We saw no churches, and met few preachers, and they were not educated. We got up at 4:00 this morning, and started to Jackson at 6:00 a. m. and by hard driving, reached here at 12:00. So our journey over the mountains is ended and we are alive.

Your sister,
Grace."(9)

The Hundredth Anniversary

The **Hazard Herald** of July 8, 1921, reports that the hundreth anniversary of the founding of Perry County was fittingly celebrated on the 4th of July (1921), the two events being combined to make both occasions more memorable. Judge Samuel Wilson of Lexington delivered the address, telling the early history of Perry County. At the end of his speech, he presented to the city of Hazard an excellent photograph of Oliver Hazard Perry, handsomely framed, and to the presiding judge of the Perry Circuit Court and to his successors in office, a gavel beautifully carved and polished. The head was fashioned from a piece of wood taken from the battleship **Porcupine,** which took part in the famous battle on Lake Erie, and the handle was made from the wood of a native walnut tree of Perry County.

Perry County Orphanages
(See Chapter on Buckhorn.)

Perry County has two orphanages; one at Buckhorn, operated by the Buckhorn School, and one near Viper. The Open Door Children's Home is located on Hall's Mountain, one mile from Viper. It was founded in May, 1947, by Mr. and Mrs. J. L. Ragsdale, who had been missionaries in

Letcher County. The Hall family was anxious to have some Christian work started on Dykes Branch, so Mr. Philip Hall and his sister, Mrs. Terry Esteppe, donated ten acres of land on which to build the home. A fire in March, 1950, destroyed all the buildings except one. It is being used at present (1951) as both a dormitory and a school; there are forty children there now, ranging in age from one to seventeen years. Three missionary teachers are now employed.

Perry County Health Department

The Perry County Health Department was formed in June, 1927, after the Hon. Herbert Hoover and Dr. A. T. McCormick inspected the North Fork of the Kentucky River area that had been hit by the disasterous flood of May, 30, 1927. Dr. A. M. Gross was appointed part-time Health Officer. The first local board members were Dr. Gross, Dr. C. D. Snyder, Dr. R. L. Collins, Mrs. Letha (Ma) Hibler and Dr. K. N. Salyers.

Immediately following the flood, 15,000 typhoid immunizations were given. Dr. R. L. Collins has been acting Health Officer since 1947, and Mr. Raleigh F. Johnson has been the administrative director since July 1, 1951.

The major activities of the Health Department are the immunization program, maternal and child health, pre-school and school program, sanitation, public health education, control of communicable diseases and a crippled children's clinic. Tuberculosis control, with an annual chest x-ray clinic, a mobile cancer clinic and a dental mobile unit are also part of the department's program.[10]

Scouting In Perry County

Arthur Wrightson, the Field Scout Executive in the Hazard District during 1950 had this to say of scouting in Perry County:

"The Boy Scouts of America has been very active in Perry County. In 1912, the first Scout troop was organized in Hazard under the leadership of Curt Feltner. Some of the members of this first troop were Carl Combs, Dewey

Combs, Lawrence Davis, Joe Feltner, Francis Baker, Howard Johnson and J. C. Eversole, to name a few. The troop was very active, and one of its projects which is still used is a walking path the troop members dug to Peter's Peak near Hazard. **The Hazard Herald** of 1912 carries an account of the organization of a Boy Scout troop by William Fitzpatrick as Scoutmaster. They had fourteen members and met at H.B.I.

In November, 1924, a troop was sponsored by the Christian Church, of which Rev. A. C. Brooks was pastor. In November, 1929, Troop 90, sponsored by the Presbyterian Church, was organized with J. W. Crouch as Scoutmaster. The troop has been active to some extent ever since. This troop has been handicapped from the start because there was no organization from which it could get help and guidance. However, Robert Foreman was the first Scout to receive his Eagle rank, which shows that the troop was active and doing good work.

In order to find out more about scouting, and to get help in training and guidance, several men petitioned the National Organization to form a Council in this area and in January, 1934, the Lonesome Pine Council was organized with P. T. Adkins of Norton, Virginia, as its President. A Perry Countian, H. E. Greer, Sr., served as its President from 1939 to 1948. Executive head of the organization was Horace Williamson and Field Scout Executive over the Hazard District was Charlie Hudson. Mr. Hudson served in this capacity for five years, when he became Scout Executive. Others serving in this area have been Harold Hayes and Estille McIntyre.

Several local men have been awarded the Silver Beaver Award for distinguished service in Scouting to the youth of this area: H. E. Greer, Sr., in 1936; R. L. Gordon in 1938; John G. Green in 1940; J. Foley Snyder in 1942; Dr. A. B. Morgan in 1944; G. A. Weatherton in 1944 and Charlie Johnson in 1945.

One of our Perry Countians, H. E. Greer, Sr., has been recognized for his distinguished service to the youth of three states, West Virginia, Kentucky and Ohio, in Scouting. He received the Silver Antelope in 1948. "Mr. Scouting" in Hazard and vicinity, H. E. Greer, Sr., was responsible for the organization of Troop 90 in 1929 and has been active ever since as Troop Committeeman, Council President, and is now active as National Representative and Honorary President.

Scouting today is providing an interesting, character building program for over 400 boys in Perry County and vicinity. Today, through the good work of Guyn Haydon, W. R. Peyton, Kenny Brashear, Claude Morgan, Ward Tayloe, and Cecil Bartlett, all of Hazard and vicinity, the boys of Hazard are taking advantage of this program to the fullest extent possible. At Buckhorn, Dr. E. E. Gabbard realizes the value of Scouting and has been responsible for the organization of one of the largest troops in this area. Under the good leadership of Roy York, the Buckhorn troop, though recently organized, is making steady progress. At Chavies, Elmer Eversole has been responsible for a wonderful program for the boys—in a recent flood, his boys were ready and willing to help to the extent of their ability, thus proving that Scouts are prepared for emergencies and are willing to help out. Other localities in Perry County that have troops are: Leatherwood, Whitt Cinnamon, Scoutmaster; Hardburly has two troops, Karl Gettman is Scoutmaster of the white troop, and Leo McBee, Scoutmaster of the Negro troop; Tribbey, Earnest Messer, Scoutmaster; Montgomery Creek (Kodak and Barridge) Truby Hall, Scoutmaster; Allock, Robert Taylor, Scoutmaster; Town Mountain (Hazard, Negro) Calloway Combs, Scoutmaster; Hazard (Negro) Walter Drake, Scoutmaster, and there is at present one Cub Pack in Hazard, of which Beecher Scutchfield is Cubmaster. Several other troops are under organization in the county, including Daisy, Slemp and others.

Many boys have attained the rank of Eagle Scout, and have testified to the wonderful help Scouting gave them in World War II. At present there are three active Eagle

Scouts in the Hazard District, all of them from Troop 90, Belvin Ewen, Franklin Brabson and Eddie Grigsby.

Much optimism is felt for the future of Scouting in this area because under the excellent leadership of the present Scout Executive, John I. Dan of Pikeville, the council is showing great gains. With the leasing last summer of a new Council Summer Camp, on the new Dewey Dam Reservoir in Floyd County, the Scouts of this area will have, in a few years, one of the finest summer camps in this part of the country. Yes, Scouting has played an important part in the history of Perry County."

Charlie Johnson, a Kentucky Colonel, of Hazard, Kentucky, was recently named chairman of the Kentucky River District of the Lonesome Pine Council of the Boy Scouts of America. Colonel Johnson was at one time a miner in Perry County coal mines and was injured in a mine accident in 1929. Since that time he has been confined to a wheelchair, from which he has conducted many worthwhile civic and business activities.

Perry County Red Cross Chapter

A charter was granted on May 5, 1918, to the Perry County Chapter of the American Red Cross, with M. E. Brown as Chapter Chairman and Miss Kittie Read (Mrs. H. C. Powell) as the first Executive Secretary. The second was Miss Eva Smith and the present Secretary is Mrs. Allie D. Gorman, who has held this position since 1945. This is the only paid office, all other workers serving on a voluntary basis.

Major activities during the past years were the care given to more than one-third of the population who were incapacitated by the influenza epidemic of 1918 and the valuable assistance given the people who were made homeless by the devastating flood of May, 1927. The needs of the armed forces were met in every respect in both of the world wars, and in the present Korean conflict.

The chapter made history in the drive for funds when on March 13, 1947, the goal of $9,000.00, plus an additional

$3,000.00. was raised between the hours of 9:00 a. m. and 6:00 p. m. The late F. L. Cisco, Fund Drive Chairman, assisted by Lee Crutchfield, secured the cooperation of radio station WKIC, and also of its advertisers in the matter of time on the air. Throughout the day, lawyers, clergymen, business men, laborers, teachers, civic leaders and housewives appealed to the public for contributions.

In the past year, the chapter has participated in the blood program. The first visit was made by the mobile unit on February 20, 1952. One hundred and twenty workers were trained throughout the county to help with this work, and during the summer, nine high school and college girls have been trained as staff aids.

The following have served as Chapter Chairmen: M. E. Brown, W. E. Faulkner, the late G. M. Saufley, the late Jesse Morgan, the late Eli H. Brashear, the late E. B. Lovern, who served fifteen years, Dewey Daniel, M. C. Napier and the present Chairman, Roy G. Eversole.

Other early workers were the late William Engle, the late Dr. A. M. Gross, W. W. Reeves, Mrs. C. B. Luttrell, Miss Bertha Lyttle, the late Mrs. R. L. Goad, the late Mrs. L. C. Hibler, Mrs. Rose Foreman, J. M. Johnson and John Baker.

Future Growth

The hoped-for growth of Perry County in the future may be expressed by quoting William Sturgill, Executive Secretary of the Hazard Coal Operators Association in a talk reviewed by the **Hazard Herald** of August 13, 1952: "The Hazard market must be broadened if we are to have a prosperous field . . . Hazard has only one marketing area. the corridor north and west of the Ohio River. To broaden the markets it is necessary to get into the south where five million tons were consumed last year, and not a pound of it mined in Perry County. We must, through some medium, place Hazard coal at the Tidewater, where we might get foreign export trade."

To bring this about, the mountain section needs lower freight rates, improved facilities on the Kentucky River for shipping and a direct railroad connection with Southern lines.

CHAPTER IV

FOLKWAYS AND CUSTOMS
Edna Ritchie

Perry County has a rich heritage of folkways and traditions, some of which are still common today, and some of which are dying out. There are various local versions of "set-running," which is a Kentucky form of the square dance; there are dozens of play-party games the early settlers used to enjoy at their parties; there are ballads, there is the dulcimer, a native mountain instrument; there are the log-rollings, corn-hoeings, bean-stringings, quilting parties and all the various forms of the "working" which literally turned working into play.

In many local communities, set-running is almost a thing of the past, but on some of the remote creeks, the young folk still gather in each others' homes and go through the figures of the old time square dance. The dance usually begins with the introductory figure, "Circle Left." Some of the figures are "Shoot the Owl," "Lady 'round the lady," "Ocean wave," "Little side door," "Right hand shake" and "Ladies, bow, Gents know how" and dozens of others.

Play-party games with singing accompaniment were very popular in earlier times, especially in groups where fiddle or banjo music was not allowed or not available. Many of these were "choosing-in" games, and were played as many times as there were couples in the ring, until each boy had a partner. Some of the games were kissing games; others were more related to the dance, either longways or in circular formation. Some, such as "Charlie" and "Going to Boston" were done in both the circle and longways positions in turn.

Many of the ballads sung in Perry County are the ones brought directly from England by the early settlers. For a long time they were not written down but were handed on by oral tradition, which caused them to become somewhat changed in repetition, but they still tell the same story. Many of these ballads have been collected and put into book form. Folk songs are classified in various ways.

Probably the two most prominent types are the regular ballad, or long narrative poem which tells a story—often tragic, and the Southern folk-hymn, or white spiritual which is still sung in Primitive and Old Regular Baptist churches. Other divisions might be work songs, courting songs, nonsense songs, songs of deserted love and children's songs. The traditional folk ballad is characterized by having short four-line stanzas, with the fourth line sometimes repeated. The melody is usually simple, and often in a minor key. Some of the best known ballads are "Barbara Allen," "The Turkish Lady," "Lord Randall," "Edward," and "The Demon Lover."

Songs such as the following one are still sung in some of the local county churches.

> "Guide me, O Thou Great Jehovah,
> Pilgrim through this barren land
> I am weak, but Thou art mighty
> Hold me with Thy powerful hand.
> Bread of Heaven, feed me till I want no more,
> Bread of Heaven, Bread of Heaven,
> Feed me till I want no more."

The melody used by the Old Regular Baptist Church for this hymn is one of the oldest of Southern folk hymn-tunes. It is in a minor key, and is sung slowly, which makes it both mournful and hauntingly beautiful. It is only one of many such melodies sung today. The preacher, or leader "lines out" the hymns, that is, he says a line then the congregation sings it. They use no accompaniment, but the sound of their voices embellishes the melody with quavering sounds impossible to write into music.

Probably the best instrument for accompanying folk songs is the dulcimer, a native mountain instrument. It has three strings, and is lute shaped. The tone is soft and delicate. The player slides a smooth stick up and down the frets with the left hand (using the first string only) and picks all three strings with a sharpened goose quill held in the right hand. Perry County has produced one dulcimer-maker, "Uncle" Will Singleton, of Viper, Kentucky, who died at the age of ninety-one, in 1950. Dozens of his dulcimers are in use, not only in the mountains, but all over the county. Other well known dulcimer makers live in nearby counties.

The following is a good description of a country "working." One neighbor has a field of corn that needs hoeing out, so he asks all his neighbors to come and help him. They all go, taking their plows, mules, horses and children. All the men and young folks who are big enough help plow or hoe the corn while the women cook dinner—and what a dinner! There are chicken and dumplings, "shucky beans," green beans, potato salad, turnip greens, onions, cornbread, sweet potatoes, roasting ears, jam, jelly, egg-batter, cakes, pies, puddings and plenty of strong black coffee to wash it down. The men and boys eat first so they can get back to work; the children and young people are served and finally the women gather around the table and have a good visit while they eat, as they don't have to hurry. When they finish, they leave the food on the table, and wash up the remaining dishes. It doesn't take all of the women to wash dishes, so some of them go to work on a quilt, made of hundreds of brightly colored squares and triangles. The underside, or lining, of the quilt is made of feed sacks that have been dyed a bright color. Between the top and bottom there is a thin layer of cotton padding to make the quilt soft and warm. Much talk, laughter and gossip have been exchanged over a quilt. There is always a new baby to be welcomed, an operation to be described or a school problem to be discussed. As soon as the corn field is hoed out, the men and boys eat supper then hurry home quickly to do their chores and "spruce up" for the party. It is customary for the man holding the "working" to let the young people play at his house. Meanwhile the girls are flying around, giggling, singing and getting dressed in their clean starched dresses. On the edge of dark, they gather again. One room is cleared of furniture. Someone says, "Let's play 'Susan Girl,'" so the young folks join hands in a circle. One girl gets in the middle while the others circle and sing:

1. Golden ring around Susan-girl (3 times)
   All the way around Susan-girl.

On verse 2, the circle turns back to the right.

2. Pretty little black-eyed Susan-girl (3 times)
   All the way around Susan-girl.

On the third verse, the center girl does a right and left hand swing around the circle.

3. Break that ring to see her swing (3 times)
   All around Susan-girl.

Then someone suggests "Cedar Swamp," so the young people line up in a long-ways formation and do a reel similar to the Virginia reel as they sing:

"Way low down in Cedar Swamp
Water's deep and muddy
There I spied a pretty little miss,
There I kissed my honey;

Swing a lady up 'n down.
Swing a lady home,
Swing a lady up 'n down,
Swing a lady home!"

The door opens and in comes Jake with his fiddle and Tom with his banjo. "Git yer pardners, boys, and let's get a set a-goin'!" "In a short time about six couples are on the floor, shuffling their feet, waiting for the call. The caller, who is the leading man in the set, calls, "Circle left," as the musicians pitch into "Cripple Creek" or "Turkey in the Straw." After a few introductory figures, the caller and his partner lead off into

"Lady 'round the lady and the gent also,
Lady 'round the gent and the gent don't go"

Each couple in turn does the same figure, after which the leader does a new one. It is said that folks could dance all night and not repeat a figure.

During the dancing, the older folks have probably gathered on the front porch or in another room—usually telling "hant" tales. Someone always tells about the "hant" that would jump up behind a horseback rider and ride "a piece" with him, then disappear.

Other forms of the "working" are the stir-offs, apple-peelings, bean-stringings, and corn huskings, which usually take place after supper. Probably the most familiar one in this section of the country is the bean-stringing. If the beans are to be canned, the strings are pulled from them and they are broken into small pieces. If they are to be dried, the strings are pulled off and they are strung with a needle onto a large twine string and later hung behind the kitchen stove to dry and become "shucky beans." After the beans are strung, the youngsters are allowed to have a fight with the strings.

In winter the candy-pullings are popular. Partners generally pull candy together. Most of it is eaten before it is finished!

Hunting is still popular, but it is not done in large parties as much as formerly. In the old days, groups of people, young and old, would follow the 'possum dogs into the woods, sometimes catching several 'possums in one night. According to the "Ground-hog Song," the whole family enjoyed the sport. Probably no other song is so full of Kentucky mountain flavor. Following are the words of this ballad:

"THE GROUND-HOG SONG"

1. Whet up your knife and whistle up your dogs,
   Whet up your knife and whistle up your dogs,
   We're off to the woods to hunt ground-hogs,
   Whack fal doodle all day!
2. Too many rocks and too many logs (repeat)
   Too many rocks for to hunt ground-hogs
   Whack fal doodle all day!
3. Over the hills and through the bresh (repeat)
   There we struck that hog-sign fresh,
   Whack fal doodle all day!
4. Work, boys, work as hard as you can tear (repeat)
   The meat'll do to eat and the hide'll do to wear
   Whack fal doodle all day!
5. Up stepped Berry with a ten-foot pole (repeat)

>'Rousting around in that ground-hog hole
>   Whack fal doodle all day!
6. Up stepped Kate and stood right there (repeat)
    Till Berry twisted out some ground-hog hair
        Whack fal doodle all day!
7. Work, boys, work for all you can earn (repeat)
    Skin him tonight and tan 'im in a churn
        Whack fal doodle all day!
8. Kate and Berry kept prizin' about (repeat)
    Till at last they got that ground-hog out,
        Whack fal doodle all day!
9. Took him by the tail and wagged 'im to a log (repeat)
    Swore, by grab, he's a very fine hog
        Whack fal doodle all day!
10. Put 'im in a pot 'n' the younguns begin to smile (repeat)
    They et thet ground-hog fore it struck abile
        Whack fal doodle all day!
11. Up stepped Sal with a snigger and a grin (repeat)
    Ground hog grease all over her chin
        Whack fal doodle all day!

There are efforts being made to preserve the best of the mountain traditions. Some of the less desirable ones are going out, along with feuding and the one-room log cabin (many modern writers intimate that all mountaineers still live in one room log houses and wring out meagre sustenance from a rocky hillside; actually one room log houses are becoming increasingly scarce in Perry County). By supporting and encouraging worthwhile organizations such as the Council of Southern Mountain Workers, The Southern Highlanders Handicraft Guild and the Berea Mountain Festival, much can be done towards preserving, utilizing and enjoying our native mountain culture.

CHAPTER V

Industries

SALT

Eunice Tolbert Johnson

Salt making was the first industry of Perry County. A road law of January 28, 1817, mentions salt works on the North Fork of the Kentucky River. [1]

The first post office in Perry County was located at Alexander Patrick's salt works in 1822. In a mortgage of 1832-1834 he mentions his "bored salt well and 55 kittles" on it. The court records show that in 1833 he had a grist and saw mill on Troublesome Creek. In the November term of court in 1836 it was ordered that a road be surveyed from Patrick's salt works to the mouth of Troublesome Creek and in 1836 he received land grants on Lost Creek, Lost Fork, Caney Creek and Troublesome Creek. Therefore, from the above information his salt works must have been located near the mouth of Troublesome Creek which was then Perry County. A settlement was already on Troublesome Creek when Perry County was formed and it is reasonable to believe that the post office and the salt works were both located at that point.

It is fairly certain that Henley Haddix owned the works on Troublesome Creek which were situated one and one-half miles upstream near the mouth of Lost Fork, since the Haddix family has always lived in the area surrounding the mouth of Lost Creek. A motion was made in Perry County Court in November, 1832, to change the road to run from the mouth of Troublesome Creek to Henley Haddix's Salt Licks "as it would be a great convenience to the people traveling there to get salt." In 1838 this well had a daily capacity of ten bushels. The brine obtained at 240 feet produced a bushel of salt from 100 gallons of water. This is probably the establishment referred to in the census of 1840 as in Breathitt, with a production of seventy bushels and three men employed. [2]

In September, 1833, the court ordered that a road be

surveyed from the mouth of Troublesome to George Calimeese's salt furnace. This was to include all the land from the mouth of Francis Branch, and all the land on both sides of the river, to the upper end of Joseph Spencer's field.

In 1836 the Kentucky House Journal[3] refers to a number of salt works then operating in the Kentucky River Valley, among which were two located near the mouth of Lick Branch and one near the mouth of Troublesome Creek.

Also mentioned in the 1836 House Journal was one salt works at the mouth of Leatherwood Creek and a well partly bored at Hazard. Elijah Combs owned the well at Hazard. It was located where the Central Hotel now stands and the furnace and kettles for boiling it down were in the lot beside the hotel. An excellent brine was obtained at 400 feet, yielding a bushel of salt from 85 gallons of water but "the manufacture was short-lived because of local competition."

The works at Leatherwood were opened in 1835 by General White and Colonel Brashear and for a time produced 250 bushels a week, which was considered ample for local demand. In 1838 there was a capacity of fifty bushels a day and sufficient water for a yield of three times that amount. In 1840 it represented a capital investment of $18,000. Eleven men were employed and there was an annual output of 7,000 bushels.

In 1854 salt was reached at the mouth of Leatherwood at 100 feet, but not very strong; the borings were afterwards sunk by Brashear to 410 feet, at which depth a fine brine was yielding, when economically worked, a bushel of salt from 65 to 70 gallons of water.[4]

W. J. Cope owned and operated one on Troublesome in 1860. Mr. Ward and Wiley O. Davis went to Lost Creek in Breathitt in 1860 and made salt. Mr. Ward sold his interest to Mr. Davis and went back to Virginia, as talk of war began. Mr. and Mrs. Walter Nichols had salt works on Leatherwood about this time.

These establishments on Leatherwood and Troublesome were opened occasionally until the railroad came into the valley, but the production was never more than sufficient for local demand. Until the railroad reached Jackson, the price of salt in this section was at times one dollar a bushel.

Around 1900, most of Perry County obtained salt from Goose Creek in Clay County, where salt of the best quality had been manufactured since 1800. A man would ride his horse, leading several others behind him, to Goose Creek and return with each horse bearing a load of salt for his neighbors.

The first road was opened from Hazard to Manchester so people could go for salt. Bates salt works in Clay County was particulary known to residents of Perry County, as he had a bull known as "Bates Bull" which was used to pull his customers out of the mud. Salt-making lasted longer in the Kentucky River Valley than in any section of the state.

LUMBER

Eunice Tolbert Johnson

When the early settlers came to Perry County, they found trees of all kinds native to Kentucky growing in abundance. Unfortunately, to the pioneers of Perry County, as to the pioneers of any other frontier, they were an obstacle that had to be cleared away before the land could be used, and since there was no market, the finest old trees were burned to make way for farming. Old settlers can remember today seeing great piles of black walnut and tulip trees being burned, simply because that was the easiest way to get rid of them. Then, too, it made them feel safer from attacks of the Indians and the wild animals to have clearings between their homes and the wilderness. The clearing of land for farming and the burning of timber caused the greatest waste of the forest. Early mining operations used very little timber, but as mining increased the toll grew larger. Early logging operations destroyed many of the young trees in the injuries they received and the fires that followed. The pioneers let the livestock forage in the woods, trampling down the young trees, and also burned the woods in the winter in the belief that it improved the growth of spring grasses. — (Kentucky Resources, chap. 4.)

Fire had become such a menace in some counties of Kentucky that early in the nineteenth century laws were passed applying especially to these counties. By an Act approved February 22, 1834, the setting on fire of woods in Perry, Clay and adjoining counties imposed as penalty for such an offense a fine of forty dollars, if a free man and a whipping not to exceed 39 lashes if a slave. In spite of these laws, fires continued to occur.

Mr. Walter Green, District Forester, has this to say of the work being done in Perry County today to protect the timber lands, which are in a depleted condition: "The first organized Forest Fire Control work in Perry County was started in 1947. In 1948 the Perry County Fiscal Court voted county-wide forest fire protection agreement, under the Enabling Act, passed by the 1946 General Assembly. Under this agreement, the county paid one cent per acre on 169,459 forested acres in this county, and this amount was matched by State and Federal funds. The cost of perfecting an adequate organization greatly exceeded this amount. The excess cost was borne by the Division of Forestry. A new county-wide five-year agreement took effect on July 1, 1949. This agreement was negotiated under a new law enacted by the 1948 Legislature. The yearly cost of protection was increased to two cents per acre; this is about one-fourth of the actual cost of adequate protection. In 1948, the Buckhorn Forest Fire Protective Unit was formed, this unit consisting of Perry and Breathitt counties with a total area of 417,759 acres.

The present fire control organization in the county consists of a Forest Ranger, one Seasonal Guard, two Improvement and Maintenance men, three Lookout Tower watchmen, and about 40 Forest Wardens. The Seasonal Guard, I&M men and Tower Watchmen are employed 6 months out of each year. The Forest Wardens are public spirited citizens, particularly interested in forest protection, who receive only a small hourly wage for the time they are actually fighting fires.

The three Lookout Towers are located on the highest points in the county, and overlook the entire county. Lost Mountain Tower is located at the head of Lost Creek, near Harveyton, Kentucky; Dixon Branch Tower is at the head of Dixon Branch, near Fusonia, Kentucky, and Jack's Point Tower is at the head of Big Willard Creek on the Perry and Leslie county lines.

In order to get our land back in timber, some reforestration should be done. But in most cases, cleared land will reseed from natural reproduction, if it is kept free from fires."

It is estimated that nine out of ten forest fires today are caused by carelessness; other waste that continues is that land much too steep for cultivation continues to be cleared for farming.

According to Mr. Paul Keen, the county agent, a program to improve reforestration started in 1949. Last year (1952) a total of 32,000 pine, walnut and locust seedlings were planted by the farmers and the 4-H Clubs. Homeplace had a reforestration project eleven years ago and set out around 2,000 pine seedlings.

The First Tax Book of Perry County at the Kentucky Historical Society shows that as early as 1822, land in Perry County was selling for $2.00 to $10.00 per acre. This was probably in the valleys, as most land grants were for level land only. In 1836 the Perry County Court was authorized by the state to sell all vacant lands in Perry County. These were called Kentucky Land Warrants; tracts of 50 acres were sold for $2.50 and 100 acre tracts brought $5.00. These tracts were mostly in the mountains.

In 1837 and 1854 good timber land could be bought in Perry County for $5.00 to $10.00 an acre.[1] In 1854 Collins History of Kentucky in the sketch of Perry County says that vacant land in Perry belonging to the state was reduced to $2\frac{1}{2}$ cents an acre.

The Federal Census taken in 1870 at the end of the first half-century of Perry's existence as a County showed that Perry had 254,571 acres at the average value of $1.29 per acre.[2] Around 1897, farming and logging employed the most labor and average wage paid was from $15.00 to $20.00 a month.⁽³⁾

In 1896, land around Hazard sold for around $5.00 an acre; the settlers wanted it for lumber, for even though they knew the value of its mineral rights, they did not expect it to be developed in their time.

In 1945, the value of farm lands, including woodlands (not the acres in the towns) sold for the average price of $26.46 per acre, according to the United States agricultural census. Today (1951) timber land in Perry County sells from $10.00 to $100.00 per acre. Most of the hardwood in the accessible areas of Perry County has been cut. However, the Ritter Lumber Company, one of the largest in the South, is in full operation on Leatherwood Creek. More timber has been sold in Perry County since 1945, the boom year, than in all its history, according to Mr. Paul Keen, the present County Agent.

The latest survey shows that Perry County now (1950) has 219,520 acres. Seventy-seven per cent or 169,459 acres of this is in timber. Perry County has an area of 343 square miles.⁽⁴⁾

It is not known when the first logs were taken out of Perry County. In 1835 the Board of Internal Improvement shows in their report that there were from 3,000 to 5,000 logs shipped from the vicinity of the three forks of the Kentucky River.

A trip into Perry County when all the land was still virgin timber, and just what kinds of lumber were being sold is best described in the words of T. E. Moore, Jr., of Hazard, who made his first trip into Perry County in 1896, on horseback.

"I was sent on my first trip to Perry County in July, 1896, on horse back by J. M. Thomas of Paris, Kentucky, for the purpose of viewing some timber on Leatherwood, and if I desired to purchase any for him, to examine the titles. Mr. Thomas had come into Perry in 1880 and purchased in fee about 15,000 acres of virgin timberland on Leatherwood and its waters at about $1.00 an acre, which he afterwards sold to the Kentucky Union Land Company.

J. M. Thomas was an experienced lumberman; he first operated a sawmill in Clay City, which he sold. About 1888 he acquired the Ford Lumber and Manufacturing Company, at Ford, on the Kentucky River in Clarke County, which he operated until his death in 1905. His mill sawed about 100,000 poplar logs annually. Also at that time there was a larger saw mill at Ford owned by the Burt-Brabb Lumber Co. Floyd Day was president and had control of a large saw mill company which operated mills in Jackson, Beattyville, and Clay City under the name of Swan-Day Lumber Co. It bought and sawed around 200,000 logs annually at its three plants. There were other mills at Valley View and Frankfort. The saw mills bought only poplar timber, which was floated in loose logs on the tides down the river and caught by the purchasers at their mills in log booms. These booms would hold from 20,000 to 50,000 logs. That was cheap transportation. Practically no oak timber was sold and little sawed. Oak could only go to the mills in rafts; one poplar log between two oak logs throughout the raft would float, otherwise oak was too heavy and would sink.

These rafts were run down the river as the tide began to recede. The poplar logs were sawed in 12, 14 and 16 foot lengths and were graded in two classes, depending upon the measurement of the logs, which were measured by Doyle's Rule, according to the least diameter at the small end of the log inside the bark. If the log had no defects or only one knot and was 24 inches or larger, it was graded as first class. Anything below 24 inches, to 18 inches was second class, even though it was a perfect log. The second class logs were cut for defects and crooks. When measured according to Doyle's Rule an allowance was made for slabs and sawdust, therefore a log gained at the mill over and above its actual content.

In 1896 first class logs were $9.00 a thousand feet and second class logs were $6.00. Around 1900 these prices were raised to $10.00 and $7.00 per thousand feet, and in 1903 the prices rose to $11.00 and $8.00. They rose to higher values, but by that time the great body of poplar had been cut or was owned by some company.

In 1890, John D. White, of Clay County who was at one time a Congressman from this large Eastern Kentucky District, purchased 10,000 poplar trees on the waters of Leatherwood and Line Fork for $1.00 each. These trees belted seven feet and up, inside the bark, and three feet above the ground on the upper side. Later the Ford Lumber Manufacturing Company purchased these trees at $5.00 each. In 1889 he also purchased one-fourth interest in 1600 acres of land in fee on Lotts Creek, which he afterwards sold to the Kentucky River Coal Corporation.

Charles W. Bowman, who was a well known resident of this county, was the buyer for the Burt-Brabb Lumber Company in Perry County. As I recall, Richmond McIntyre was the Representative for the Swan-Day Lumber Company for purchasing and measuring its logs.

W. J. Roberts, who was known as "Son Roberts," father of Mrs. E. C. Wooton, also bought a great many logs which were sawed at Frankfort. He was the son of Farmer Roberts, who lived at the mouth of Big Creek in Leslie County.

The purchasers of these logs made separate contracts, generally, with each individual land owner, but there were some exceptions. The firm of A. B. Asher and Henry Hensley bought a great many logs by making contracts with the land owners and then had contracts with the mill companies at $1.00 per thousand higher than the price they paid the land owner. The Ford Lumber and Manufacturing Company bought 10,000 to 20,000 logs a year from that firm over a period of seven years.

The rafts were a very small per cent of the logs that were sawed and were not purchased by the mill companies until they arrived at the mill. There was always some uncertainty about whether or not the rafts would get there, moreover the mill companies were not anxious to bother about the rafts; they were principally interested in the loose logs. These companies bought a great many standing trees, nearly always poplar, lynn and cucumber, and then made contracts to have them logged. About the only oak taken out of this country before the railroad came was what the citizens called "square sticks." These were cut from the very best white oak trees. A tree had to be straight and of perfect body, and the square stick was hewn from the trees and floated to Jackson. There it was loaded on trains for Quebec to be used in ship building.

Each saw mill had its own brand, which was on a large hammer. These brands were registered in each county wherein they purchased logs, and every log, when bought by the company, was branded with this brand for the purpose of identifying the logs when they floated down the river to the mills. For instance, the Ford Lumber and Manufacturing Company used a large white F painted on each end. The Bert-Brabb Lumber Company's brand was a circle-four and they also painted a large white circle on each end."

Not all logs were sent down the river loose; many of the settlers took them in rafts. The men would then walk back home, the trip often taking a week. They would be eagerly awaited, for they brought news from the outside world.

When all the poplar was gone they turned to white oak, using second class poplar to float the oak logs. Mr. R. O. Davis, who floated many rafts out, says that his grandfather, Elijah Cornett, took rafts down the river and had a steam saw and grist mill as early as 1875. This was probably the first steam mill in Perry County. He brought it to his farm, 3½ miles south of Hazard (near the Glomawr bridge), on push boats.

It is tradition in the Cornett family that a man from Mason's Creek was bringing corn to be ground when he heard the steam whistle blow, and he became so frightened that he collapsed when he reached the mill. He had not known about the new mill, and said that he thought it was Gabriel blowing his horn, and the Judgment Day had come.

J. L. Johnson brought the first steam mill with circular saw into Hazard in 1894. He had moved his mill from

Paintsville with oxen, up the creek beds and located at the mouth of Odgen Creek in Knott County. When he finished his contract to saw walnut logs for the Singer Sewing Machine Company, he moved to the mouth of Lotts Creek in Perry County. In 1897, W. O. Davis and D. Y. Combs, seeing the great need for lumber, persuaded him to move to Hazard. He set his mill up on Main Street and his lumber yard reached from the bridge on the river side of Main Street up to where the Major Store now stands. He built kilns and seasoned the lumber by stacking it and building fires beneath. He sawed all the lumber that built early Hazard. He was the founder of what is now the Home Lumber Company.

Today lumbering in Perry County ranks second only to coal in cash income.

COAL

Jane McKenna Gallaher

Discovery of Coal

Coal in what is now Perry County might have been discovered by Christopher Gist in his famous exploring expendition in 1751 when he came into this country as a land scout for the newly organized Ohio Land Company of Virginia. In his journal under entry of March 27, 1751, he records, "On all branches of the little Cuttaway River was great plenty of fine coal, some of which I brought to the Ohio Company."[1] The Cuttaway River was possibly the North Fork of the Kentucky River, and this being true Gist was most likely in what is now Perry County.

Just when the first coal was mined in Perry County is unknown. The settlers who first reached this area no doubt used some of the natural outcroppings in their domestic affairs. A lack of industrial development and transportation facilities left the big scale development for the future. Early records indicate a consciousness of the existence and value of the rich coal deposits. An early deed recorded in 1824 in Perry County Deed Book describes a land transfer from Jeremiah Combs to Samuel Combs as "being on the north side of the North Fork of the Kentucky River beginning in the middle of a certain coal bank . . ." This land was near the Grand Vue Drive-In on Highway 80. Other early deeds contain the same type of descriptions.

Coal Boats

Construction of coal boats was an art within itself. Large poplar logs were sawed in halves and fastened together to form rafts on which sides were erected to a height of 6 to 8 feet. The whole boat resembled a floating box car when completed. These boats were caulked with tow, being the refuse from flax, and the sides of the boat were reinforced with heavy "post timbers" and baled with heavy flax and hemp ropes. The boats varied in size, but most were 60 to 70 feet long, about 8 feet deep and 14 feet wide, holding from 1,750 to 3,000 bushels of coal. In the **Senate Journal** of Kentucky, 1838-1839, page 258, Mr. W. W. Mathers states 30 bushels of coal equal one ton. A cat-walk was constructed around the sides of the boat where three to ten men would stand with poles and oars to guide the boat down the river; usually one man on each side with poles and one at back with an oar were sufficient. The occupation of boat construction and coal digging was carried on in the fall and winter when there was no farming to be done. When the coal boat was loaded, it was anchored securely, awaiting the spring floods and swift current to "ride" the boat all the way to Clay's Ferry —some went to Frankfort. Under normal conditions the boats would average 4 to 5 miles per hour and make the run to Boonesboro or Clay's Ferry in 24 hours. The boat was sold with the coal and the men walked home! The river was full of rocks and debris and some boats wrecked before they had traveled far. No person was ever remembered to have drowned in such accident. At the most, 5 or 6 boats met such fate on the North Fork of Kentucky River as best as anyone remembers. The early settlers had their slaves construct and man these coal boats, but after the Civil War this work was carried on by only a few men so skilled. It seems a part of the boat was constructed bottom upwards and then turned into the river for completion. "Boat turning" became quite a social event after the Civil War. All the men for miles up and down the river gathered to help the builder turn his boat. All the friends then were feted with apple brandy and moonshine and all the news, gossip and jokes were exchanged. John Hensley, who lived on Second Creek at the time of this interview, said he had just married and was living on First Creek where the Kentucky Block mine was later opened when "Lurenzy" (Lorenzo) Combs built his last coal boat about 1881 or 1882 and he attended this boat turning and what a time nearly 50 men and boys had! To aid the boats through the shoals in the river, farmers who lived in the vicinity would pull the boats through with their oxen, as the oxen did not slip on the rocks.

First Mines and Primitive Methods

Dr. Josiah H. Combs, writes, "I've a hunch that Henry (Harrison) Combs, one of the eight brothers, moved the first coal down the river. He was a river man, building and running flat boats, even making improvements on them. Old Henry ran boats as far as New Orleans! And it must have been before 1828, as Henry moved to the mouth of Troublesome that year." The coal taken to market by Henry was mined from the montain side just across from the Airport on Highway 80. A. B. (Bige) Combs of Combs, Kentucky, said he could point out the old workings in the mountainside there. Another "mine" worked by the Nick Combs family at the same time is near the present Engle Mine on Highway 80. The old working can still be seen. This mine is mentioned on Page 117 of the **Journal** of the Senate (Ky.) 1838-1839, Report of W. B. Foster, Jr., resident engineer, to Sylvester Welsh, Esq., Chief Engineer of Kentucky, dated Frankfort, Ky., November 22, 1838:

"**North Fork of Kentucky River**—The point of commencing the survey being fixed by your instructions at the mouth of Leatherwood Creek, from the exit was continued down to the mouth of Middle Fork—a distance of 121.3 miles. The coal mines now opened and from which the principal shipments are made on this Fork are located

at the 22nd, 62nd, 66th, 74th and 81st mile respectively from the commencement of the survey. The first of these is situated on the south side of the river and about 60 feet above the plane of low water. It is 3½ feet thick and has been worked about 40 feet under the hill . . ."
The old workings still visible at the present Engle mine are exactly 22 miles from the mouth of Leatherwood Creek. Further in his report to the President of the Board of Internal Improvements, Mr. Foster elaborates:

"Coal is now carried out of this river in flat boats, some from a mile near Hazard (Elijah Cornett's mine) and from several points below . . ." These were the Combs, and further on the Duff and Johnson mines. Ira Duff of Chavies can point out the old pits where Major Duff's slaves extracted the coal. It was years later that the coal was mined near the same section by Thomas Johnson.

Coal was first mined by hand pick, as far back as a man could extend the pick to dig. Maybe several slaves would be used to dig the seam perhaps for fifty feet along the side of the hill. A cut was dug first under the seam and then a similar cut made at the top of the coal seam; then wooden wedges were driven in the top cut to break the coal down. The seam was worked no deeper into the side of the mountain than light and air could travel. As the working advanced the men on their knees loaded the coal onto little wooden wagons which had wood runners instead of wheels which were called sleds. The wagons were drawn out of the opening by the men and the coal dumped down a wooden chute into the coal boat. To aid the sight of the miners, big fat tallow candles, made at home, were used, a sharp contrast to modern electric miners' lamps. It is surprising to find on Page 39 of the **Senate Journal** of Kentucky, 1835-1836:

"Reports of the Assistant Engineer of his operations in 1835 to the Board of Internal Improvements, dated Frankfort, Kentucky, 12-27-1835: The explorations which have already been made of the minerals with which this neglected region abounds have discovered coal, salt, nitre and copperas in such vast quantites that the future supply of them might be enumerated by the word inexhaustible. The coal region commences a few miles below the Junction of the Three Forks and extends up along and beyond the heads of each of them. The principal veins that are now mined and which have ineffectually supplied the markets of Lexington and Frankfort are near the mouth of the South Fork, near the mouth of Troublesome, 60 miles up the North Fork where it is found in better quality than in any other part of the United States, and near Perry Court House (Hazard), 50 miles higher up the same Fork. The quantity of this article brought to market during the last boating season amounted to 75,000 bushels and sold for nearly $9,000. Signed N. B. Buford, Civil Engineer."

Not every man was adept or capable of handling these coal boats. While there may have been others, it seems that Henry, Danger Nick, Bird-eye Nick and Jeremiah Combs were the first to mine coal and Henry and Bird-eye took it down the river to market. Alex, Bird-eye's older son learned this business. Alex lived near Combs, Kentucky, his house having stood on the site of the Manuel Combs property. After Alex grew older, his son, Robert, ran a few coal boats. "He lived just above the site of the present lumber mill at Combs, Kentucky," said John Hensley. Ike Hurt would dig the coal for Robert from an opening on George's Branch and William, Benton and Ray Combs would help Robert build and load the boats. Also about this time Lorenzo, Alex Combs' youngest brother, became a great boatman. He was known all over the river for his expertness in handling these coal boats. He was aided in the construction of his boats by his cousins, Shelby Combs of Big Creek and Thornton Crawford. Lorenzo took a boatload of coal out to market each year for thirteen years; the last boat was taken to market about 1882.

Mrs. Mary Combs, who lives with her daughter, Mrs. Liza Grigsby, on Lotts Creek, remembers that her husband, Elhanon S. Combs, dug one boatload of coal out of Spruce Pine Mountain (near Combs, Ky.) which he took to market in 1873. He sold the boat and coal in Frankfort for $50 and walked home!

Farther down the river, Major John A. Duff, who settled at Chavies, ran a few coal boats to market long before the Civil War. Ira Duff of Chavies can point out the old pits worked by Major's slaves. Later Alex Duff, who lived on Sam's Branch just above Napfor, took one or two boatloads of coal down the river about 1875.

In the upper part of the North Fork of the Kentucky River (near Glomawr) Elijah Cornett, grandfather of Mrs. A. N. Peters, was the only man in that section to mine and ship his coal down the river. Just when he began or when he stopped this enterprise is not certain, but he was born in Perry County in 1821 and died in 1916, so no doubt he and Alex and Lorenzo Combs met on the river many times. He is supposed to have been the last man to take a boat of coal to market. John "Tight" Combs said a coal boat "Lige" took down the river hit a snag and wrecked, but no one was drowned. Lige's sons, Ben and Dan helped their father.

In the **Senate Journal** of Kentucky, 1838-1938, W. W. Mather wrote his report to Governor Clark, dated December 28, 1838:

"The coal formation occupies about 7,000 square miles in the eastern part of Kentucky. 200,000 bushels of coal descended the Kentucky River to Frankfort and other towns on the river this past year. Coal averaged in price 10 cents per bushel . . . Each boat averages 3,000 bushels of coal."

Before the Civil War little cash outlay was necessary to get a boat of coal to market, so the profit was a handsome return of the owner's natural resources. After the War, when wages of 2½ cents per bushel were paid to mine the coal, $1.00 per day for sawing the necessary timber, etc., and boat construction, the profit dwindled. The river shipments of coal reached their maximum in 1847, dwindling to almost nothing in 1880 and ceasing altogether in 1884 due to the fact that the Louisville and Nashville Railroad Company had completed its extension, connecting Cincinnati, Lexington and Knoxville and opening up the market to those Tennessee coal mines.

Surveys

Unknown to most residents of Perry County in 1838, the eyes of the State were already focused on this area. On February 16, 1838, Governor James Clark approved the Senate resolution establishing the first Geological Survey, appointing William Williams Mather the first State Geologist. Mather made a reconnaissance of this area that summer. The general industrial and financial depression of 1839 and 1840 plus the war with Mexico interrupted this enterprise and it was 1854 before the Second Geological Survey was undertaken by Dr. David Dale Owen. He traveled up the North Fork sometime during the summers of 1854-1855. Dr. Nathaniel Southgate Shaler was the third State Geologist. He surveyed this territory in 1875. The work done by these men was more or less preliminary and it was not until 1884 when James M. Hodge working under the State Geologist John Robert Proctor made a thorough investigation of the coal in Perry County. John B. Eversole says there was great excitement in Hazard when this Survey arrived. Mr. Eversole was about ten years old at the time and remembers the geological party spent the whole summer and way into fall going over every inch of the territory, up and down the mountains on every creek and branch. Mr. Hodge came back in 1907 to check the details of this survey but for some reason his report was not published until 1910. Also in 1879 the United States Army Engineers surveyed the waters of the Kentucky and its tributaries. They saw coal in the beds of creeks and the outcrop of veins in the hills as recorded in Report of Chief of Engineers, U.S.S., 1879, pp. 1411-16.

Leases and Land Companies

The early surveys and the incorporation in 1851 of the Kentucky Union Railway Company, proposing to build a line from Winchester, Ky., to Abington, Va., started a flurry of land patenting. The Civil War curtailed interest and it was in the early 1870's before actual sales of lands in 100,000 acre tracts began. According to Deed Book D of Perry County practically worthless land was sold in 1872 and 1874 for 26½ cents per acre. The surprising thing noted in these transactions was that the buyers as well as the sellers in most instances lived outside Kentucky—in fact several deeds covered sales made by owners living in England. A farseeing resident of Louisville, Ky., purchased 95,000 acres on November 7, 1874. However, a native Perry Countian, Elijah C. Morgan, the father of Mrs. A. M. Gross and Jesse Morgan, was County Surveyor at the time and he had the foresight to patent thousands of acres of "undesirable" hills which had been lying unwanted and unclaimed.

The first purchaser of mineral rights in this county was W. J. Horsley, who came to Hazard the summer of 1885. He was the most widely known, best remembered person. He was an imposing man of pleasing personality and about forty years old. Everyone remembers he had the handsomest head of thick, dark brown hair. He rode a fine, bay horse and carried two of the largest saddle bags ever seen in this section. He stayed at Combs' boardinghouse on Main Street and was aided by a Colonel Salyers. Horsley hired Lee Daniel, who was just a boy at the time, as courier and had the Court appoint him Deputy Clerk. During the two summers at this work, Horsley, agent for a group of Virginians and Tennesseans headed by T. P. Trigg of Abington, Va., obtained some 125 options and deeds at 50 cents per acre. The next summer, 1887, Mr. Trigg came with a corps of engineers, stenographers, legal counsel to execute deeds for these options. "The manner in which these sales were handled caused the French-Eversole Feud", according to A. R. Eckert. Thus Trigg and his associates acquired approximately 60,000 acres of coal lands and mineral rights which were deeded to their newly formed land company. This transaction increased the value of land in Perry County about $6.00 per acre. This land company by reorganization and expansion later became the present Virginia Iron and Coal Company.

The two men whose investments and influence were most instrumental in opening the Hazard coal field were C. Bascom Slemp, U. S. Senator from Virginia, and John C. C. Mayo, Paintsville, Ky. Their insistence that the L. & N. Railroad Company extend its line from Winchester, Ky., to their coal mine at McRoberts, Ky., brought transportation through Perry County. These men and others, individually and through their agents had acquired huge acreages of mineral in this area. Many land companies were organized from these holdings and, since the Slemp and Mayo holdings, were so extensive, these gentlemen became officers and stockholders in the larger percentage of the land companies. It was evident from the beginning to these gentlemen what legal entanglements this would arise and Mr. Slemp tried to organize a huge syndicate to purchase all these mineral rights in Perry County. That attempt failing, he did succeed in combining Kentucky River Consolidated Coal Co., Haly Coal Company, Slemp Coal Co., Rockhouse Realty Co., Hamilton Realty Co., Lost Creek Coal Co., Henry Coal & Coke Co., Tennis Coal Co., and a few smaller ones and forming the Kentucky River Coal Corporation in 1915 with W. S. Dudley as President. In 1928 this corporation acquired the large holdings of the Kentucky Union Railway Co. on Leatherwood and the acquisition in 1945 of the Swift Coal & Timber Co. lands on Leatherwood and Line Fork added considerable acreage to its holdings, making it the largest land company in this area. The other land companies currently leasing mineral rights to operating mining companies are: Virginia Iron and Coal Company, Hazard Coal Corporation, Alimar Coal Corporation and Nelson Coal Corporation; Fordson Coal Company, Peabody, Ky., Kycoga Land Co., Ashland Ky.; Vizard Investment Co., Birmingham, Ala.; Montgomery Coal Corp., Bristol, Va.; Grant Coal Co. and Chamberlain & Warren, Three Oaks, Mich. Besides these holdings, there are many thousands of acres of coal lands retained by their individual owners; some of this land is under lease to mining companies, while some is still undeveloped, due mainly to the inaccessibility of the coal land to railroad or highway. Due to physical conditions, some coal lands can never be mined for economic reasons. No U. S. Geological Survey has been made of Perry County, but plans for this work are being made at which time it will be estimated the number of tons of coal in Perry County and the percentage recoverable will be ascertained. At the present time there are approximately two hundred thousand acres of coal under lease by mining companies from the land holding companies and in addition there is a considerable acreage under lease by mining companies from individual owners.

Wagon Mines

To supply the townspeople, several men engaged in digging coal on their property in the early 1870's and hauling it to Hazard in wagons. Vard Duff and Ike Hurt "raised" the coal for W. J. Combs on his farm near the mouth of Lotts Creek during the winter months of the years 1882 to 1885. Jerry Walker, who lived where Columbus Mining Co., Allais, Ky., is now, "Babe" Turner who lived on Highland Ave., mined coal and also had an ice plant at the foot of that street; John B. Eversole says his grandfather mined a little coal at the mouth of Messers Branch (where Blue Grass is now) and his father mined coal for their own use at home and sold a little to local trade. This coal was taken from the hill across the Kentucky River opposite the Lincoln Hotel. Also I. J. Francis had a mine for years on what is now Liberty Street; some of the workings are still evident. Jim Combs mined coal farther up on East Main Street—the old entrance to the mine is plainly visible back of the Gulf Station. Grant and John "Tight" Combs were great teamsters and hauled most of this coal at $1.00 per load. At first the coal sold at the mine for 5 cents per bushel, but from 1898 to the beginning of the railroad mines, the coal price was $1.00 per load plus $1.00 haulage.

Early Coal Operators

About 1910 many men, later identified with various coal mining companies in the field, came to Hazard to prospect and negotiate leases. Among these were John Gorman, J. Tim Moore, W. E. Davis, William Ellison, Jim Morrison, Jim Hoge who represented Congressman Slemp, J. B. Allen, engineer for Slemp; Walter Hull, representative of Virginia Iron and Coal Co.; P. T. Wheeler, Bailey P. Wooton, engaged in abstracting titles.

In 1912 E. G. Speaks and his two sons, James W. and E. L. Speaks arrived in a jolt wagon to open up a mine on Rev. A. S. J. Petrey's property in the Backwoods (Cedar St.). The Hazard Herald of April 11, 1912 carried this account:

"Messrs. E. G. Speaks and sons of Fonde, Tenn., have leased mining property at the edge of Town Branch to take effect May 1. They expect to be able to supply local demands and by the time the railroad reaches us the mine will be able to put quite a force to work."

This mine was a crude, hand-dug pit, using donkeys to pull the wooden sleds on which the coal was loaded inside. The coal was hauled as orders demanded by the Combs' brothers. It was soon discovered to the disappointment of all concerned that the railroad would never reach this section and the lease was soon abandoned. In the meantime, the railroad company bought considerable loads of coal to fire their engines used in completion of the line beyond Hazard. Also with the aid of the Combs' brothers wagons one railroad car was loaded with coal from this mine, described by Hazard Herald of October 7, 1912, as follows:

"The Speaks Coal Company is entitled to the credit of being the first coal company to make a coal shipment by rail from the Hazard field. It was a 40-ton car and billed to J. M. Kennon, a manufacturer at Clay City, Ky. It will not be long before the coal from this city will be counted by the trainloads instead of the carload."

This mine has been operated at various times by various men as a wagon or truck mine. It has not been worked in recent years, but the old workings are still visible behind Backwoods Grocery on Cedar Street.

The Hazard Herald on July 4, 1912, reported S. A. D. Jones had leased coal land from Leslie J. Combs. Under date of July 25, 1912, this same paper had this to say:

" S. A. D. Jones began work the first of the week erecting buildings and otherwise preparing for the coal operation which he and his brother, Will Jones, are putting in at the mouth of Gregory Branch, two miles above town. Prof. Jones is ambitious and a hustler and everyone will wish him every measure of success. He is the first local man to assume the arduous undertaking of installing and operating a mine and will put forth his very best efforts to make a go of it."

This mine was called Raccoon Coal Company with Post Office named Douglas, Ky., which was changed to Christopher when Columbus Mining Company bought this mine in 1915. Raccoon was the second mine in the Hazard field to have shipped a railroad car of coal to the outside world. Mrs. S. A. D. Jones, now residing in Pompton Lakes, N. J., had this to say of the operation:

"We used donkeys to pull the coal out of the mine,

dumping it onto the tipple which had no screen and then into the railroad cars. The depression was very bad in 1914. I have stood on the railroad track myself and flagged down a train to pull our coal when an order would come in. I ran the whole mine while my husband went on the road to sell coal. We were glad to sell Run of Mine coal that year at 90 cents per ton."

The third mine to ship a railroad car of coal to outside markets was Hazard Coal Company, organized by John Gorman, W. G. Polk and associates. J. Tim Moore had been successful in securing this lease for these men from Mr. and Mrs. J. L. Johnson (parents of Howard and Charlie) and Mr. and Mrs. J. E. Johnson, Sr., on April 29, 1913. Mr. Polk was General Manager and Perry Gorman, Superintendent. Mrs. Perry Gorman said she went as a bride to live at that coal company camp, which was just above the present location of the L. & N. Depot at Hazard. Several years later this mine was combined with its next-door neighbor, Hazard-Dean Coal Company, becoming Hazard-Blue Grass Coal Company, under the operation of J. E. Johnson, Sr. The Hazard Coal Co. mined its coal by air-driven punchers; ventilated by furnace and used mules to transport its coal from the mine to the tipple. It shipped its first coal in 1913 and soon had its own power plant which furnished electricity for its operation. In short it was the first electrically operated mine in the Hazard field and the first mine, therefore, to ship the prepared (screened) sizes of coal.

The fourth mine to start shipment of coal in the Hazard field was Kentucky Jewel Coal Company on a leasehold secured by W. E. Davis and Harry Bullock from Slemp Coal Company. This news was printed in the Hazard Herald of January 23, 1913. Kentucky Jewel Coal Company was fortunate to be located three miles from East Tennessee Coal Company, Glomawr, Ky., (now Eblen Coal Co.) being installed by Mr. W. E. Davis, and which had completed a power plant of sufficient capacity to sell power to Kentucky Jewel mine. Thus, Kentucky Jewel Coal Company was the first in the field to operate by electricity from its installation. It began to ship coal shortly after October 3, 1913. This company had a very long storage track; so more for a stunt than anything else, Mr. Bullock held up the shipment of his coal until he had a full trainload (about 30 cars) of coal on his storage track which shipment was pulled from his mine on April 1, 1915. In 1917 this mine was sold to the Pritchard interests and the name of the mine was changed to Algoma Block Coal Company under the able management of Dave Pritchard.

Many mining companies were organized in 1912, but it took time to construct a power plant, erect dwellings, install machinery; they did not begin shipments of coal for several years. Among these were Hazard-Dean Coal Co., organized by W. R. Marsee, S. R. Jennings, W.M. Jones, C. R. Luttrell; Himyar Coal Co., incorporated by T. L. Young, Louis des Cognets and others; East Tennessee Coal Company already mentioned; Ashless Coal Corporation organized by L N. Buford, Alvah Stone, Hugh Buford, D. T. Mitchell and others. Statistics at the end of this Chapter show the year in which the first companies began production.

The First Creek Branch line from Typo to Harveyton was not completed till 1916. Harvey Coal Corporation, Kentucky Block Coal Co., Blue Diamond Coal Co., First Creek Mining Co. (later acquired by Blue Diamond) and Crawford Coal Corporation began shipments over this line in the order in which they are listed.

In 1948 there were only three of the early coal operators continuing coal production; namely, W. E. Davis, H. K. English and J. E. Johnson, Sr. Mr. Johnson has the further distinction of being the only native Perry Countian to produce coal continuously through this period.

Each succeeding year saw an increase in the number of mines till 1922 when 65 mines reported tonnage to the State Department of Mines. However, the 65 mines produced only 4,280,981 tons of coal that year. The maximum tonnage was reached in 1926 by 50 mines producing 6,647,807 tons. Comparison of these figures shows that practically all mines had passed the development stage and were in the swing of full production. And strange as it may seem to those of us who saw the rush for coal, heard the hue and cry for coal during and after World War II, this tonnage produced in 1926 is the all time high production from the railroad mines in Perry County.

Truck Mines

During the great demand for coal, truck mines mushroomed over night it seemed, till in 1947 a total of 259 truck mines were reported in the Annual Report of Kentucky Department of Mines and Minerals for that year. This is a great increase over the first available report of that Department, dated October 10, 1889, covering the inspection of 28 mines in Perry County that year. Today, however, the output from truck mines is handled in new style. Until the last war, truck mines sold their coal for domestic use. Now, the truckers sell it to small railroad mines who ship it. Some mines almost exhausted found it more profitable to cease mining their own coal, buy from the trucker and run it over their tipple for loading into railroad cars. Other men bought abandoned mines for the tipples for screening and loading coal brought from trucks. Figures set down for comparison tell that, as this truck mine tonnage rose from 14,378 tons in 1940 to 856,887 tons in 1947, the running time and tonnage of the railroad mines decreased. In order to serve every shipper of coal on the line, the L. & N. Railroad Co. had to more or less pro-rate its supply of empty cars among all its customers. In the coal business, history repeats itself many times; down through the years, whenever the demand for coal was good, the reports disclose a distressing number of days of work have been lost for both the mines and men who work at them due to insufficient railroad car supply.

Statistics

The car loading reports of the L. & N. Railroad Co. show 1947 to have been the year of maximum car loading in the history of the Hazard field. Examination discloses this tonnage was not all produced in Perry County—Cutshin Coal Company and Smith Coal Company are in Leslie County, as so reported by the Kentucky Department of Mines and Minerals. The coal produced by these mines is trucked to Combs, Ky., in Perry County to the railroad, and thus counted in the L. & N. Railroad reports as coal loaded in Perry County. In 1947 the tonnages were accounted for as follows:

Loaded by railroad mines in Perry County, tons	5,895,894
Mined by truck mines in Perry County and sold to ramps for loading in railroad cars	856,887
Tons	6,752,781
Mined in Leslie County and trucked to railroad in Perry County	539,401
Tons	7,292,182

Due to mechanization of the mines and improvements in mining equipment, there was a great increase in the production per railroad mine over the 1926 tonnage. In 1947 only 27 railroad mines produced the 5,895,894 tons of coal. Reading some of the reports on the early mines' development, expenditure of $200,000 to install a mine seemed exorbitant. Today just a tipple costs millions of dollars.

Coal in Perry County is mined from the Nos. 9, 8, 7, 6, 5-A and 4 Seams of coal. Due to natural conditions, all of these seams are not found in every section of the field.

STATISTICS
COAL MINE PRODUCTION

Year 1912	Raccoon Coal Co., Hazard, Ky.	400 tons
	Bowman & Speaks	1,000
		1,400 tons
Year 1913	Hazard Coal Co., Hazard, Ky.	6,716 tons
	Ky. Jewel Coal Co.	3,203
	North Fork Coal Co.	750
	Raccoon Coal Co.	14,963
		25,632 tons
Year 1914	Hazard Coal Co., Hazard, Ky.	53,468 tons
	Hazard-Dean Coal Co., Hazard, Ky.	21,381
	Himyar Coal Corp., Domino, Ky.	54,313
	Ky. Jewel Coal Co., Hazard	49,957
	North Fork Coal Co., Lennut	35,913
	Raccoon Coal Co., Douglas	17,758
	Ross-Petrey Coal Co., Hazard	10,871
		243,661 tons

Year 1915 Ashless Coal Corp., Lothair .... 74,261 tons
Blue Grass Coal Corp. (succeeded Haz.-
    Dean) 56,217
Columbus Coal Co. (succeeded Raccoon). 16,365
Daniel Boone Coal Co. (succeeded N. Fork
    & Ross-Petrey) 46,888
East. Tenn. Coal Co., Glomawr 23,915
Hazard Coal Co. 70,341
Hazard-Dean Coal Co. (Jan. to Apr. in-
    clusive; succeeded by Blue Grass Coal
    Co.) 14,168
Himyar Coal Corp. 96,918
Ky. Jewel Coal Co., Lothair 104,009
North Fork Coal Co. (Jan.-Apr. inclusive;
    succeeded by Dan'l Boone 29,669
Raccoon Coal Co. (Jan.-Apr. Inclusive; suc-
    ceeded by Columbus Coal) 5,955
Ross-Petrey Co. (4 months; succeeded
    by Dan'l Boone Coal Co.) 7,538
                                            ———
                                       546,244 tons

The figures above were taken from the Reports of the Inspector of Mines, Lexington, Ky., for the years indicated.

Coal Production in Perry County, Ky., from Annual Reports of the State Department of Mines, Lexington, Ky., and Minerals Yearbook of U. S. A. for the respective years:

	RAILROAD MINES				TRUCK MINES	
Year	No. of Mines	Tonnage	Average selling price per ton (R.O.M. basis)	No. days worked	No. Mines	Tonnage
1912	2	1,400	$1.50			
1913	4	25,632	1.13	109		
1914	7	243,661	1.18	189		
1915	9	546,244	1.12	188		
1916	14	995,091	1.39	242		
1917	26	1,616,557	2.78	205		
1918		2,120,223	2.59	221		
1919		2,712,043	2.62	169		
1920	39	2,966,426	4.69	163		
1921	55	4,235,278	2.56	152		
1922	65	4,280,981	2.93	144		
1923	60	4,895,434	2.52	140		
1924	61	5,229,066	1.79	182		
1925	51	5,932,258	1.75	181		
1926	50	6,647,907	1.82	227		
1927	56	6,378,895	1.73	206		
1928	45	5,806,710	1.57	221		
1929	43	5,760,881	1.57	228		
1930	37	5,325,910	1.44	170		
1931	40	5,100,837	1.14	161		
1932	35	4,322,893	.93	160		

1933	33	3,852,557		155		
1934	32	3,369,790	1.11	149	10	1,822
1935	30	3,651,757	1.71	165	4	2,015
1936	30	4,457,718		181	14	12,552
1937	31	4,342,697	1.71	162	8	4,538
1938	28	3,632,362		131	10	8,047
1939	27	4,028,878	1.77	154	7	6,951
1940	27	4,629,499		169	18	14,378
1941	27	5,459,467	2.32	200	27	22,570
1942	28	6,252,586	2.51	236	16	24,490
1943	27	6,270,375	2.90	278	16	46,917
1944	27	6,055,850	3.18	272	17	165,585
1945	28	5,873,145	3.33	246		
1946	28	5,712,341		200	34	513,752
1947	27	5,895,894	4.80	206	259	856,887
1948	26	5,547,760	5.92	201	140	697,650
		154,176,983				2,378,154

Note: The very great demand for coal suddenly slackened in July, 1948, causing a number of truck mines to close, due to fact that domestic market called for prepared, washed coals.

First Laws Governing Mines

The first Kentucky law pertaining to the operation of coal mines was the bill passed May 18, 1886, providing for check weighman where there were as many as 20 miners employed and the majority of these demanded such service.[2] In 1887 a law was passed regulating ventilation of mines.[3] In 1898 a law was passed requiring coal mining companies to pay their employees before the 16th of the month following the month in which the service was rendered.[4] The employment of children in Kentucky coal mines became somewhat general in the late 90's and in 1902 the Child Labor Law passed, making it illegal to employ a child under 14 years of age; in 1906 this law was amended limiting the labor hours and employment of children under 16 years of age.[5] In 1908 a law required mine forement to pass an examination held by Chief Mine Inspector.[6] Today these and additional laws abide.

Organizations

The Kentucky River Mining Institute was organized December 10, 1925, at a meeting at the Combs Hotel, Hazard, Ky. This was an organization of coal officials, mine foremen, superintendents, electricians, etc., for the purpose of promoting safety, instructions in first aid and the study of mining methods. Many mining men have given time and effort through the years in behalf of this Institute. George P. Fitz was the first Secretary; J. B. Allen served in that capacity from about 1934 to 1947. Robert Dickson is the very able Secretary at the present time.

The Hazard Coal Operators' Association was formed by the operators just previous to World War I to meet the unusual conditions confronting the coal industry in the Hazard field. Through the years this organization has continued to widen its scope and assume more responsibilities to better serve its members and the Hazard coal industry as a whole. The following men have served as President: John Gorman, Calvin Holmes, George Barker, E. L. Douglas, A. L. Allais, J. E. Johnson, Sr., J. T. Hatfield, W. J. Brown, Jr., Henry Phening, W. W. Miller, J. B. Hilton, W. E. Davis, John P. Gorman, F. M. Medaris, D. T. Pritchard, Wm. Burlingham, George P. Fitz, C. Prewitt Gum, M. K. Eblem. The Secretaries were: R. A. Hord, J. E. Johnson, Sr., C. B. Rose. A. E. Silcott, Louis Hopper and W. B. Sturgill.

CHAPTER VI

COMMUNITIES AND THEIR GROWTH

BUCKHORN

Agnes Gabbard Kirby

Buckhorn is in Perry County, Kentucky, 137 miles southeast of Lexington and 238 miles from Cincinnati. It is located on the Middle Fork of the Kentucky River where the waters of Squabble Creek tumble over their rocky bed into the larger stream.

Legend has the settlement of Buckhorn made by one Jerry Smith, who is said to have come from Tennessee after serving in the War of 1812, though no service records for him have been brought to light. Not later than 1816 he is said to have built a pen of chestnut rails to serve as shelter while building his house at the Buckhorn Spring. "Uncle John" Gross, who married one of Jerry's granddaughters, Ella Riley, quoted Jerry as saying that when he came to Buckhorn all the bottoms were filled with big poplar and walnut trees with grape vines as "large as his thigh." [1]

One night Jerry's wife (Elizabeth Jones, daughter of Milton Jones) heard the calf which they were keeping in the pen with them bawling. She jumped up, grabbed a battling stick, and went to the calf, finding that a wolf had crawled through an opening and had the calf by the leg. She, in turn, took the wolf by the leg, jerked it loose, and killed it with the battling stick.

Such stories of the early days of Jerry and his wife with their tribe of ten children, three boys and seven girls, would indicate that they were hewn of strong pioneer stock, as they would not otherwise have survived the life of rugged hardship which was certainly theirs. Bears and wolves were prevalent in the vicinity, as well as roving parties of Indians who were hunting in the wilderness around them.

Jerry, once while hunting, walked into an Indian camp before he realized what he was doing and was then afraid to run away. He decided to act friendly, and was pleased to find that the chiefs in the group did likewise. Not so did the young braves, however, who eyed him with hostility; as Jerry's story goes the young braves acted "mighty cat like." They had a horse's ham over the fire broiling with the hoof still on it. He had to stay for supper, but, in recounting the day's experience, said that the horse meat and the meal coffee they served with it tasted "right good." When he was ready to leave, the chiefs escorted him part of the way to protect him from the young braves and when out of sight he said he "did his best." (Presumably ran as fast as his legs would carry him.) (2)

It is from Jerry Smith's descendents that we have the story of the naming of "Squabble Creek," though the name in itself does not leave much to the imagination. He said that his brother and others living up the creek and on Gays' Creek killed a lot of game and had a squabble over the division, calling the "creex" Squabble Creek.

The last story about Jerry has to do with a farewell sermon, which he ordered a certain Bob Burton to preach for him when he was an old man. All of his children with their family connections were present, and he counted 104 grandchildren and great grandchildren. At the time he told them of his naming of the Buckhorn Spring, which he did after killing a foursnag Buck and hanging his horns over the spring. Before the sermon started, Jerry called Bob Burton in and told him to "do his damndest." (3)

There must have been other settlers on Squabble Creek and Bullskin before Jerry Smith built his lean-to at Buckhorn. Louise Saunders Murdoch, in her charming story, **Almetta of Gabriel's Run,** introduced her heroine with a background sketch of the history of Squabble Creek, which she called "Gabriel's Run," and the legend of the naming of the "Run" is more picturesque than the picture of Jerry Smith and his cohorts squabbling over game. Her story was the result of many years of visiting with old families living on the creek, and the grave of Gabriel Recording Angel, of whose family she wrote, may be seen today in the "Luce

Angel" Cemetery near the head of Squabble Creek.

Mrs. Murdock told of Gabriel Recording Angel's trip from "Carliny" through the Gap. "He came in quest of deer and bear and wild honey. Finding them in abundance, with wild turkey and other game, he settled on a large creek in the wilds of the Cumberland Mountains.

"On his return from his second trip back to the settlement with pelts and honey, he brought a young wife to his half-camp in the deep woods of Kentucky. This 'camp' was a rude shelter of three log walls and a split board roof without either chimney or flue. The ash cakes were baked and the venison spitted at a fire built upon the ground just outside the open end of the camp." (4)

Later, after the young wife's brother and family had come to join them in the wilderness, and two log cabins had been built to house the neighboring families, the incicent occurred to give the naming of the creek.

"It was the first winter in the new cabin that a huge brown bear came between Rec and his rifle in one of his rare unguarded moments and gave him the chase of life. Indeed, he was only saved by the timely intervention of his wife, who checked the beast upon the step-block at the door with a dash of boiling suds and slammed and barred the door during the recoil of the animal; and so the creek came to be known as 'Gabriel's Run' among the settlers who were coming every year in great numbers." (5)

Among the families prominent in the early days of the settling of the Buckhorn area may be listed the following names: Johnson, Amis, Anderson, Baker, Barger, Bowling, Burton, Callahan, Deaton, Fox, Gay, Gross, Hacker, Lewis, McDaniel, McIntosh, Riley, Sebastian, Smith, Turner, White and York. In 1927, Asbury Johnson, while a graduate student at Peabody College in Nashville, Tenn., started work on a paper entitled, "A Brief History of Various Families around Buckhorn, Ky." and work was ceased because of his ill health and subsequent death. Before the death of Luther Johnson, his brother, in 1951, the material became available for study in regard to the early settlement of the Buckhorn community. An interesting story is told of the pleasant relationship between Jerry Smith, of Buckhorn, and Nelse (Nelson) Gay, of Gay's Creek, which is six miles above Buckhorn on the road which now leads to Hazard, via Chavies and Grapevine Creek. It seems that Nelse Gay had a drum at his home on Turkey Branch, just above Gay's Creek, and Jerry Smith had a bugle at Buckhorn. The two men used to signal to each other these six miles until "Marshall's Rebels" took Nelse's drum during the Civil War.[6] Anyone who is familiar with the winding terrain of the area with its turns and gulleys would not doubt the possibility of such an arrangement between the two men.

Until the beginning of the twentieth century, comparatively untouched by outside influences, generation succeeded generation in this small community with little change of mental outlook since the days when the first tide of immigration flowed over the mountains from Virginia, the days when Daniel Boone roamed the forest of Kentucky.

To the people in Buckhorn, time did not stand still, but moved slowly. Primitive conditions prevailed, and until the Brainard Memorial Hospital was built there in 1909, there was no hospital within one hundred miles. In 1901, the nearest railroad was 25 miles away, there was no highway, and the roads ran across the mountains along the creek beds, being impassable except when the streams were dry, or the water low.[7]

On April 2, 1901, a young minister serving as assistant in the Lafayette Avenue Presbyterian Church in Brooklyn, N. Y., heard a plea for the neglected regions of the mountains of the border states. The young man was Harvey S. Murdoch, a native of Mississippi and a graduate of Colorado State College and Princeton Theological Seminary. He had heard Dr. Edward O. Guerrant, one of the most colorful figures in the history of the American Church, when he made a plea for evangelism and education in the Southern Highlands, and he had accepted the position of

Field Secretary of the Society of Soul Winners, Dr. Guerrant's organization.(8)

To a group of men in the Lafayette Avenue Church, Mr. Murdoch said: "If you will help me, I will go down where the need is vastly greater than it is here." They promised their support, and he made an exploratory trip South. On this trip into Kentucky he was brought into contact with Rev. Miles Saunders and his daughter, Louise, who were mission workers at Laurel Point, at Buckhorn, where Sunday School and preaching services were held under an old tent. Dr. Miles Saunders, a veteran Presbyterian minister, had come with his daughter from the Blue Grass and they were giving this summer of 1902 to Christian work on Squabble Creek and other stations on the Middle Fork of the Kentucky River.

It was evidently a case of love at first sight with Mr. Murdoch, who fell in love with Buckhorn and its people as well as with "Miss Louise" Saunders. Dr. Guerrant had been heard to say of the two that, "She would not have any man and he was a confirmed bachelor." That was before they met each other in the chapel at Laurel Point, where Mr. Murdoch had come to preach one Sunday morning. The Buckhorn people had erected this small structure on Laurel Point and had named it "Louise Chapel."

The young minister's survey revealed that here at Buckhorn was a place where a church and a school would meet urgent needs. Each of the two workers had dreamed of a school for boys and girls of this great part of the Cumberlands, and early in September of that year Mr. Murdoch called a meeting of the heads of families in the John Gross home, and secured subscriptions "toward the erection and equipment of a Christian College in our community."(9) The October issue of the **Soul Winner** 1902 (the publication of Dr. Guerrant's organization) gave further information concerning the enterprise:

All who are interested in the mountain people will be glad that the good people at Laurel Point, in Perry County, Kentucky, have determined to build a college with the help of the Society of Soul Winners. The people are too poor to give much money, but they have subscribed 400 logs, twelve thousand feet of lumber, all the shingles to cover all the buildings, coal enough to heat it 'for good', nine acres of land, and $150 in money and 125 days work. (10)

General Howard, Dr. Guerrant, his daughter, Anne, and the photographer for the **Christian Herald** arrived at Buckhorn the week following this important meeting in the John Gross home. Meantime "Brooklyn friends had underwritten the young missionary's salary of $50 per month" and "gifts of exactly $240 provided capital for the beginning of the work." (11)

By April, 1903, work had progressed with this account from the **Soul Winner**:

This new institution for the mountain boys and girls will be opened on the 29th of this month. It is built in Buckhorn in Perry County. It was begun only last Fall, and in spite of the bad weather and many obstacles in the way of building 25 miles from the railroad across rivers and mountains, the devoted people have pushed the work to this happy conclusion.

The institution will be called Witherspoon College in honor of the great teacher and preacher and soldier and statesman, John Witherspoon, President of Princeton College, member of the Continental Congress and signer of the Declaration of Independence. (12)

From the same issue of the **Soul Winner** a brief editorial note:

The many friends of the mission will be pleased to learn of the marriage of our Field Secretary, Rev. Harvey S. Murdoch to Miss Louise Saunders, who has done noble service in the Cumberland Missions of the Society, and she has been her father's able lieutenant. They will all return to the mountain work.

An interesting report of the Log College finds place in The Soul Winner for February, 1905:

Our enrollment is now 187, about thirty of whom are preparing to teach in the public schools. They come from Cane Creek and Long's, from Lost and the lone Troublesome, from Squabble and mouth of Leatherwood, from Rush and Buffalo, and Canoe Fork, from the Middle Fork, the North and South Forks, from Indian Creek, Gay's and Bull Skin, from creeks, coves, brooks and branches without name or knowledge.

Our beautiful Louise Hall is already over-crowded. As

many as five student in one room, and even then we are compelled to send students elsewhere for accomodations. We turn away students every day. We could easily fill another building the size of this. In fact, if we had the accomodations for them I believe we could get one hundred more boarders. The refectory is an attractive two story four room building.(13)

The annual trips which Mr. Murdoch made to Brooklyn provided the capital so necessary to the operation of this growing enterprise. Among the early friends of Buckhorn was the late John T. Underwood, who with his wife, the former Grace Brainard, gave encouragement and interest as well as financial support to the new "college." The fact that his school never became officially a college did not trouble Mr. Murdoch then or later. The fact that there were at the time a thousand children of school age in a radius of 12 miles of the institution seemed to be the most important factor involved.

By 1908, the Buckhorn school was known as the "Log College" and consisted of five large buildings, two hundred students, and five professors, under Mr. Murdoch, who taught the classics and whatever other subjects were necessary.

A young girl's visit to the "Log College" at this stage of its growth is related in Grace Guerrant's letter to her sister Anne written from Buckhorn:

"We had to climb a mountain called Bunker Hill, which was the worst I ever saw. At 9 o'clock I reached the Log College, and it is beautiful. It sets on a mountain brow, opposite the church on Laurel Point, with a lovely valley between. Mr. and Mrs. Murdoch, with Mrs. Gordon live nearby, and Dr. and Mrs. Saunders occupy a room in the college. I wish you could see those Highland boys and girls. They come jumping out of the bushes and crowd the chapel and sing for all they are worth.

"Papa preached every morning at 8 o'clock in the college chapel and at night in the church. You never saw such a path up the mountain to the church, before they made a new one. It was like climbing a tree. But they all got there and crowded the church. Would you believe it, I found a little namesake of yours up here at Mr. Jack Gross' between two big mountains. They call her Annie

Guerrant and all say she looks like you. Of course, she is a beauty.

"I stopped to see a woman who weaves blankets on a big loom in the front porch. It was a curiosity.

"The men were building the new girl's dormitory out of great hemlock logs, all sawed square. It will be beautiful. This is the only college in this big country, and the people are very proud of it. One day four hundred crowded into the chapel to hear the exercises.

"Well, we started home at 6 o'clock in the morning on two mules. You ought to have seen me. I know I looked like a horsefly on that big mule, but I stuck to him, and he brought me through all right."(14)

In the **Soul Winner** for August, 1914, Dr. Guerrant describes a recent visit to Buckhorn accompanied by Dr. Frank DeWeitt Talmage:

Evening brought us to Buckhorn. I could hardly believe it was the same place where dear Dr. Saunders and Miss Louise taught a score of children, under an old tent about a dozen years ago. Now a great institution fills the beautiful campus with twelve handsome buildings where 369 Highland lads and lassies are trained for time and eternity. . . .

A thriving village surrounds the College where a few years ago "Uncle Jimmie" Sandlin raised his corn and sweet potatoes. A church of 400 members. . . . a large college building, two large dormitories, a well furnished hospital, a children's home, and handsome buildings for a new kindergarten and manual training, and for the president, a church edifice, and one for teaching agriculture.

I was compelled to leave early Monday morning, but not until I saw 146 Highland youths enrolled the first morning of the session and had the pleasure of saying a word to them. . . .(15)

One of the students of Witherspoon who heard Dr. Talmage and Dr. Guerrant was Elmer E. Gabbard. When Mr. Murdoch died in October, 1935, The Buckhorn Association, the governing board of the Buckhorn Institution, turned to Rev. Elmer E. Gabbard, D.D., pastor of the Northside Church of Chattanooga, Tenn. Dr. Gabbard, after preparation for college under Mr. Murdoch, at Buckhorn, graduated from Berea College and the Louisville Theological Seminary. He served for six years as associate in the Buckhorn work before accepting a pastorate at the Fifth

Avenue Presbyterian Church, in Knoxville, going on later to Chattanooga.

On his return to Buckhorn, in 1936, in an evaluation of the program and plans for the future, Dr. Gabbard found that in the 35 years of the Buckhorn work the sum of $203,000 had been spent on land and buildings, more than 4,500 students, within a radius of 50 miles of Buckhorn had been enrolled in the school and that approximately 600 had become teachers in the Public Schools of Kentucky. [16]

Dr. Gabbard is now pastor of the large Buckhorn Presbyterian Church and President of the Buckhorn Association, which comprises school, hospital and homes for children, and holds title to 1,400 acres of forest, coal and even level land for farms and gardens. [17] Buckhorn is now known as the "Buckhorn Schools" as the accredited high school is partly supported as far as teacher's salaries are concerned by the Perry County Public Schools. There is a total enrollment of about 300, and the emphasis is in the Christian spirit on vocational training in industrial arts, domestic science and agriculture. The care of homeless children in Worthington Home for Girls and the Boys' Cottage is considered to be one of the most vital parts of the work, and the Synod of Kentucky, of the Presbyterian Church, makes an annual contribution toward the support of the orphanages. Louise Hall, the large dormitory for boys, was destroyed by fire early in 1945, and this building was replaced with a modern stone fireproof building with accommodations for 60 boys and two apartments for teachers and workers. The new building, of native stone, is an interesting contrast on the campus to the older log structures which gave the school its name of the "Log College." A disastrous fire on February 14, 1953, destroyed Worthington Home for Girls on the Buckhorn campus. The building was a three story log structure built in 1913 at a cost of $10,000. Twenty-eight girls were left homeless and bereft of clothing, but appeals throughout the state for aid brought wearing apparel. The valiant efforts of volunteer workers made possible the evacuation of all the children without injuries, though most of the contents including appliances, sewing machines were burned.

The Buckhorn Church, the building which was the gift of Mr. and Mrs. Edward F. Geer, of Brooklyn, N. Y., is regarded by many who have seen it as one of the most beautiful rural churches in America. It is constructed entirely of logs, the interior finished in natural wood with amber hand blown glass panes for the windows. The seating capacity is for six hundred. For many years the Buckhorn Church has been the largest rural congregation in the Synod of Kentucky. During the winter of 1951 the building was seriously damaged by flood waters and the question of moving it was considered. Community sentiment was so strong, however, that a temporary war surplus barracks building was constructed to use for services to continue while plans for rehabilitation were made. By May, 1953, services will be continued again in the Buckhorn Church. Since the erection of the Church Bell Tower, the "Angelus" or "Prayer Bell," as it is known in Buckhorn, has been rung each evening at twilight for a minute or so to call all within sound of the bell to pause for evening prayer. This bell was rung for many years by "Uncle John" Gross or his wife "Aunt Ella" in whose home Louise Saunders had her first dreams of a school and church at Buckhorn. After their deaths the bell was rung each evening by a member of their family, and the custom is continued. It is more than the bell tone which echoes through the valley on Squabble Creek at dusk each evening. The campus below Laurel Point seems "encompassed about with a cloud of witnesses" as the Buckhorn people pause to remember the past and plan for tomorrow.

CORNETTSVILLE

Irene Ison Minniard

Cornettsville is a small railroad station on the North Fork of the Kentucky River, eighteen miles south of Hazard, which has a post office, depot, two stores and about twenty houses. It was originally named Salt Creek, from the salt wells at the mouth of Leatherwood. The name of Cornettsville was chosen by John B. Cornett, the first postmaster and storekeeper in 1924. It was well named, as all the residents were descendants of the early settler, William Cornett.

The present post office, of which M. J. Dixon has been postmaster for 25 years, has four star-routes and the services of the new Highway Post Office. Two of the star-routes are operated by horse-back. One mile from this little village is the Cornett Cemetery, which contains some of the oldest graves in Perry County, among them that of William Cornett, Revolutionary War veteran and early settler.

DWARF

Eunice Tolbert Johnson

Dwarf, altitude 834 feet, a small village of about 300 people, is located north of Hazard at the intersection of Highways 15 and 80. The chief occupation is mining, although there are no mines in the vicinity. It has 46 families, four stores, one church (Baptist), two garages and one graded school.

Dwarf is the site of Old Tunnel Mill, on Troublesome Creek, near the horseshoe bend. The tunnel was built by Sam and Felix Combs, sons of Lydia and Mose Combs, and grandsons of George Combs, one of the eight Combs brothers.

Jason Combs, Sam Combs' son, owns half interest in the old mill and lives across from it on the old farm. The other half is owned by the heirs of his brother, Jordan Combs. Jason Combs is now 76 years old, and he says that the mill was built before he was born and that grinding started during the "hard summer." Old timers say that it was built in the early 1770's.

It took the Combs brothers four years to tunnel through the mountains to make a space large enough that the force of the water would be sufficient to run the mill. They built a saw mill, a carding mill and a grist mill but only the grist mill remains. It has five to seven foot fall in the water. They charged $1.00 for sawing 100 feet of lumber, one inch thick, and $2.00 for 100 feet two inches thick. Corn was ground for a toll of one gallon to the bushel. They had three machines for cotton, one picked it, one made the bats and the third made it into rolls. The grist mill was in use for grinding corn until 1945, the start of World War II, when it closed for lack of help to run it. It is badly in need of repair, and unless the foundation is fixed, it will soon collapse. It is the only mill of this kind in Perry County. The tunnel is 172 feet long and the opening is 4 feet square. It is cut through solid rock; hand-operated drills and gunpowder were used in making it. The tunnel is still in good condition.

The first post office was established at Dwarf on July 24, 1878, and was then called Tunnel Mill. Joseph Hall was appointed the first postmaster. The second appointment was Newton Smith in 1880. Tunnel Mill post office was discontinued July 22, 1881.

On July 13, 1883, a post office was re-established there with Thomas W. Gibson as postmaster. It was named Dwarf for "Short Jerry" Combs, an early settler. Around 1,500 people in a radius of four square miles receive their mail at Dwarf. The Engles, Combs, Fugates, Ritchies and Owens were among the first settlers on that part of Troublesome Creek.—(Jason Combs, J. B. Campbell, J. D. Smith.)

THE GROWTH OF HAZARD
Myrtle Ward Gabbard

When Perry County was formed, the site where Hazard now stands was a farm owned by Elijah Combs. Referred to as Perry Courthouse in the early records, the county seat was formed in 1821. At that time, many Kentuckians had fought under Oliver Hazard Perry in the Battle of Lake Erie. Admiral Perry died on August 23, 1819, only a few months before the passage of the act creating this new county (November 2, 1820) and at the request of the people, the legislature named it in his honor. The first meeting to decide on the location of the county seat was held in the home of Elijah Combs, its founder, and for long years a leader in the public life of the town. In the December term of court, 1836, John A. Duff, surveyor of Perry County, reports the survey of a ten-acre plot of land that had been deeded by Elijah Combs and his wife, Sary Combs, to the trustees of the town for a county seat. This land was part of the tract on which Elijah Combs' home was built, and in outlining the boundaries, the distances from his chicken house is given. This survey was acknowledged by Jesse Combs and A. C. Godsey, S.C.C.

This ten-acre plot was subdivided into Main Street, lots and a public square. In 1833, the trustees of Hazard sold some lots by number. Lot No. 13 was sold to Nicholas Combs for $16.00 (Deed Book B. p. 2). This lot is the plot near where the Masonic Building now stands. In 1833, Jeremiah Combs sold to John D. Pace lot No. 8, containing one-quarter acre, for $25.00 (Deed Book B., p. 227). Jesse Bowling, John Duff, Robert Brashear, Elijah Combs, and Jeremiah Combs were the first trustees for the town of Hazard. (Deed Book B., p. 2). Surveyors for that year are given in the Perry County Court records as Andrew F. Colwell, Ezekial Brashear, and A. C. Godsey.

The Kentucky Historical Society states that Hazard had two taverns as early as the year 1821. Elijah Combs and John Craft paid tax on taverns that year. Sessions of court were held in Elijah Combs' house.

The period before the Civil War was another time of growth in the town. Several more lots were sold, and the name of the post-office was changed to Hazard in 1854. Mr. J. H. Lacy was the postmaster at that time. In 1851, Mr. Lacy purchased lot No. 5, one-quarter acre, about where the Hurst Hotel now stands. (Deed Book C, p. 336). In 1853, A. C. Godsey purchased lots No. 1 and 2, for which he paid $100.00. This site is the corner of Fleet and Main Street and the Salyers Building. In 1854, lot No. 7, also one-quarter acre, was sold by Elijah Combs to H. G. Crook for $30.00, with "enough timber to build a house 32 feet by 16 feet to come off my land." Also in 1854, John W. Combs sold to J. H. Combs and Ira Davidson lot No. 11 in the town plat on the west side of Main St., for $45.00 (Deed Book H, p. 250). Engle Hardware and Florist stand today on part of lots No. 11 and 12.

Lots No. 16 and 17 were sold April 27, 1854, by H. G. Crook to John Morgan for $106.00 (Deed Book C, p. 336). In 1891, Josiah Combs sold L. H. Salyers lot No. 6, described as being on the southwest side of Main St., for $150.00. (Deed Book J, p. 452.) In 1893, Josiah Combs and Polly Ann Combs sold lot No. 4 to Jesse C. Boggs for $300.00. (Deed Book L, p. 30.) (See town plat.)

In 1850 Elijah Combs still operated his tavern. Hopes aroused by the promise of new roads and better mail service probably were in part responsible for the growth of Hazard at this time. However, with its few homes clustered in the valley, the town seemed destined to remain a small trading-center and stopover for travelers The difficult methods of travel and slow and hazardous means of transportation of supplies are certainly responsible for the belated development of the resources of the Upper Kentucky River Valley of which Hazard is the center.

In the years just preceding the Civil War, I. J. Ward carried the mail from Hazel Green to Hazard. He later described his first view of Hazard, with "Elijah Combs' peach orchard on Graveyard Hill in masses of pink bloom, forming a lovely background for the village nestled below."

During the war between the states, Hazard suffered from guerilla warfare raids from wandering bands of soldiers. Dr. E. O. Guerrant tells in his diary of passing through this area with Morgan's Raiders. Some of Hazard's families were slaveholders and there was the same division in families and bitterness between neighbors that was found throughout the borderline states of the South. Robert Combs, a Confederate soldier and one time jailer of Perry County, often recalled the condition of Hazard when he returned from the war. He described the neglected farms, the roads and paths overgrown with weeds and almost no business of any kind being carried on. Many people in the mountains have felt that some of the feuds developed as a result of the guerilla warfare. Old grievances over livestock driven off, or beehives that were destroyed by soldiers could not easily be forgotten, especially when a neighbor was recognized among the offenders. By 1874, Hazard was described in Collins **History of Kentucky,** as a small village.

In 1884, Hazard was incorporated, with a population of around 100. The trip from Jackson to Hazard in 1892 is described by Dr. E. O. Guerrant in the following excerpt from The Galax Gatherers. The time is in the month of August.

"I started at 6 a. m. for ten miles up the beautiful Kentucky River, between her palisades of paw-paws and her colonnades of wild cucumbers or wahoos under the cool shadow of the mountains was a delight. I hardly saw a soul save a few bare-footed children going to school.

Ten miles above Jackson, I came to the mouth of Troublesome. Up Troublesome one mile my road turned up Lost Creek for nineteen miles.

I stopped at the post-office, at the Mouth of Lost Creek, to write a postal card home.

I traveled with Judge Strong up Lost Creek. Several miles up Lost Creek I met a Mr. Nipper or Napier and travelled with him to the mouth of Ten Mile Creek. All the rest of the way I travelled alone with God and the mountains.

The shadows of the mountains were falling over the valley when I reached Lotts Creek. I rode into the little mountain town of Hazard at 7 p. m., about as weary as my horse. It had taken three days hard riding to make the trip.

Hazard the only town in Perry County, consists of a court house, a jail, four stores and seventeen families. There is no church or schoolhouse. I am trying to preach in the Courthouse."

The French and Eversole feud retarded the growth of Hazard and brought death, destruction and desolation to the enterprising village. After the fighting in Hazard in 1889, one of the most bitterly fought conflicts of the feud, one-half of the houses were unoccupied and only about 70 inhabitants remained. For years the newspapers carried sensational stories of this feud, the courthouse was burned and many of the town's leading citizens lost their lives. Scars left by the feud could only be dimmed by time and the great economic changes that have come with progress. (1)

Hazard experienced a struggling but very real growth in the 90's. The railroad reached Jackson after long delays and resulted in a small boom as far away as Hazard. There were many changes and a population increase. Natural resources began to be tapped and a sense of expectancy prevailed. Some coal lands were being leased and the lumber business was booming. Many stories are told of the "log runs" and thousands of logs were taken out on the "tides."

In 1892, Granville Cornett lived in the house in Big Bottom built by Henry Combs, and Joe Eversole's home was the first house in the lower end of town where the swinging bridge crosses to the mouth of Tan Bark Branch. Other residents were Will Martin Combs, Eli Couch, Drew Combs, Leah Feltner, J. H. Combs, W. J. Combs, Felix Feltner, Jerry McIntosh, R. F. Fields, Em Smith, D. Y. Combs, L. H. Salyers, Alex Duff, Robert Combs, Sally Davidson, Lige Davidson and John Baker. At this time there were D. Y. Combs' store, Baker's sawmill, Eversole's store, Field's hotel and the famous old log house which had been built by Elijah Combs. (2)

Dr. E. O. Guerrant in his diary tells of the beginning of the first church in Hazard. Until his coming, all religious services were held in the courthouse. Judge Josiah H. Combs gave a site in town, overlooking the valley and the village for the erection of a church building and gave the timber for the building. Dr. Guerrant states that when the church was organized in 1892, there was not an organ in the county. A Mr. Mickel was teaching the county teachers institute and preaching occasionally.

The need for new homes in the town brought J. L. Johnson from Magoffin County with his saw mill. His was the first circular saw in the county. This was the beginning of what is now the Home Lumber Company. Rev. A. S. Petrey, who came to Hazard in 1897, said of J. L. Johnson,

"No man ever helped more in the building of Hazard. His saw mill and his generosity helped greatly in the buildings going up at the time the Baptist Church was being erected."(3) I. J. Ward also came to Hazard from Magoffin County and later built a home in the Backwoods where the Catholic Kindergarten now stands. Mr. Ward built many of the houses in Hazard and Perry County and figured prominently in the promotion of the Masonic organization.

Bailey P. Wootton came to Hazard as a teacher in 1894. He became one of the leading influences in the life and development of Hazard. In 1900, he and Jesse Morgan opened a law firm and the two men became prominent in the practice of law in Eastern Kentucky and were known throughout the state. Mr. Wootton helped establish the first telephone system in 1903, and he led in a campaign for good roads that resulted in the first blacktop that was put on Route 15 from Winchester to Hazard, when he was Attorney General. He was responsible for the first movement in the interest of a library for the city, and always interested in the improvement of the school of this area.

At the turn of the century, still striving for better roads and the railroad, Hazard had some important developments under way. In 1898, Rev. A. S. Petrey came to Hazard. By 1902, under his leadership, an organized movement was under way for the founding of the Hazard Baptist Institute. This soon became a reality when some of the leading citizens of the area joined his efforts and regardless of denominational affiliations erected the institution for "the good of the community" which was to be maintained and promoted as a "public service enterprise." A brief biography, **The Prophet of Little Cane Creek,** written by Harold Dye, and published by the Mission Board of the Southern Baptist Church presents the life and ministry of Mr. Petrey. He came to Hazard at a time when his leadership and inspirational service was needed by the community and the value of his part in the development of Hazard is inestimable.

In 1903, Bailey Wootton, Charles G. Bowman and

Jesse Morgan organized the Hazard Bank, with J. B. Cornett as president. In 1906 this became the First National Bank, with C. G. Bowman as president.

During the Civil War and subsequently Hazard had several doctors. Dr. Jasper Stewart lived in Hindman but was often called to Hazard. He is remembered especially for his work during the terrible typhoid epidemic. Dr. Jesse Combs, son of Jesse, Sr., has a record of operations performed to assist in cases of shooting, stabbing and accidents. Dr. John Marcus Daniel practiced during the Civil War and Dr. W. T. Wilson, Dr. Stout, Dr. Henson and Dr. Mason were here in 1890 and are remembered by some of today's older citizens.

By 1900, Hazard had at least three doctors: R. R. Baker, J. C. Sumner, and E. H. Kelley. Dr. Kelley came to Hazard in 1900 and established the first modern drug store with a soda fountain. (4) By 1912, Dr. A. M. Gross, Dr. Taylor Hurst, Dr. Sam Ritchie, Dr. C. A. Eversole, Dr. Cecil Young and Dr. M. E. Combs had also begun to practice in Hazard.

The court house was used for various purposes, such as Sunday School, day school, church services and public gatherings of all types. Christmas entertainments attracted large crowds, and box suppers were held there to raise money for the local baseball team. A service that became widely known was a monthly meeting held in the court house by Rev. Ira Combs (Uncle Ira) of the Old Regular Baptist Church

In spite of the difficulty in getting supplies from Jackson to Hazard in these days, the town grew steadily in these years. Supplies brought up the river by freight boat were sometimes delayed by too severe weather, or low water levels in the summer. The transportation situation was eased somewhat by livery stables that provided horses for local trips. Stables were kept by D. Y. Combs and Wootton and Morgan. On June 22, 1911, the **Hazard Herald** carried this statement: "Several traveling men spent Sunday in Hazard at the D. Y. Combs Hotel. Hazard is the central point of Eastern Kentucky and there are always plenty of strangers in town."

In July, 1911, the court house burned and five months later the entire block of business houses opposite the court square was swept by flames. The **Hazard Herald** commented at this time "Hazard is in the path of the march of progress and will emerge from her ruins to proudly take her place in Eastern Kentucky as queen of the mountains." Hazard's more modern buildings date from this disasterous fire. A building boom started in 1911 when the Jellico Grocery Company's Office and Business Building was built, Wootton, Morgan and Bowman erected a fire-proof building and the R. C. Newberry and John Watts Building was constructed. The Baptist Church was built, the Jones Building and the Perry County State Bank were erected and residences sprang up rapidly. Ike Ritchie's home in Big Bottom, Dr. C. A. Eversole's on High Street, Judge W. C. Eversole's house on Lower High and many other residences were built, according to reports in the **Herald** during September, 1911. A Big Bottom lot sale, in which the Hazard Brass Band participated is described in the October, 1911, **Herald,** with George W. Humphrey as Band Director.

On June 22, 1911, the **Hazard Herald** carried the following items indicating the beginning of a busy city as the present-day Hazard:

"Doug Hayes and Ned Grigsby are getting along as fast as possible with their new building on High Street. They hope to occupy it in a month or so."

"R. C. Newberry and William Feltner are completing this week the addition of their store building which doubles their store room capacity and provides for business on a much larger scale."

"Richmond Combs and James Davidson have greatly improved the appearance and convenience of their places of business with new and substantial porches."

"Progress and improvement are the order of the day."

"Lee Daniel and J. D. Davis, Circuit Court and County Court clerks respectively, have returned from a visit to Garrard County where they had an opportunity to see some real Blue Grass farming."

"Professor S. A. D. Jones left last week on an extended

trip to rest up after a long hard year as head of the Hazard Baptist Institute."

Among the advertisements in this same issue were D. Y. Combs, General Merchandise, James Davidson, Barber Shop, and the Kelley-Engle Drug Co. Professional cards displayed were those of W. F. Hall, Ryland C. Musick, C. M. Horn, Jesse Morgan, H. C. Eversole, S. M. Ward, E. E. Hogg, J. E. Johnson and Bailey P. Wootton, Attorneys, and H. B. Maggard displayed a Dentist's card.

At this time the railroad was under construction from Jackson to Hazard, and on March 21, 1912, the first steel rails were laid within the borders of Perry County, thus fulfilling a dream of many years.

Hazard's real growth began in 1912. July 18 of that year, the **Herald** carried notice of horses and carriages for hire from James Holliday's Livery Stables. C. M. Horn owned a furniture store, D. Y. Combs and W. O. Davis had hotels and R. F. Field's built a new hotel to be lighted by electricity as soon as the new power plant was completed. East Hazard's building boom started in May, with a new store and a dozen new houses being built. On August 6, Cedar Heights property owned by Miss Bertha Lyttle sold 62 lots. A bridge was planned across the ravine leading to this section. The Hazard band furnished music, and 100 gallons of "Kentucky Burgoo" drew the crowd. In 1912, Hazard celebrated the Fourth of July, by having an old fashioned Barbecue dinner served to all. People came from all over the county, the band entertained and a wagon was used as a stand for the speakers. The food was served on the picnic grounds at Cedar Craig.

A Boy Scout troop was organized in 1912 by Scoutmaster William Fitzpatrick. They had fourteen members and met at H.B.I. The Woman's Civic League was organized in 1911 and the Commercial Club about this time. These clubs met at the Lyceum Theatre. Electric lights were assured by May 15, 1913. The plant was located across the river at the mouth of Messer Branch. In 1913, water works were installed.

The new Perry County Court House was dedicated

on February 14, 1913. The Hazard Lumber and Supply Co. was incorporated for $20,000 on August 5, 1914. Some of the stock holders in this company were J. E. Johnson, George Wolfe, and J. L. Johnson, President. This company later became The Home Lumber Co.

Dr. D. R. Botkin established the first hospital, later erecting a building purchased around 1920 by Drs. A. M. Gross and R. L. Collins which they named the Hazard Industrial Hospital. In April, 1947, the hospital then called Hazard Hospital was purchased by the Benedictine Order of the Roman Catholic Church and became known as Mount Mary Hospital. At present, it has an 85-bed capacity. The Hurst Hospital was founded in 1927 by Dr. Taylor Hurst and reorganized in 1930 as the Hurst-Snyder Hospital with Dr. Dana Snyder as co-owner. It is a smaller hospital, of 25 beds.

In 1920 Hazard had a population of 4,348. By 1940 the population had increased to 7,397, and by the 1950 census it is nearly 7,000 today. It is estimated that Hazard has a trading population of about 100,000. The bank deposits in 1915 were $157,000. In 1920, they had grown to more than $1,000,000. The combined deposits of the two banks amounted to more than $10,000.00, to June 30, 1952.

The Perry County Times, a 21 page paper printed in 1906 was probably the first newspaper printed in this county. W. C. Fugate was editor of this paper, and its presses were operated by foot power. It is not known when **The Mountaineer** was started, but it ceased to exist on June 20, 1911, when the late B. P. Wootton bought controlling interest in **The Mountaineer** from J. B. Hoge and founded the **Hazard Herald,** with E. C. Wooton as part-owner until 1943.

Prior to 1922 the **Herald** was published in the basement of the building where the Major Store is now located. It was published as a weekly until 1939, when it became the first daily newspaper in Perry County, with Charles Wooton as editor at this time. In 1951 it was was purchased by the B.M.G. Broadcasting Co., with Fred Bullard as Editor. **The Hazard Herald,** at the end of its first year,

1912, had 500 subscribers; today its circulation is estimated at 4,000. It was difficult for the paper to grow, with its antiquated printing methods. With power still not available in 1911, a two H.P. gasoline engine was installed to run the press. After 1912, electricity was available and the changeover was made.

In 1939, Mr. and Mrs. E. T. Sparks started a newspaper which they named **The Union Messenger** and which soon absorbed two small papers, **The Plaindealer** and the **Hazard Leader**. The **Messenger** is still a weekly publication and has a circulation of 2,165.

Early theatres during 1912 were "The Hip," Theodium and Lyceum; owned by Charlie Morgan, B. F. Creech, Colson Duff, Montgomery Horn and a Mr. Garnett. Announcements of the shows ran in the **Hazard Herald** in August, 1912. Miss Jessie Patton played the piano while the pictures were being shown. The machines were cranked by hand and had ether lights. In early 1914 Tony Zoellars bought "The Hip" renamed the Perry, later the Family. The Perry was the first to be operated by electricity. Today, Hazard has three theaters, the Virginia, the Family which are owned and operated by L. O. Davis and Tony Casinelli, and the Grand-Vue Drive-In, erected in 1950 by Richard Johnson and Gene Combs, on the river road between Hazard and Combs.

The City of Hazard, large mines nearby and the surrounding communities are served by the Kentucky and West Virginia Power Co. Transportation today is by the Louisville and Nashville Railroad, several bus companies and by automobiles on the good highways that now lead from Hazard. There are two wholesale grocery companies, two wholesale dry goods companies, one wholesale hardware concern and the usual up-to-date retail stores usually found in a city the size of Hazard. There is adequate fire protection, and plans are under discussion for an improved and enlarged water plant.

Churches of seven leading denominations serve the city and Hazard takes pride in its attractive homes. The civic clubs include the Rotary, Lions, Kiwannis, Chamber of Commerce, and Jaycees. There are also active organizations of the Business and Professional Women, Garden Club, Parent-Teachers Association, D.A.R., several Home-makers organizations and Church-Women's groups.

In 1938, the people adopted by vote the City Manager form of government and in the same year, the city hall was built. This hall houses the offices of the city administration and also the Perry County Health Department. An Army Recruiting Office, Social Security, Internal Revenue, offices of the Veterans Administration and certain offices of the state government are maintained in Hazard. Hazard was made a third class city in the spring of 1951. The first government owned building in Perry County was the postoffice, completed on July 1, 1936. Mrs. Anna M. Moore was appointed postmistress on April 4, 1936, and the Hazard postoffice received a First Class rating in 1945.

The Bobby Davis Memorial Park was given to the city of Hazard by L. O. Davis in memory of his son, Robert Oren Davis, who was killed July 13, 1945, at the age of twenty in a railroad collision on the French-German border.

The park covers four acres of landscaped mountainside. The Library is the central point of interest in the park. It is built of Perry County sand stone. It now has over 11,000 books and is growing rapidly towards its ultimate capacity of 22,000 books. A second feature of the park is its swimming pool. In the summer of 1951, 17,000 people used the pool, which charges no admission. Swimming classes are held each summer, and a life guard is always on duty. At 4 o'clock p. m. each day the pool is turned over to reserved parties of adult groups for combined picnics and swimming parties. The pool is used in the afternoons by reservations only, but is available at no charge.

A third feature of the park is the landscaping. Native growth predominates the 400 varieties of plant life. A large rose garden affords fresh cuttings for the Library. A gardener is on duty throughout the year.

The fourth feature of the park is the Memorial to the 196 boys from Perry County known to have lost their lives in World War II. It is located in a sunken terrace near the Library. In the center is a reflecting pool of crystal clear water. The terrace is bounded on each side by walls of large sandstone blocks, and in each of these blocks in one tier is attached a bronze plaque bearing the name of the fallen soldier. Under each plaque is planted an azalea, which is always in bloom on Memorial Day.

The park was built at a cost of $200,000. It is under the supervision of the Park Board of Hazard and the Garden Club of Perry County. It is truly a living memorial.[5]

As traffic increased in and through Hazard, Route 15, the highway running from Winchester, Ky., through Jackson, Hazard, Whitesburg and Jenkins, presented increasing problems for the Hazard area. This highway traverses Main Street, Hazard's one street which runs through the heart of the business section of the city. On normal days, traffic on this street became heavily jammed and on weekends and special occasions the jams would sometimes last for hours.

The task of providing relief for this traffic situation required a major engineering effort at great expense. Through a group of influential citizens headed by Dewey Daniel and Senator W. A. Stanfill, the Highway Department of Kentucky gave assistance in the construction of a By-Pass costing around $555,000. It was completed in the fall of 1950 and was opened to the public for use by Governor Weatherby and other state officials with appropriate ceremonies and a picnic followed in honor of the occasion in the newly completed Bobby Davis Park.

The Construction of a Memorial Gymnasium is a true portrait of the present-day Hazard spirit. The sacrificial effort and cooperative generosity shown by the leaders and the people in this enterprise are the things that make a great community; the story of this achievement was given in an editorial in the **Hazard Herald** on Tuesday, September

11, 1951, with a sixty-six page edition dedicated to this project. The following excerpt summarizes:

"The clamor for an adequate gymnasium and community center in Hazard has been voiced in varying degrees over a period of several years. It is probably true that the first realization for the need by the public generally resulted from the editorial efforts of Leslie Wilson, a former **Herald** sports writer. His continual challenge to replace the 'cracker box gym' gained public support, but the Hazard Board of Education was not in a position to satisfy the demand for a new gym.

"The persistent efforts of the Hazard Junior Chamber of Commerce which began in 1947 was the advance guard of a movement which reached its culmination in the memorial gym project.

"Few, if any, individuals in our community possess the talents, ability and vision of Lawrence Davis. Fewer still would give themselves so wholeheartedly and sacrifically to a civic undertaking as Mr. Davis has done in the building of this memorial gymnasium. Throughout this edition of the **Herald** and on many other occasions much tribute has been paid this philantropic man. It is worthy praise for a deserving citizen. Always generous with his means and ever self-giving, Lawrence Davis has built enduringly that Hazard might be a better place to live.

"Great service was rendered to the Gym project by the late John Green. He was especially valuable to the progress of the building during the months that Mr. Davis was away from Hazard. We join with others in expressing regret that an untimely death removed him from our midst before he was able to see cherished dreams come true. Mr. Green's civic effort did not begin and end with the Gym project. He gave liberally to the Buckhorn School, the Red Cross and other worthy organizations as well as to hundreds of individuals and families whose needs were deserving."

Governor Lawrence Weatherby in his expression of praise for the co-operative efforts of the people of Hazard and Perry County in the raising of funds for this great building, stated "America's greatness is to be found in the self-reliant effort of its people.

Radio Station WKIC began operation November 23, 1947. It is a 250 watt full time station and a member of M.B.S. It is owned by Fred Bullard, Charles Metcalf and Richard Goodlette.

Elijah Combs, founder of Hazard, is buried in Hazard's oldest cemetery, overlooking the city. The land was planted with his orchards and was a part of the home he had built in the wilderness. Many of Hazard's early families are buried on this hill and a grandson helped to build the first Presbyterian church ever erected in Hazard near this spot. Perhaps some civic group will one day undertake to erect a suitable monument to Elijah Combs' grave, and honor the founder of this city which now surrounds his wilderness home.

HOMEPLACE

Miss Lula M. Hale—Director

Homeplace, owned and operated by the E. O. Robinson Mountain Fund, without the aid of any county, state, or federal funds, is a small rural community center located on Highway 15 between Jackson and Hazard, sixteen miles from railroad or telephone. It was established in 1930 by E. O. Robinson of Cincinnati and Ft. Thomas, who had extensive lumber operations in Eastern Kentucky. Mr. Robinson wished to return in some educational service part of the fortune which he had made. Unfortunately, he did not live long enough to see the fruits of his hopes, but we have kept on working steadily, missing his counsel, but trying to remember the things that he told us, particularly that "Girls and boys are my hobby, not fine horses or yachts." Visualizing Homeplace as a kind of human link between the existing governmental agencies in the community and the people, he planned for it to supplement, wherever possible, the work of these agencies. So, in a sense, it is an educational institution—though having no formal school with an exact enrollment and plainly labeled "graduates."

Homeplace's program may be roughly divided into five parts. First, there is the farm itself, serving as a home-base for all our activities and also as a gathering place for many group meetings. Although it is not called a model farm in any sense of the word, it does carry some type of special demonstration each year. The rural home-making classes, the travelling library, the wood-work shop and the medical program are the other main activities.

When the various "occupations" here were counted, there were about twenty jobs in evidence. This does not mean there are twenty workers doing a specified thing eight hours a day, then punching the time clock and going home. It means that there is a variety in our work and an overlapping of our jobs requiring constant personal adjustments to fit each day's needs. Here is, in part, what is done:

The farm of 48 acres was purchased in 1930, and since that time a little more than 150 acres have been added.

Actually there are only eleven acres which are level or which have slopes gentle enough to be safe from erosion, and much of that is taken up with buildings; they are the Log House, Cottage, Community House, Shop, garage and milk house, barn, canning house and chicken houses. The carpenters and masons—local men—who have erected the buildings are genuine artists. Of the Log House, the first structure built, Allen Eaton in his book, **Handicrafts in the Southern Highlands,** says " . . . one of the most attractive houses in the highlands." On our farm, a permanent hillside pasture has been established for our herd of Jersey cows. (The men who operate this little dairy boast of the cleanest milk in the county . . . in the state! However this claim has not been checked since the beginning of the war and may not be true now.) From the beginning, the poultry project has been successful and other similiar projects in the community have been started. Cartons bearing the label "Homeplace Eggs" and "Homeplace Neighbor Eggs" commanded top prices on the Hazard market. The eggs still sell, but with the war and the shortage of paper, the cartons are not so dressed up now.

Back in 1930, the neighboring farmers around us were not planting certified potato seeds or using commercial fertilizer, but now it is the accepted practice. A small vineyard, and orchard, and berry patches have been established. We are never able to grow all our feed, and since the beginning of the war with its increasingly high feed costs and shortages of labor, the farm has not been able to make as good a showing.

However, the books for 1948 show farm sales to the amount of $8,500.00. Very little of that was profit. Aside from actual sales, the staff of eight persons who live on the place has been provided with fresh vegetables, milk and eggs throughout the year.

In 1930 there were no high schools conveniently located for children living on Troublesome Creek in Perry and Breathitt counties. In the eighth grade along that creek were many girls between the ages of fourteen and eighteen who were just repeating the grade to remain in school. We employed a Home Economics graduate who experimented with classes in homemaking for those girls. For two hour periods each week she rented kitchens from farm women who lived near the county schools in which to conduct classes. The girls were so enthusiastic that in 1937 another home economics teacher was employed, which made it possible to have eighteen groups, totalling 176 girls. In the home-like surroundings of the rented kitchens, using equipment with which the girls were familiar, they were taught to cook. Most of the foods used in the classwork were grown on the Homeplace Farm. At the present, there is only one home economics teacher, but the plan is the same. Variety in the diet and generous use of milk and eggs and vegetables are preached. Gardens are glorified; fruit jars are filled. Pupils learn better ways to prepare food, better ways to clothe themselves, and better ways to live. Always present is the personality of the teacher—her remarks, her attitudes, her manner influencing the girls throughout the year as she meets with them. These classes, though unconventional and given for no visible credits, are welcomed by the teachers and the county school superintendents. In 1940, a high school was erected nearby, so one of the Homeplace teachers followed the girls to it, giving them "credit" for the work done. By 1943, Perry County had accepted full responsibility for this teacher's salary and equipment. Then with the coming of consolidated schools and the establishment of Breathitt County High, the need for this work was not as great. The present plan is to discontinue this type of teaching with the close of this school year. There is no way to measure results, but sixteen years of this unique school will undoubtedly influence the homes of tomorrow.

In a tiny room of the Community House is the home and workshop of the Homeplace Library of about 5,000 volumes. The reading rooms are the schools and homes dotted up and down the creeks and hollows in Perry, Breathitt and Wolfe County. The loan desks and stacks are on wheels—of two book-mobiles that fairly groan with age now, but still manage to climb hills and follow creeks over paved, gravel and dirt roads. One year they checked out 48,000 books as they traveled on their weekly schedule. "Book day" is often reported by the children as the best day of the week. Hopes are to continue this service until the state and counties furnish these children with reading material.

The shop consists of one large room of electrically-operated Yates-American machines, one room with benches for hand tools for beginners, and a finishing room. The boys from the near-by high school, carried by county bus, take up half of the teacher's time, while the other half is given to building furniture for sale or helping men who live on the creeks to build kitchen cupboards and cabinets for themselves.

This happens to be one of the spots in Eastern Kentucky where goiter is rather prevalent. The County Health Department co-operated wonderfully with Homeplace in holding monthly or bi-weekly pre-school or prenatal clinics. Dr. Howard P. Fishback of Cincinnati volunteered to give a goiter clinic, which proved so helpful that he eventually held other types of clinics here. Through him and one of the foundation trustees, arrangements were made with a Covington, Kentucky, hospital, and later, one in Cincinnati, whereby people who had been unable to obtain long-needed surgical attention might have it. A trained nurse was employed to follow up these clinics; at the present, Dr. Fishback has performed, free of charge, almost four hundred major operations. A doctor and a nurse are at Homeplace now, and are trying to establish a rural medical center with a prepaid membership. At present there are 120 families in the membership.

In the fall of 1948 a small hospital, built of native stone, was dedicated. It is well staffed with two doctors (a surgeon in charge), six nurses, a technician, a Business Manager, a dietician, aids, orderlies, cooks, etc.—a staff of 21 people. It is equipped with modern machines in the treatment rooms, and there are offices for the doctors,

X-ray and operating rooms. The addition of this 24 bed hospital has greatly enlarged the services of Homeplace.

Four years ago, Homeplace volunteered to sponsor a hot lunch program for the rural school house, and the women in the neighborhood took turns doing the cooking, except one year when a cook was hired. Arrangements were made whereby the teacher, whose salary is paid by the county, might live without charge. Lack of comfortable and congenial living places often prevent good teachers from accepting rural or out-of-the-way schools.

There are other activities in which Homeplace likes to help depending on the time and interests of the staff and people of the community. For instance, the large Community Room is open each Friday evening with a staff member present to direct folk dancing or group singing. Once in awhile a bit of dramatics may be attempted. The local women come for a class in Home Nursing, or the teachers for a First Aid Course sponsored by the Red Cross. We have had periods of Sunday School, 4-H Clubs, Boy Scouts, Homemakers clubs and various farm meetings.

Homeplace is indebted to a great many people for the help received here, to the Board of Trustees who have allowed the staff to go ahead with this work and to enlarge it since Mr. Robinson's death, to the Kentucky Experiment Station for plans and suggestions—too many to enumerate here—and to the Berea College teachers who have studied local needs and have sent many fine young people here who have made this work while while.

LEATHERWOOD

Irene Ison Minniard

Leatherwood is a thirteen mile creek with many small forks. It is divided into "Big" and "Little" Leatherwood Creeks. The largest part of this creek flows into the North Fork of the Kentucky River about seventeen miles south of Hazard, in the eastern section of Perry County.

Leatherwood Creek was named for the numerous leatherwood trees that were in evidence when the first settlers came here; this section of the county can boast vast areas of timber as well as coal fields.

Salt was first made at the mouth of Leatherwood as early as 1835. These wells were first drilled near the mouth of the Kentucky River by Robert S. Brashear and a Mr. White on a 1,400 acre tract later known as the Duff farm. The early pioneers would often work night and day to locate the wells by hand drilling; many men worked and fed their families on a wage of fifty cents a day.[1] The owner sold his salt to people in Virginia and Kentucky, transporting it in bags by mule and oxen for $1.00 a bushel. As much as ten bushels could be boiled down in 24 hours. The kettle in which the last salt was made remains on the original farm, now owned by McKinley McIntyre. 1892 brought the climax of the salt wells when they were swept away by the tide.

From this section, many logs were sent north on rafts to Frankfort and other nearby towns. This was a dangerous voyage, and often cost the loggers their lives.

A branch line of the L&N Railroad connects Toner, later known as Leatherwood, Kentucky, with Dent, ten miles away. Construction of this branch line cost the railroad $1,000,000, and on this line 6,000 tons of coal are hauled daily. The Leatherwood tract of coal is one of the state's largest. These 146,000,000 tons of Leatherwood coal were leased from the Kentucky River Coal Corporation to the Blue Diamond Coal Company in 1943.

Leatherwood is a modern mining camp, having around siz hundred homes, a post office, club house, grade school, theatre, recreation building and a modern drug store. These Leatherwood mines are 100% mechanized and employ approximately 1,000 men.[2]

A 2,000,000 ton of coal per year cleaning and preparation plant was completed in 1949; this plant has a 100 foot high double track bridge spanning the 700 foot gorge across Clover Fork from out-crop to out-crop of the coal seam so that trains of cars from within the mine can dump coal from either side into a 2,500 ton storage bin.

During World War II, Mr. Alexander Bonnyman, President of the Blue Diamond Coal Company made every effort possible to get this huge mine into full production; the production target set for the Leatherwood mine is 2,000,000 tons per year.

Leatherwood is noted for its thousands of acres of valuable timber. In 1927, Garrett and Walker Lumber Company bought approximately 5,000 acres of timbered land from citizens and Land Companies. Two years later, this land was sold to the Leatherwood Lumber Company, which worked it for 10 years and then sold it to the W. M. Ritter Lumber Company. This company has operated over some 15,000 acres of Leatherwood timber. Poplar, white, red and chestnut oak rank highest in sales, however, much maple, beech and basswood is finished and sold. The W. M. Ritter Lumber Company exports millions of feet of timber yearly to South America, England and various parts of Europe.

ROWDY
Eunice Tolbert Johnson

The community of Rowdy, formerly called Stacy, is in the northern part of the county near the Breathitt County line. Some of the early settlers were the Combs, Allens, Campbells and Hayes. They were of Scotch-Irish descent.

School was held in a log building on Buckhorn Creek. John Oliver and Wayne Combs were early teachers; they walked five miles twice a day to the school.

Troublesome post-office, located where Homeplace stands, was moved to Stacy, now Rowdy, about 40 years ago. Ira Allen was an early postmaster; Ance Hayes served as postmaster for 27 years. Then mail had to be brought in on horseback from London. His daughter, Mrs. Wireman Neace, is the postmistress at present. About 250 people in a radius of four square miles, receive their mail at Rowdy.

John Watts had the first store in this section. He sold it to a Holliday, who later sold it to Ance Hayes. Today there are ten stores in the Rowdy community, a Church built by the Riverside School of Lost Creek and a graded school. The old Regular Baptist Church is conducted in the school building.

SLEMP
Irene Ison Minniard

Slemp, Kentucky, a post office five miles from the mouth of Leatherwood Creek, and originally located near Beehive and Owens Branch Fork, was named around 1905 for a Mr. Slemp who came into the vast coal territories of Leatherwood buying coal land for a large coal company known as the K.U. Land Co., later owned by the Kentucky River Coal Co. Much of this land, so rich in coal, sold for as low as fifty cents per acre. Jessie, Kentucky, was the first Post Office in the Leatherwood area.

VIPER — MASON'S CREEK
Grazia K. Combs

Hallsville was the name of the first post office located in this area. It was located at the mouth of Wick's Branch on Mason's Creek and was operated by members of the P. W. Hall family. As the population increased and shifted, the need arose for a more conveniently located post office and Hallsville was abandoned. In the meantime, Enoch Campbell, a pioneer merchant and land owner, tried to have a post office established near the mouth of the creek. One day he came upon some boys admiring a large spotted viper which they had just killed. As he talked with them by the roadside, a young man, named Phillip Fields, joined the group and suggested that Viper might be a good name for the new post office. The postal authorities agreed, and when the new post office was opened, it bore the name of Viper, and the first postmaster was Enoch Campbell.

The creek, known as both Mason's Creek and Mace's Creek, gets its name from Mason Combs, one of the eight Combs brothers who followed Boone through Cumberland Gap and came to see the "Settlements" at Boonesboro. Like others who were dissatisfied with what they saw there, he chose to return to the pioneer paradise he had just passed through and came back to the Upper Kentucky River country. He settled at the mouth of Carr Creek and claimed a large boundary of land up and down the river and up Carr.

The first settler in this neighborhood was Henderson Baker, who settled at the mouth of Elk Branch just below Viper. After a few years he sold his holdings there and went to Colorado but later returned and settled in Knott County. The second settler was Hiram Combs, a grandson of Mason. He lived on the river about one mile up from Viper. Hiram had gone west as a young man and married in Missouri, but he came back to Kentucky and reared a family here. After his wife's death, he went back to Missouri.

Other early settlers in this area were the Cornetts, Halls, Farlers, Fields, Adams, Caudills, Campbells, Bransons and Brashears. John Cornett, son of Arch Cornett, married Elizabeth Holbrook and came from Leatherwood to settle on the Middle Fork. His neighbor was Woolery Campbell, a son of Billy Campbell, who lived on Line Fork. Woolery married Lucy Creech from Harlan County. Another neighbor was John Adams, who came to the creek from Letcher County. John "Bert" Henry Hall and Josh Hall settled on Holly Thicket, and P. W. Hall, a brother to "Bert" settled on the head of Middle Fork. P. W. came to Kentucky from Turkey Cove, Virginia, and had married Elizabeth Branson from Harlan County. After a few years, he sold his property on Middle Fork to James N. Brashear and bought Henderson Baker's holdings at the mouth of Elk's Branch.

Another member of the Hall family was Zeke, a cousin to P. W., who settled on Left Fork. Zeke also came from Turkey Cove, Virginia, and married a Branson. Later P. W. bought out Zeke's heirs and moved to Left Fork. Wilkinson ("Wicks") and Green Branson came to the creek and settled near them.

Early settlers on the Right Branch were the three Farler brothers John A., Farris, and Alex. John A. and Farris soon moved on to Owsley County but Alex stayed in the head of the creek and has numerous descendants living there now. Other settlers in this neighborhood were Mahlan Fields and John "Knock" Pratt. "Knock" married

Elizabeth Campbell and came to Mason's Creek from Line Fork. He lived to be 94 years old.

James N. Brashear and his wife Betty Young Brashear came from Tennessee and settled on the river, four or five miles above Viper. Some of the land in this area is still owned by their descendants.

Before the industrialists began to move in, these people lived much as pioneers elsewhere. They owned large tracts of land which provided food and timber. Their homes were simple, their wants were easily satisfied, but things were destined to change. In 1911 the railroad was begun and excited groups of spectators welcomed the first work train as it came up the line in 1912. Excitement also ran high when the first passenger train came on January 1, 1913. In the beginning, the first railroad stop was called Masu, but it was soon changed to Viper.

The railroad made industrial development possible, and business boomed in this neighborhood for several years after its construction. Mobray-Robinson Lumber Co. was quick to establish a band mill near the mouth of the creek and to build a narrow gauge road up Left Fork. Tram roads were pushed into the coves and hollows that were near the mill. In the meantime, Mason's Creek Coal Company opened a mine, but there was not enough coal in this area to make this a profitable undertaking. Until fairly recently, stave mills which operated on the head of Right Fork and in nearby Leslie County made Viper one of the most important shipping points for staves in Eastern Kentucky. In early days, some of the staves were carried across the hills on mule back to be loaded on wagons and hauled to the railroad, and many people who live in the vicinity of Viper today can remember seeing stave wagons backed up Mason's Creek for a half mile waiting to be unloaded.

During these years when lumbering, mining, and railroading were good, Viper grew into a prosperous village, boasting local doctors, a hotel, barber shops and a lodge hall. W. C. Singleton built and operated the hotel; before this he had been in the dry goods business. The most successful merchant of this era was John Watts, who later joined with Charlie Bowman to establish the Bowman-Watts Wholesale Co.; this business moved to Lothair after the 1927 flood.

When the State Legislature convened in 1916, the people of Viper had special reason to be interested; they had helped to elect G. G. Brashear a neighbor and kinsman to serve them in Frankfort. He served under Governor Stanley as Representative from Bell, Harlan, Leslie and Perry Counties in 1916-17.

At present, Viper is a very unpretentious little community. The industry and several of the buildings which characterized it a few years ago are gone. There is still a little truck mining going on but most of the people who live there either work in Hazard or in mines in neighboring communities. A non-denomiational church has been established in the community and a high school has been maintained here since about 1935.—(G. G. Brashear.)

CHAPTER VII

EDUCATIONAL GROWTH

Clarine Ross Daniel

The first attempt of the State of Kentucky toward education was made in 1794. This was to grant counties 6,000 acres of land for the building and support of Seminaries. They were to be exempt from taxation. The land, however, was usually inferior. The majority of the people settling the county were poor. The trustees of this land were not always as responsible as they should be. The citizens were faced with problems of a frontier country and were not ready to build a school system.

An Act of Legislature was passed on February 14, 1820, giving all fines and forfeitures in various counties to the respective Seminaries located within them.[1] This aid was, however, not enough and it was not possible to get legislation passed to help them, so the system was abandoned as a state enterprise.

Perry County Seminary

This Seminary was such in name only. Its history can be written in few lines, with the assurance that the story is finished. Only three legislative acts pertain to Perry County's seminary lands. This was entered in 65 tracts totaling 5,350 acres between the years 1820 and 1841 in Perry and Clay Counties.

In 1830, the County Court was permitted to sell as much of the Seminary lands as necessary to complete the public buildings of the county. The following year, the final act pertaining to this "Seminary" appropriated all the funds, resources and lands to the purpose of building a road from the Estill County line to the Virginia state line.[2] This act is unique in the history of Seminary funds, and is therefore quoted in full.

An ACT concerning the Seminaries in the Counties of Monroe, Perry, Jefferson and Simpson

Approved November 22, 1821

Perry Seminary

Sec. 2. **Be it further enacted.** That Jesse Bowlin, Charles Smith, Robert Brashears, Stephen Hogg and William Stamper, be, and they are hereby appointed trustees of the seminary of learning in the County of Perry. And the trustees in the said County of Perry, and their successors, shall have power to locate, survey and carry into grant, six thousand acres of any land which by law is subject to similar appropriations, in the names of the trustees of said seminary and their successors; and shall have power to sell and convey the said land, or any part or parts thereof.

Sec. 3. **Be it further enacted.** That a majority of the trustees for the said Counties of Monroe and Perry shall constitute a board for their respective seminaries aforesaid, to transact any business appertaining to said seminaries, and to fill any vacancy which may happen in their body.

An ACT to provide for the improvement of the road from the Estill County line, by way of Perry Court House, to the Virginia State line.

Approved January 15, 1831 (3)

Acts of 1830

Perry Seminary:

Sec. 1. Be it enacted by the General Assembly of the Commonwealth of Kentucky, that the County Court of Perry shall have the power proper, if to them it shall seem proper, to make sale of the Seminary Lands of said county, that have not already been sold, and apply the proceeds thereof to the opening of a road from the Estill county line, by way of Perry court house, to the Virginia state line.

Sec. 2. . . . pertaining to survey of road.

Sec. 3. Be it further enacted. That the funds and resources of the Perry Seminary, now in the hands of the trustees thereof, be, and the same are hereby appropriated to the opening and improvement of the road, mentioned in the first section of this act. The county court of Perry are authorized to cause a settlement to be made, with the trustees of said seminary, and it shall be the duty of the trustees, if, on said settlement, it should appear that any of the funds of said seminary remain in their hands undisposed of, to pay the same over to the said county court; and it shall be the duty of the said court to make a record on their books of said settlement, specifying the amount paid over by the said trustees, and the reception of the same by the court. (4)

During the session of 1821, the Legislature passed another general law in relation to common schools. This was known as "The Act to Establish a Literary Fund and for Other Purposes," approved December 18, 1821, which provided that one-half of the clear profits that have arisen and may heretofore arise to the State, from the operation of the Bank of the Commonwealth of Kentucky, be set apart, as a fund known as the Literary Fund, to be used in the establishment and support of a general system of education. (5)

Notwithstanding the means provided for it, this second system of popular education in Kentucky was doomed to failure. After this, the school system, if such it might be called, languished in Kentucky for many years. (6) From 1831 to 1840, there can be found no records of schools in Perry County, and it is the concensus that education for all children was more or less at a standstill. From some of the older residents of the County, we have learned that some of the families had tutors for their children, as in the case of Elijah Combs, the founder of Hazard, whose children were taught by a man from Virginia. This was stated by Aunt Mary Combs, who is still living on Lotts Creek. She says that Dr. Jesse Combs was trained in medicine by a Dr. Roberts from Virginia.

The present state public school system was founded in 1837. It was at that time a public system, but not a free school system. After the adoption of the third Constitution in 1850, during Supt. Breckenridge's administration, the schools of Kentucky were made free. From a table showing the state of education in Kentucky in 1840, Perry County ranked 89th. The population was 3,090. Revenue list was $264,960.00. (7)

The census listed children from the ages of 5 to 15 as being 1,014; children from 7 to 17 years of age 666. The share of school funds that Perry County received that year was only $266.40. One can readily see how little could be done toward education with so little money.

The first act of the Legislature of Kentucky toward establishing a system of common schools and a permanent school fund was the act of February 23, 1837. At this time, the school fund consisted of the interest at 5% on the sum of $850,000.00, which sum was to be distributed among the counties in proportion to the number of children reported to the school commissioner. No district was entitled to any part of this fund unless a school had been organized, a school house built, and a school tax levied on said district. (8)

The method of distribution was as follows: first, the entire school fund was divided by the number of children who were of school age reported to the Auditor. This gave the per capita. Second, the number of children reported by the school commissioner in a given county was multiplied by the per capita. This gave the county's share of the school fund. The school districts were to be laid off in the county by surveyors named by the County Court. No district was to contain more than 100 pupils nor fewer than 30 pupils. This provision of the law naturally delayed the adoption of the school system in many counties, and stands as evidence why Perry County was allotted such a small share of the school funds. The county was sparsely settled and so few children were of school age.

In Minute Book 6 of Perry County, on Page 139, in the year 1851, it is shown that John Hyden resigned as School Commissioner, and that, in 1853, Hiram Begley was paid $1.00 per day at the November term of court to serve as judge of the election to elect the trustees in District No. 4. This district was at that time known as Perry Court House, now the town of Hazard. In 1851 there were 796 children in Perry County of school age in the 26 school districts with only 274 children in school. The teachers were paid $477.60 for teaching a term of one to three months of school. Kentucky documents in the University Library, show that in

1854 there were 1,125 children in Perry County of school age. Highest attendance recorded was 459 and the lowest attendance 109. The average length of the school term was three months. The amount distributed that year for schools was $787.50.

Perry County Court records show that, at the June term of Court, 1855, John G. Lacy, the school commissioner for that year, produced to the court orders and receipts from the trustees of the districts of Perry County for the amount of $448.00, showing the amount paid to each district listed:

District No. 1......................$46.90
District No. 2...................... 43.40
District No. 4...................... 43.40
District No. 5...................... 39.20
District No. 6...................... 67.20
District No. 10...................... 28.70
District No. 11...................... 28.00
District No. 13...................... 46.90
District No. 15...................... 20.30
District No. 16...................... 22.40
District No. 19...................... 33.60
District No. 21...................... 35.00

The districts not listed are considered those without a school building, or with so few children in the district that they may have been sent to school in the district nearest them.

In 1855, the court records also say that Joseph Eversole was school commissioner. Minute Book No. 6, Page 43, shows that Josiah H. Combs was paid $1.00 per day for serving as school commissioner in 1859-1860.

In 1862, Eliza Lacy Combs, wife of Dr. Jesse Combs, grandson of Elijah Combs, founder of Hazard, taught school in a log house in what is often referred to as "the Backwoods section of Hazard," believed to be in the vicinity of Cedar Street.

In 1865 (as shown in Minute Book 6, Page 36), Elijah Duff, school commissioner, came into the court, made a settlement for that year (1865), and presented vouchers that were approved by the Court for the sum of $1,616.02.

Minute Book 6 reveals that in 1866 there were 34 school districts in Perry County. The highest amount paid to any district was $87.42, paid to District No. 4, and the lowest amount was $13.72, paid to District No. 24. These districts could not be located due to the fact that, when the courthouse burned, so many records and maps were destroyed.

The same year, 1865, a subscription school was held in the courthouse in Hazard. The teacher was Susan Combs, who married Joe Eversole. The only pupil remembered was Marcus Daniel.

In 1866, Elijah C. Duff was the school commissioner. The amount of school funds that year was $1,746.18. [9]

The legal session of the school term was three months. From the new system and an increase of funds, the sessions were lengthened to five months. Under the old plan, teachers were paid from $12.00 to $30.00 per month. The new wage guarantee was from $30.00 to $45.00 per month for a five months term. [10]

These excerpts from the records of Perry County Court are given to prove that some effort was made during these years to maintain schools in Hazard and Perry County.

About this time, much dissatisfaction had arisen in regard to the method of electing commissioners, and it was in 1885 that the commissioners' office was changed to that of County School Superintendent, and the number of trustees was reduced to one trustee to a district. [11]

In 1882, a Dr. Mason taught school in Hazard, and, about the same time, Mr. Lee Daniel went to school on Second Creek, opposite the farm owned by Aunt Cynthia Combs. The Hazard Bombers baseball field is built on this land now. John G. Combs, father of Rev. Henry Combs, was the teacher. In the years 1882 to 1885, records tell us that John Baker hired teachers for $20.00 a month. These schools were sometimes known as subscription schools. The tuition was $1.00 a month per child. School was conducted upstairs over a store-room, where the Citizens Bank Building now stands. John G. Combs, a man by the name of Smiley, and another by the name of Godsey were the teachers.

In 1887, Mr. Lee Daniel taught school in a log house on Lotts Creek. At that time, it was in Perry County and later became a part of Knott County. Some of the county school superintendents have been G. P. Combs, who served for 13 years and later served another term of three years; others were B. P. Bowling, John Napier, and John McIntosh, who was elected in 1910 and was succeeded by the present superintendent, Mr. M. C. Napier.

In 1891, Brother Michel was teaching at the County Teachers Institute and preaching between times at the courthouse. These county institutes were held for one week in the county seat of each county in the summer prior to the opening of school. The purpose of these institutes was to help teachers to become familiar with the textbooks they were to use. They might be called a brief training course for teachers.

In 1891 and 1892, Judge J. G. Campbell served as chairman of the school board of trustees in District No. 9 and caused to be built, despite much opposition, by local and district taxation at the cost of $800.00 the first substantial school house ever built in Perry County. In 1913, this building was still standing.(12)

The term of office of county school superintendent was changed in 1885 from two years to a term of four years. the late John McIntosh said that, when he took office in 1910, there were only four reasonably good school houses in the county. One was located at the mouth of Big Leatherwood, one at the mouth of Bull Creek, and two on Big Leatherwood. There were other make-shift schools. Some were being held in one room of a residence. These were all very poorly equipped, with wooden benches made of very rough lumber and black boards that were painted on the walls.

The Presbyterian Church school at Buckhorn was the only school north of Hazard. The county paid tuition for any child who wanted to attend Buckhorn School.

During Mr. McIntosh's term of office, there were 44 school houses built and one accredited high school. This accredited high school was Hazard High School, maintained by the County and City Boards of Education, and the building is now known as Lower Broadway. The building now is used as a grade school for grades one through five, and is referred to as Lower Broadway School.

The four school houses referred to by Mr. McIntosh were all located south of Hazard. The ones built during his terms of office were ditributed throughout the county.

The **Hazard Herald** of September 22, 1950, contained an article released by Mr. M. C. Napier, Superintendent of Perry County Schools that reads as follows: "The Perry County Schools began the 1950-51 session with an enrollment of 9,938 pupils and a staff of 301 teachers, including one supervisor. At the present, the system maintains and equips 34 one-room schools for white children and seven one-room schools for colored students, 31 two-room schools, eight three-room schools and 32 schools with four or more rooms. Eight four-year high schools are now being operated by the county, enrolling approximately 1,200 pupils. The two large high schools, the C. Dilce Combs High School, at Jeff, Kentucky, and the M. C. Napier High School, at the mouth of Lotts Creek, were open for the school term September, 1952. These two high schools take care of the eighth grade and high school students in the immediate and adjacent communities and eliminate seven old frame buildings. The new structures have modern lighting, including glass-brick windows, an intercommunication system from the principal's office to each of the 20 classrooms, tile floors, and acoustically treated ceilings. The walls are in pastel colors. Each building has a cafeteria, library, music room, study hall and science laboratory. The buildings formerly used for high schools will be used to some extent to consolidate grades in the respective communities. Plans are under way for the Perry County Board of Education to work with the City Board of Education in the vocational field of education. This will mean that all persons interested in vocational training will be able to attend school in the new vocational building under contruction near the bridge at Walkertown."

The school systems of Perry County and of Hazard

have always been closely interwoven, just how close is shown by a book published by the first graduating class of Hazard High School. To quote: "the hopes of having a school in Hazard began to glimmer when at various times a pioneer teacher made his appearance in the community. Among these early teachers were a Dr. Mason, John C. Eversole, and a Methodist preacher by the name of Shockley. School was held in the courthouse and in other places, no more suitable for a school room. In 1892, Judge Josiah H. Combs, to whom much credit is due, started the ball to rolling when he gave the school trustees permission to select a lot on his property anywhere they felt was suitable for a school house. Judge Combs was the grandson of Elijah Combs, who was one of the first settlers of Perry County. The problem was getting funds with which to build a school. At this time, Mr. W. O. Davis, for many years a trustee, did more than any one man. After getting the lot, he succeeded in getting placed in an old shed enough lumber for a one-room school. While searching for a carpenter to put up the building, the lumber was used for other purposes. A second and a third time, the same thing happened. It was then that he decided to get the carpenter first and then obtain the lumber. On hearing that there was a carpenter at Jackson, in Breathitt County, by the name of Ward, he secured the services of this man, who was the father of J. D. Ward, at one time Secretary of the Board of Education. After securing the services of the carpenter, Mr. Davis got the lumber for the building by taking logs from the river as they were being floated down stream to market, and then telling the owners of the logs how many he had taken and what they were to be used for. Mr. Ward built the first school building in Hazard. The building was built on High Street on the site of the C. B. Rose Home. The first teacher was Albert Williams, but cold weather came and he disbanded his school. In a short time, Will Ward reassembled the children and taught the remainder of the term.

"The real beginning of the graded school in Hazard was in 1893, when C. M. Horn, an alumnus of the University of

Missouri, took charge of the school. Within a few months, he was joined by Bailey P. Wootton, a graduate of Lebanon University. In 1894, Mr. Wootton was elected principal and had full charge for four years. While he was principal, he succeeded in having a second story added to the one-room structure. The money for this building was obtained by getting the Masonic Lodge to give $300.00 and the school raised $400.00.

In 1903, Hazard Baptist Institute was organized and incorporated as an academy. The board of trustees was composed of Rev. A. S. Petrey, who became the first president of the Institute, Bailey P. Wootton, Dr. E. Kelly, J. C. Boggs, J. L. Johnson, J. E. Johnson, W. H. Cornett, W. O. Davis, Rev. James Hall, Rev. W. M Baker, Pearl Combs, Judge A L. Begley, and B. P. Bowling. Cleon Calvert was the principal. The first structure was built where the Hazard High School Athletic Field now is located. Joe Blackburn, of Barbourville, was employed to construct the building, and it was finished at a cost of $5,500.00, plus $240.00 that was paid for 2.4 acres of land upon which the building was erected. In this one building, the Hazard Baptist Institute was conducted until 1909, when an adjacent plot of one acre of land was bought from Bird (E. C.) Holliday for $500.00, less a gift of $25.00 from the owner, Mr. Holliday. A new administration building was put up on this site, the work being done by hand labor at a cost of $8,000.00. Brick for both of these buildings was made by Joe E. Johnson, and Farmer Eversole. The lumber was prepared by J. L. Johnston in his saw and planing mill.(13)

The Institute included grades and high school. It graduated its first high school class in 1908. The members of this first graduating class were B. F. Cornett, Rachel Owens (Brashear), Anna Johnson (Jones) and Edmond Combs. In 1910 and 1911, the State Superintendent of Public instruction ruled that no public school could be operated in connection with a sectarian school. It was then that the district voted $12,000.00 in bonds to erect a new public school building. The public school, or Free School, as it was often referred to, was then resumed in the old building on High Street that had been used for a barn and had fallen into a terrible state of dis-repair. From there, it was moved into the building that is now occupied by Taulbee Furniture Company, and from there to a building on Broadway about where the home of Mrs. Frank Horn now stands.

At this time, through the efforts of County Superintendent John McIntosh, the Perry County Board of Education and Hazard Board of Education, it was decided to erect a joint building to be used by county high school students, Hazard grade and high school students. The contract for this building was let to B. F. Smith, of Dayton, Ohio. After getting the foundation started, misfortune caused the contractor to give up the project. The contract was then awarded to the Falls City Construction Company, of Cincinnati, and the building that is known as Lower Broadway was completed in 1913 at the cost of $30,000.00. The first trustees were W. O. Davis, J. D. Ward, B. P. Wootton, W. C. Eversole and W. C. Combs.

The first superintendent of schools for Hazard was John Wilson. He was followed by L. B. Stephens. Coming later was Mr. Hargrove, and Mr. Stephens returned to Hazard to serve a second time. When he left Hazard, he was succeeded by R. T. Whittinghill, who was followed by P. H. Neblett. When Mr. Neblett left Hazard, Mr. Whittinghill returned and remained until a few years ago. He was succeeded by the present superintendent, Mr. Roy Eversole. In 1920, the city school census showed an increase of more than 1,200 students, with accommodations for only 800.

In 1921, Superintendent P. H. Neblett proposed to the Hazard Board of Education a five-year building program which would include a two-story brick building with 10 class rooms at Allais; a modern high school building to accommodate 600 students in Hazard; a two-story brick 12 class room building at Lothair, and a building for colored children to be located on Liberty Street.

In 1923, the Allais building was completed at a cost of $15,000.00. In 1924, Hazard High School was completed at a cost of $140,000.000, including equipment. The census report sent out by the Kentucky State Board of Education shows that no city in the state has equalled the increase made by the Hazard school.

In 1920, the enrollment had increased from 1,250 students to 2,482. These figures show that Hazard City Schools lacked only 18 pupils of having a 100% increase in a five-year period.

The Lothair school, a ward school, had been housed in a very inadequate building near the bank of the river in Lothair. The new building was completed and ready for use in 1928.

The Liberty Street School was completed in 1936. The plan to contruct this building was not carried out under the building program that Mr. P. H. Neblett had proposed, because of lack of money. The colored children went to school in a two-room building that was on Liberty Street, and, while Mr. Neblett was superintendent, he added another room to that building. In 1924, the enrollment of the colored school was 115 students, taught by three teachers.

In regard to colored schools, it will be necessary to go back as early as 1874. The General Assembly passed, in February of 1874, a school law for the benefit of colored people. At this time, the colored school fund consisted of revenue tax of 45 cents on each $100.00 worth of property owned by colored people, a tax on each colored male over 21 years of age, all taxes levied and collected on dogs owned or kept by colored persons, all fines, penalties imposed upon or collected from colored persons due the state. The assessors were to keep separate lists of property of colored citizens, ages of children from six to 16 years. There were to be three trustees to a district, and later, when the law was changed to one trustee to a district, it applied to colored trustees as well as white trustees. (14)

There were no schools for colored children in Perry County until Mr. John McIntosh became Superintendent, and, during his term of office, there was one school house built on Town Mountain. A report of the State Department of Mines of Kentucky, for the year 1924, page 120, shows that there were three colored school districts in Perry

County, five school buildings and an enrollment of 573 colored school children.

The first colored school teachers remembered in Perry County were named Olinger and lived on Browns Fork. Susie Puryear, wife of the principal of Liberty Street School, and Nannie Cornett are members of the same family.

A colored preacher by the name of E. Williams came to Hazard from Cynthiana, Kentucky, and taught school in Perry County. He married Eliza Combs. After the completion of the Liberty Street School, it was opened not only to colored boys and girls of Hazard who were in high school, but was also opened to county students.

This year, 1950, there were seven graduates of Liberty High School. They have an enrollment of 285 pupils and employ eight teachers. There are now seven schools in Perry County for colored children.

In 1929-30, the Hazard Baptist Institute found itself heavily in debt and it was decided to turn the school into a Junior College. This project functioned for two years, and the board found that, in order to be an accredited college, they had to reach and maintain a standard that was out of the question for so small a group of sponsors. Rev. Petrey made an appeal to the Baptist Educational Society in Louisville, in 1936, for aid but the appeal failed. The board of trustees had no alternative but to close the doors of the Hazard Baptist Institute. The property remained closed until it was sold, in 1941, to the Hazard Board of Education for $19,000.00 and is now used for a Junior High School.

At the opening of school on September 4, 1950, the records show that the Hazard school system reported an enrollment of 2,073 pupils for the year, according to Superintendent Roy Eversole. Sixty-seven (67) teachers are now employed by the Hazard Board of Education.

On November 7, 1950, the voters of Hazard voted a bond issue for $59,000.00. The money is to be used to build a four-room addition to the Allais school and for repairs on the present school building.

The **Hazard Herald,** published October 29, 1949, tells

of Dr. R. L. Collins swinging a pick into the ground, before some 500 cheering spectators, to start work on the Memorial Gymnasium to be built for Hazard through the generosity of Hazard and Perry County people, under the supervision of Lawrence Davis.

In summing up the enrollment for the year, we find there is a total enrollment of 12,031 children in Hazard and Perry County schools from grades 1 through 12.

CHAPTER VIII
RELIGIOUS GROWTH
Allie Daniel Gorman

When the first settlers came into Perry County to establish homes, they immediately started planning for a place in which to worship God.

In 1789, Jacob Eversole, a Baptist minister, settled in what is now Perry County, and it is related in "The Ebersol Families in America, 1729-1937," by Charles E. Ebersol (owned by Roy G. Eversole, Hazard) that because he could not speak English plainly his congregation left him and members of his family organized "The Old Grapevine Church" where he preached many years. He lived to be 100 years old.

In 1790, Richard Smith, a Baptist minister, came to Perry County from Virginia. He preached in Perry and in what is now known as Breathitt County.

In 1807, Electious Thompson, a Baptist minister, came to Perry County originally from North Carolina and preached among these settlers. In 1808 he settled near the mouth of Rockhouse, now located in Letcher County. In 1809 he was joined by Elder William Salisbury of Floyd County and later Simeon Justice another minister of Floyd and these three constituted the Presbytery that organized the first Church. They were from the North District Association which was organized the first Friday in October, 1802, at the Unity Meeting House, Clark County.

These pioneers journeyed by foot, horseback or ox cart through almost unbroken wilderness covering hundreds of miles attending associations, funerals and Church appointments. These early ministers were called Elders.

These early settlers were very devout and deeply consecrated, permitting only those things in their homes which led to higher and nobler living. They worshipped in homes, under trees, in old log school houses and open spaces until church buildings could be erected. In some communities the church was built first and served also as a school. The first churches were constructed of logs and sometimes called "Meeting Houses." (Minute Book A, p. 202 and Deed Book

13, p. 448.) The first church established in what was later Perry County was the Indian Bottom Church.

THE INDIAN BOTTOM CHURCH

In 1810 some twenty Baptists assembled in the home of Isaac Whitaker about two miles up the Kentucky River from where Blackey is now located near what is known as the Indian Bottom (where Indians had camped) and organized the Indian Bottom Church. William Salisbury and Simeon Justice of Floyd County and Electious Thompson formed the Presbytery. Some of the early members were: James Webb, John Adams, Benjamin Webb, Electious Thompson, John Dixon, Isaac Taulbee, James Harris, Stephen Caudill, Sarah Caudill, Rachel Adams, Mathias Kelley, Amy Kelley, James Caudill, Mary Caudill, Benjamin Caudill, Spencer Adams, Isaac Whitaker, Archelous Craft and John Bunyard.

Electious Thompson was chosen pastor and Isaac Whitaker clerk. These settlers brought their letters from the churches where they had belonged back in Virginia and North Carolina colonies. In 1811 this church was received into the Washington Association which was composed of churches in the southwestern part of Virginia. Regardless of distance, these early churches were represented at the annual Associations. In 1814 Elder Daniel Duff was known to have preached where Whitesburg is now located (then Floyd, later Perry). In 1815 on a return trip he was accompanied by two other Baptist ministers, William Wells and John Flannery. The latter was pastor of Deep Springs Church, Lee County, Virginia. Duff once lived on the river above Blackey, Kentucky, and came down into what is now Perry County in 1818. His preaching tours covered not only Perry, but records show that the Presbytery which organized the Oven Fork Church in 1820 was composed of Elders Daniel Duff, William Wells (who later settled in Hazard) and John Flannery.

GRAPEVINE AND CAMPBELL BEND

The Grapevine Church was organized on the fourth

Saturday in April, 1815, by Abel Pennington and John York. It was reorganized the third Saturday in September, 1855 at the Mouth of Wolf Pen Branch by Irvin Eversole, James B. Noble and Sam Smith and was named "Old Campbell Bend." This is the record given by Reverend Taylor Hamblin, present pastor of the "Old Campbell Bend Church" at Dunraven, Kentucky, and Scott Campbell, Clerk.

The record given by Grover Day, present clerk "Old Grapevine Church" states this church was organized June 15, 1915, by Abel Pennington and John York, and was reorganized September 1, 1872, by James Napier and Zack Fugate. This Church has held to the old name. It is located on Highway 28 near the Davidson School house where services are held at the present time.

A site was donated by Dr. H. P. Duff and a new modern church building now under construction is almost completed. In an interview with Nancy Ann Davidson, eighty-five years old, wife of the late Shade Davidson stated she had lived in this vicinity sixty-four years and that she and her late husband had served as deacons of this church for fifty-four years. The Reverend Elias Mullins who served this church as pastor sixty-four years told her this was the oldest church in what is now Perry County. Reverend Mullins died in January, 1951, at the age of ninety-four.

The early Minister Daniel Duff lived near the site of this church between 1818 and 1834.

Reverend Brach Feltner is the present Pastor.

SANDLICK CHURCH

This Church was organized August 13, 1815, at the home of Stephen Caudill near the mouth of Sandlick, and named for the Creek near by. The Presbytery consisted of William Salisbury, Electious Thompson, and Simeon Justice. Other visiting elders were Daniel Duff, William Wells and John Flannery. John Adams and Benjamin Adams were elected deacons and Spencer Adams was received as an elder, having been ordained by the Indian Bottom Church. Simeon Justice was chosen pastor followed by Spencer Adams.

CARRS FORK CHURCH

This Church was established in 1827 by members from the Indian Bottom Church. Among the 13 Charter Members were John Smith, John Bunyard, Thomas Francis, Joseph Mullins.

AN EARLY RECORD

"The second Saturday in April, 1830, the Baptist Church of Jesus Christ on Troublesome, Perry County, Kentucky, this is to certify that our Beloved Sister, Phebe Fugate is in full fellowship with us, and is dismissed from us when joined to any other Church of the same faith and order, signed by order of S.D. Church. William Miller, C.C."
—(George Campbell, Hardshell, Ky.)

LIBERTY CHURCH

Established in 1852 by ten members from the Carrs Fork Church. Elder Jordan Ashley, Minister. Early Members were B. Hall and N. W. Cornett.

LOTTS CREEK CHURCH

This Church was in existence in 1860. Some of the early members were Thomas Keathley, Alexander Combs, and Thomas Grigsby.

MINUTES OF THE MOUNTAIN ASSOCIATION OF REGULAR BAPTISTS, HELD WITH SWIFT CAMP CHURCH, WOLFE COUNTY, ON FRIDAY BEFORE THE 2d SATURDAY IN SEPTEMBER, 1860, AND TWO DAYS FOLLOWING.

FRIDAY, Sept. 7th., 1860—1st. Introductory Sermon by Elder Jos. Spence, from Hebrews, 10th chapter, 16th and 17th verses.

2d. Letters from the different Churches called for and read, and the names of the Messengers and Churches enrolled, as exhibited in the following table.

Names of Churches	*Messengers' Names*
Lotts Creek	John Grigsby and Ben Grigsby
Mount Zion	Not Represented
Buckhorn	Alfred Combs
Swift Camp	John Wireman, Franklin Spencer and J. H. Senter
Spencer	Eld. J. D. Spencer, Eld. Wm. Boothe and W. T. Spencer

Quicksand	Elder Joseph Spence, Wm. Taulbee and W. J. Cope
Liberty	James Oaks and W. G. Noble
Holly Creek	Not Represented
Baptist Union	Elder J. W. Moore, Thos. Handy and Elias Moore
Mountain Chapel	Robert Boyd, Robert Burgy and James Smith

3d. The Association then chose Elder James W. Moore, Moderator, and W. J. Cope, Clerk.

4th. The Association then opened a door for the reception of Churches. There came forward Mountain Chapel of Regular Baptist faith and order, and offered a letter by her messengers, Robert Boid, Robert Burgy, and James Smith, which was received and her messengers invited to take a seat.

ORDAINED PREACHERS

James Napper, Samuel Smith, J. Campbell, T. Holiday, J. W. Moore, J. D. Spencer, Wm. Boothe, E. N. Baker, Joseph Spence, P P Napper, J. W. Moore.

LICENSED PREACHERS

Zach. Fugate, I. Smith, Wiley Roberts, Dick Johnson (a Slave), J. H. Robinson, John Brown.

CIRCULAR LETTER

To the Churches and Members of the Mountain Association of Regular Baptists:

DEAR BRETHREN AND SISTERS:—My wish is that grace, mercy and peace may ever abound amongst you. We hope the Lord will ever direct you in that way that shall be best calculated to promote his own glory and your happiness; and as we know of no subject from which we can derive more comfort to ourselves than that of Christian fellowship, we offer you a few thoughts on its nature and importance. All those who believe that it comes from God, will readily admit that its nature is divine, for, says the Apostle, "Have fellowship with us, for truly our fellowship is with the Father and with his son Jesus Christ." From which it appears we have no right to expect the fellowship of others unless we give some evidence that we have fellowship with the Father and his Son; or, in other words, to give them evidence that our legal hope has been slain by the law, and our present consolation and good hope is through grace, not that the Law was made Sin to us, but that we were made sinners by its revelation, first in our nature by Adam's transgression, as our practice is as bad as his was. Hence we may as well expect the body to live when the spirit is absent, as to expect Christian Fellowship in the absence of religion. We should therefore try to distinguish, Brethren, that which is real and that which is seemingly. As fellowship consists of union of soul in proportion to the faith we have in each other, it becomes the more necessary that we examine ourselves whether we be in the faith, and that our endeavors should be to give to others those evidences that correspond with the obedience of faith, by being often engaged in labor of love, and as we can only love those as the children of God that we believe to be born of his Spirit of Christ, he is none of His; and such as deny his divine operation we believe to be yet in their sins, having neither fellowship for Christians nor a right to Christian Fellowship, for it is impossible for those who do not believe our Lord Jesus Christ to be their only Saviour to have fellowship for those that have no other hope for salvation.

The Glory of God and the advancement to his Kingdom should be our main object in all our religious acts. It is therefore important at all times, for Christians to attend to good order and discipline in the house of God, which is the guardian of our peace, without which there can be no union among the professed followers of the meek and lowly Jesus, for a neglect of discipline in the churches is a certain road to discord and confusion. So that we ought not to neglect to meet at our stated Church Meeting, for we are commanded not to forsake the assembling ourselves together, for we are bought with a price, therefore we ought to glorify God by attending to all the ordinances of His house, and adorn the doctrine of our Saviour by obeying his commandments. This is his commandment, that we should love one another. Dear Brethren, let us not deceive ourselves hoping that we love God if we love not the Brethren. Be ye therefore followers of God, as dear children, and walk in love, as Christ loved us and gave himself for us to redeem us from all iniquity, and purify to himself a peculiar people zealous of good works, which God hath ordained that we should walk in them. From the coldness in the several Churches composing our body, we fear there has been a neglect of our duty that is justly due to God, and a want of faithfulness to one another as Brethren. The Apostle admonishes us to hold fast the profession of our faith without wearying, for he is faithful that promises. And, above all things, have charity among yourselves which shall cover a multitude of sins.

Now, may the God of all grace shine into each of our hearts to give the light of the glory of God as it shines in the face of the Lord Jesus, who is the great Shepherd of his sheep. Yours in bonds of love. Farewell.—(Minutes secured by Eva Smith.)

BALLS FORK CHURCH

Established in 1861, Elder Sam Maggard, Pastor. Early members were James Stewart, William Huff, J. W. Moore, G. W. Moore and M. Hughes.

(Information on the above early churches was contributed by the late Rev. G. Bennett Adams, Whitesburg, Ky., Regular Baptist Minister before his death in 1950.)

THE JOHNSON UNITED BAPTIST CHURCH

The Johnson United Baptist Church was organized from the Grapevine United Baptist Church, Perry County, Ky., in 1869 by the Rev. Matt Cannagin, Rev. Jimmy Gunn and Rev. Elias Morris as Moderators. The Ministers who served from its date of organization 1869 to 1944 were Robert Burton, Robert Bowling, George Johnson, Levi Robins, Wm. Baker, Lewis Little, W. M. Baker, M. A. Petrey, I. H. Gabbard, Edd Gabbard, Squire McIntosh, T. G. Bates, Squire M. Riley, W. M. McIntosh, O. J. Amis, Cam Johnson, Ed Amis, and Eli Turner.

The Johnson Sunday School was organized in 1889 by R. R. Baker, W. M. Amis, Polly T. Johnson, I. D. Johnson and others.—(The late Luther Johnson.)

BIG LEATHERWOOD CHURCH

On the second Saturday in July, 1871, a group of members from the Indian Bottom Church met under a large woodshed at the home of Anderson and Susanah Cornett and organized the Big Leatherwood Church. Elders John A. Caudill, Wiley Morris, Samuel Combs and James Dixon formed the Presbytery. The Charter Members were Rhoda Pratt, Archibald Cornett, Polly Brashear, Cindy Caudill, Eli Callihan, Wm. R. Stamper, Clemat Shepherd, Susanah Cornett, Mary Holcomb, William Holcomb, William Campbell, Isom Caudill, Nancy Caudill, Elizabeth Caudill, William McIntyre, Dianah McIntyre, Elizabeth Brashear, Robert S. Brashear, Sally Brashear, Lou Anna Combs, Mary Ann

Brashear, John D. Combs, Elizabeth Hall, John H. Hall, Mary Fields, Charles L. Cornett and James Stevens.

Hiram Pratt and William Brashear were ordained as deacons, and Charles L. Cornett, Clerk. James Dixon was chosen Pastor.

The Church was admitted to the New Salem Association organized in 1825.

Some of the other early members were Anderson Cornett, Jonah Ison, Edward Griffith, Matilda Ison, Judy Ison, Abagail Hall, Theophilus Woods, Cindy Woods, Roger Cornett, Samuel Brashear, Ira Combs, John Jent, Elizabeth Griffith, Cynthia Combs, Polly Ann Boggs, John B. Cornett, and Elizabeth Cornett.

Early Deacons were Robert S. Brashear, Anderson Cornett, Jonah Ison and Matilda Ison, J. B. Cornett and Elizabeth Cornett.

Elder Ira Combs was baptized into this Church October, 1873, and ordained a Minister July, 1879. He was called as Assistant Pastor in October of the same year and in 1886 he became Pastor where he served until his late eighties.

Other early Ministers who came out of this Church were William Brashear, ordained July 1879; Hiram Fields, ordained 1882 and became Assistant Pastor July 1888; J. M. Hall, ordained December, 1887.

A site for the Church Building was donated by Anderson and Susanah Cornett in the lower end of the field of their farm, where the Ritter Lumber Company pond is now located. The first Church, which also served as a school, was a large one room structure of logs with an immense open fireplace. On May 5, 1894, a site below the old road near the mouth of Big Leatherwood, was purchased from Eli and Jane Cornett and a new frame structure was erected. With the coming of the Railroad it was moved to its present site at the mouth of Little Leatherwood adjoining Denver Miniard's farm, and under the leadership of the present Pastor, James Pratt, a new Church is being erected.

Ministers who have come out of this Church are Eli

Pratt, Bee Ison, B. Cornett, Granville Riddle, L. C. Riddle, G. M. Caudill, J. W. Pratt, Dixie Ison.

Above information was taken from the original record. —(Floyd Huff, James Pratt.)

CLEAR CREEK CHURCH

Established in 1872. Some of the members were Elders Samuel Combs, Felix Combs and Wm. Campbell.—(The late Bennett Adams.)

AN EARLY RECORD

The Sandlick Association was organized in 1876 in the name of "Regular Baptist," in 1893 it was recorded as "Primitive Baptist," and in 1894 is was recorded as "Regular Primitive." The original record is in possession of Steve Fairchild, Whitesburg, Ky. Rev. Odis Smith, Regular Primitive Baptist Minister of Dwarf, Ky., states there was a division during this time and some of the Churches took the name of Regular Primitive. In 1894 the Sandlick Association held their annual meeting with the Lotts Creek Church which was numbered with the Regular Primitive Churches.—(Rev. Odis Smith, Steve Fairchild.)

HUFF ISLAND BAPTIST CHURCH

This Church located on Campbell's Creek was organized January 25, 1885, by Irvin Eversole and Isaac Hamblin.—(Reverend Taylor Hamblin.)

IRA COMBS MEMORIAL CHURCH

Many will remember that Church Services were held regularly the first Saturday and Sunday of each month in the Court House by Rev. Ira Combs, a pioneer Old Regular Baptist Minister, who was known to all as "Uncle Ira." For many years it was a custom for some of the Churches to dismiss their Sunday Morning Service and attend his Meeting at the Court House. Rev. Sam Combs of Jeff, Ky., stated:

On the second Saturday in August, 1909, the Big Leatherwood Church granted permission for a Church to be established in Hazard, Kentucky. Rev. Hiram Fields was appointed to assist Rev. Ira Combs, and letters were granted to the following charter members: Ira Combs, Hiram Combs, Elzira Combs, Polly Ann Crawford, Susan Tyree, Joseph Cornett, Morgan Cornett, Chester Combs, Polly Ann Boggs, Mary Combs, Aly Walker, Sally Davidson, Sally Ann Adams, Margaret Cornett, Cinthia Combs, Jasper Cornett, and Polly Ann Cornett.

The Church was named Little Zion, Rev. Ira Combs was chosen Pastor, and Joseph Cornett, Clerk.

In 1910 a lot on east Main Street near where the Seale Motor Company is now located was purchased from John and Maulta Ward, the Church building was erected and dedication services were held August 6, 1911. (Hazard Herald, August 10, 1911.)

In 1921 Little Zion Church was moved to a new church building that had been erected on Uncle Ira's old homestead on Highway No. 15 at Jeff, Ky., where he continued as Pastor, preaching regularly, until around three months before his death which was one month and twenty-one days before his ninetieth birthday. Following his death Elder Watson Combs became Pastor and served until his death in 1944. Rev. Sam Combs, present Pastor and son of Rev. Ira Combs, was elected Pastor and under his leadership the old Church Building was replaced by a new modern building and the name was changed to "Ira Combs Memorial Church" in memory of his father. It was dedicated on Easter Sunday, 1952.

Rev. Ira Combs was born at Jeff, Ky., 1844, son of Elizabeth Ison Combs and Talton Combs. He was one of Perry County's most loved and respected Minister and Citizens. He died April 8, 1934, and was buried in the family graveyard on his old homestead.

BOWMAN MEMORIAL METHODIST CHURCH

The Methodist Church had its beginning in the early days of Perry County. A marriage return in the Perry County Clerks Office is recorded as follows: "R. W. Landrum was marriade by me C. Babbit 18 August 1836."

Rev. A. C. Watts, retired Methodist Minister living in Simpsonville, Ky., relates records show Carlisle Babbitt was placed in charge of the Kentucky Mission in 1834, including this portion of Kentucky. Ruben Washington Landrum, born in Clark County, began preaching at an early age and was admitted to the Kentucky Conference of the Methodist Church. In 1834 he was assigned to the Mt. Vernon Circuit and in 1835 assigned to the Hopkinsville Circuit. During this time he married Margaret (Peggy) Brashear, daughter of Robert and Polly Everage Brashear who lived at the mouth of Little Leatherwood. He was appointed to supply Hazard 1872, and Breathitt Circuit 1875, later settled on Lost Creek, Breathitt County. Rev. M. T. Chandler appointed to Hazard and Whitesburg, 1881. Although assignments were made to this area, there are no records of any activity in the community.

Rev. Geo. O. Barnes, independent Presbyterian, sometimes termed "Mountain Evangelist" held a meeting at the Court House July, 1881. Rev. Barnes describes his stay as follows: "A place was prepared for us, the congregation this P.M. looked a welcome, no scowling, nor hardness in any face, it inspired me at once, had an excellent congregation at night, very attentive, no drinking visible, no swearing audible, quiet and orderly a place as we have found."

The Hazard Methodist Church was organized in 1887 with the Rev. James B. Shockley and twenty-eight charter members. Some of these members were Isaac Baker, Eliza Baker, Zachariah Morgan, Louisa Morgan, Ella Morgan, Emily Morgan, Robert Combs, Eliza Combs, Robin M. Baker, Maragret Baker, Reuben Messer (Minister), Celia Davis, Mary Ward. Other early members were Lee Daniel, Dr. J. P. Boggs and Araminta Ward. Rev. Shockley served as Pastor for eight years. In 1895 he became critically ill and Robin Baker arranged for him to be taken down the river on a raft to Jackson during a tide. He died in a Lexington Hospital six weeks later.

The Church was abandoned for thirteen years and the

members worshipped with the Baptist and Presbyterian congregations. Rev. W. P. Fryman, Present Pastor of Park Methodist Church in Lexington, Kentucky, stated that in the early part of 1908 while he was serving the Hindman and Whitesburg Churches he came into Hazard and preached at intervals in the Presbyterian Church. Many of the members had died and by this time the Church was greatly impaired and could not be used. In the summer of that year, Rev. Gillis and Rev. Guise walked into Hazard from Wilmore, Ky., to hold a meeting in the Church. They were directed to the home of Robin and Margaret Baker, known to everyone of "Uncle Robin" and "Aunt Mag." Before returning to Wilmore Prayer Meeting was held there on the front porch of Uncle Robin and Aunt Mag's home. A house to house solicitation of funds and anyone who could use a hammer or saw was made by Aunt Mag. Soon the Old Church was repaired. Rev. Fryman arranged for Rev. Allen and Rev. Overly to hold a meeting in the fall. Many were added to the Church. Among these were Charley and Elvira Bowman. Under the leadership of Rev. Fryman and with the combined efforts of the old pioneer members, the Bowmans, and many others, the Church was reorganized and became very active. Rev. Fryman continued as part time Pastor until 1909. During Rev. Fryman's Pastorate services were held in the Church on Saturday Evening for the colored people.

Rev. Walter V. Cropper was Hazard's beginning full time Pastor, serving from 1909 to 1913. Under his leadership the Church continued in its steady growth. The old building was replaced with a beautiful new structure along with the Pastor's home adjoining the Church which was given the name of "Bowman Memorial Methodist Church." Charlie Bowman donated $26,000 cash to this building, was a day laborer on the job and also donated the lot for the parsonage. Services were held in the old skating rink where Wells Paper Shop now stands while the new building was under construction. Other Pastors following were C. P. Pilow, I. R. Hollon, R. A. Selby, E. L. Griffey, R. F. Jordan, E. K. Pike, W. B. Garriott, J. W. Crates, C. L. Bohon, A. E.

Smith, A. R. Perkins, G. D. Prentiss, Frank King, G. M. Rainey, J. Ralph Wood, Albert G. Stone, R. F. Ockerman, and Ralph P. Mirse, present Pastor. Young Men in the Ministry who have gone from this Church are Clyde Boggs, now Pastor of Methodist Church at Mt. Gilead, North Carolina, and Charles W. Boleyn, Pastor of Bethany Methodist Church, Atlanta, Georgia.—(Mrs. James Garnott, Rev. W. P. Fryman, Rev. A. C. Watts.)

LOTHAIR METHODIST CHURCH

In the summer of 1920 a Mrs. J. H. Burke, better known as "Mother Burke" of Richmond, Kentucky, Miss Effie Hahn and Mr. J. R. Parker both students of Asbury College, Wilmore, Kentucky, came to Lothair, Kentucky, with a tent and held a revival. Prior to this the late Thomas D. Walters and the late W. B. Wise had been conducting Sunday School and Church services in the school house. The late Jesse Morgan of Hazard, Kentucky, donated a plot of ground. The late E. K. Pike then Pastor of Methodist Church in Hazard, is largely responsible for the erection of this church. Mr. and Mrs. Charles Walls, Mrs. Maggie Hall Coleman, Herschel Walls, Mrs. Ernest Fritts (Miss Effie Hahn) and Mrs. Lika Mullen were some of its charter members. The Church was finished in 1924 and was dedicated in 1935. Rev. Leslie M. Rogers was Pastor at the time of dedication. Some of the Ministers that have served as Pastors were the late Thomas D. Walters, late Proctor S. Elam, Rev. David Kingler, Walter B. Garriott, W. B. Conn, Leslie M. Rogers, Herbert Henry, Howard Coop, T. H. Bandy and Rev. Roberts.—(Mrs. Ernest Fritts.)

PHILLIPS TEMPLE METHODIST CHURCH (Colored)

In the spring of 1937 a small group assembled in the home of Louie and Inez Davis and the Phillips Temple Methodist Church was organized. Charter Members were Hattie Adams, Louie and Inez Davis, Arzo Brown, Will Harding. Early Members were Julia Razor, Clarence Nunn, Jesse Richardson. An appeal was made to Bishop C. H. Phillips in Cleveland, Ohio, for a Pastor and Rev. Warr was given the assignment. There was no money for the Pastor's salary and he was given a place to live in the home of Louie and Inez Davis. Services were held in the homes until funds were raised to start the Church. Through the cooperation of Dr. J. P. Boggs sufficient funds were raised to finish paying for the building. Liberal contributions were made by the Members of Bowman Memorial Methodist Church. A lot on Peach Street was purchased from Estill Combs for $200.00 which was donated by Bishop Phillips. Members and friends prepared the ground for the contractors and the first services were held in the new building November 23, 1937. Pastors were Rev. W. W. Warr, S. L. McGee, I. H. Harris, J. J. Manna, H. G. McGee, and M. J. O'Hara.—(Clarence Nunn.)

CHRISTIAN CHURCH

The Christian Church is one of the oldest congregations in Perry County. A marriage record in the County Clerk Office states that: On May 17, 1866, James Campbell married to Rebecca Campbell by the Rev. W. R. Hoskins.

Nora McIntosh Campbell says that Samuel Standafer, James Oliver, and W. R. Hoskins were Ministers of the earlier days of the Christian Church in Perry County, preaching mostly in the rural area. A. J. Witt residing in Krypton, now in his eighties, stated that in his boyhood days he attended Church on Willard at the home of W. R. Hoskins (better known as Uncle Billie) and in the school house. The Willard Church was established and church building erected during the ministry of W. R. Hoskins, where he served as Pastor for many years.

In an interview with Sarah Baker Hill, former resident of Perry County, now living in Utah, she related that Isaac Baker was an early Minister of the Christian Church, preaching in Perry and Leslie Counties.

An item in the Hazard Herald—March 27, 1913, and April 10, 1913, states that the Rev. R. A. Zahn, noted evangelist and Pastor of a Louisville Church, held a meeting in the Court House and a Christian Church was organized

April 17, 1913, with twenty resident members. However, nothing more was ascertained from this meeting.

Dr. C. B. Combs stated that the Rev. George Woodard, colored Christian Minister, accompanied by Dan Olinger, a teacher, came into Perry County from Virginia around the year of 1886 and preached among the colored people on Browns Fork. Services were hold in the home of his father, Jack Combs. Rev. Woodard returned two or three times a year from Virginia riding over Black Mountain to hold services. He continued these visits for six or seven years. Although a Christian Church was never established by this group, many were baptized by Rev. Woodard. Among these were Jensey Combs, Harriet Combs, Lizzie Ison, Vina Combs, and Sarah Combs.)

HAZARD CHRISTIAN CHURCH

The Hazard Christian Church had its beginning on the fourth day of November, 1915, when four ladies, Mrs. Will Cook, Mrs. D. H. Goodlette, Mrs. H. C. Faulkner and Estelle Grace, met in the home of Mrs. Will Cook and organized a "Ladies Aid." Mrs. Will Cook was chosen President, Estelle Grace, secretary, and Mrs. D. H. Goodlette, treasurer. They sought other members of the same faith to join them and work toward the organization of a church in Hazard. On December 12, 1915, an evangelistic meeting was held at the Court House with Rev. J. Ross Miller as evangelist. During this meeting the Church was organized and the charter members were Mrs. H. C. Faulkner, Mr. and Mrs. John McIntosh, Alma Faulkner, Mrs. D. H. Goodlette, Estelle Grace, Mr. and Mrs. Monroe Nichols and Ira Nichols. John McIntosh was first Sunday School Superintendent, Monroe Nichols, teacher of Men's Class, Mrs. H. C. Faulkner, teacher of Women's Class. Rev. Garrett Combs served as part time Pastor. First Elders were Joe Alloway, C. E. Bullard, W. E. Faulkner, Dr. John Hoskins and John McIntosh. The group met at various times in the local theater, the school building, and the court house and in December of 1916 called the Rev. John H. Allen as Pastor. He remained with the congregation until January of 1918. The exodus of people from the community during and following the war took with them many of the members of this church and another pastor was not called to succeed Rev. Allen. In 1916 six lots were purchased from Miss Bertha Lyttle, they hoped to erect a Church but these were sold in 1919 for $1,250.00 and the money was invested in Liberty Bonds. The Church met in private homes during 1921 and 1922. During the summer of 1923 Rev. W. J. Clarke, Secretary of the Kentucky Christian Missionary Society, assisted in reorganizing the Church at a meeting held in the home of Mr. and Mrs. L. H. Stiles. A revival was held at the Courthouse during November of that year and the reorganized Church started out with one hundred and twenty-eight charter members. From November to the following June the congregation was ministered to by visiting clergymen until Rev. A. C. Brooks could come to Hazard. He served until September, 1928. During his Ministry the present Church Building was erected. The dedication services were held on November 28, 1926, with the Rev. Allen Wilson, Secretary of the Kentucky Christian Missionary Society, delivering the principal address. Rev. Russell Osgood of Louisville followed. During his Ministry which closed on February 1, 1931, a portion of the building indebtedness was paid off. A Sunday School was established at Ajax. Rev. Ruben H. Stewart began his work on February 1, 1931. Through a ministry of eleven years, five thousand dollars was paid on the building indebtedness. The Rev. C. Duke Payne came to Hazard on July 15, 1942. Prior to his coming the Church purchased the home to the Southeast of the Church as a parsonage. During Rev. Payne's Ministry the last remaining debt on the church and parsonage was paid, the chancel and chapel rearranged and newly furnished. The last debt was paid on December 31, 1944. Rev. Herbert T. Chase followed and took up his responsibilities on November 10, 1949. In the fall of 1952 Rev. William Brizendine assumed the pastoral duties after Rev. Chase's departure for ecumenical work in South America.—(Mrs. D. H. Goodlette, Mrs. John E. Campbell, Rev. H. T. Chase.)

CAMPBELL CREEK CHRISTIAN CHURCH

This church was organized in the school house on Campbell Creek in 1930, and church was built in 1932. Some of the charter members were Taylor Witt, A. J. Witt, McKinley Campbell and M. C. Howard.—(M. C. Howard.)

HAZARD PRESBYTERIAN CHURCH

It was during the Civil War that Dr. Edward O. Guerrant, a young lieutenant who was well educated and a practicing physician in General Morgan's Army, found his duties led him into the remotest sections of the Appalachian Mountains. Here he came to know and love the people of the mountains. After the war was over he returned to not only heal broken and sick bodies but to minister to their spiritual needs. In August, 1892, Dr. Guerrant rode horseback from Jackson to Hazard and a meeting was held in the court house with 38 professions. He had made friends earlier with a physician, Dr. W. T. Wilson, whom he felt was the only Presbyterian in Perry County. On August 31, 1892, Dr. Guerrant with Josiah H. Combs, Dr. W. T. Wilson, and Jeremiah McIntosh met in the dining room of the Palace Hotel and the First Presbyterian Church was organized. Charter Members were Polly Ann Combs, Curtis Combs, Ellen Campbell, Mr. and Mrs. Wm. Stout, Marshall Combs, Josephine Stout, Dr. W. T. Wilson, Farmer Eversole, Sara Ellen Edwards, Jeremiah McIntosh, John Sexton, John B. Eversole, Polly Stout, Alfred Feltner, Nancy Ann Campbell, Nancy Ann Stacy, Josiah H. Combs, Susan Eversole, Mr. and Mrs. Eli Couch, Kate Morgan, Lula Sexton, Sara Jane Combs, Lucinda Couch, Charles Morgan, Asberry McIntosh, Susan Asher, Roscoe Little, Emmet Stout, Mr. and Mrs. Tom Smith, Nancy Sexton, Armelda Asher, Emily Morgan, and Finley Sumner. First Elders elected were Josiah H. Combs, Dr. W. T. Wilson, and Jeremiah McIntosh. John B. Eversole was the First Deacon. The First Trustees were Josiah Combs, Jr., and James O. Combs. The First Pastor was Rev. Matt R. Sawyer. After Rev. Sawyer's arrival the membership began making plans for a building.

Josiah H. Combs gave the lot on which the building was to be erected. The location is where Dr. J. P. Boggs now lives.

The second Pastor of the Church, Rev. J. H. Wallins served 1895-1897 and the Church on the hill was completed in 1895. Services were held in the homes and in the Courthouse until the Church was built.

Felix G. Begley, Elder and Sunday School Superintendent for sixteen years and his wife, Margaret Boggs Begley was instrumental in holding the Church together during the time when there was no Pastor.

Other Ministers who followed were Rev. Charles Farnsworth, J. T. Mitchell, Rev. Tupple and Rev. Witherspoon assisted during summer months.

On March 22, 1904, the Church on the hill was blown down by a wind storm, services were then held in the old school house on High Street. Rev. J. A. Thompson was the Pastor at that time. Rev. A. D. Boggs, Chairman of Evangelism in the Synod, assisted in holding the Church together. The lot was sold on the hill and another purchased from John and Maulta Ward on High Street in 1905. J. E. Johnson furnished the lumber and a new building was erected the first service being held on Sunday, January 7, 1906. Much credit is due Margaret Begley, Lizzie Combs and Angeline Dixon for their untiring efforts to raise funds to furnish the Church.

Rev. Allen Jones came in 1912. During his ministery the manse was built on Hall Street. Following Rev. Jones, Rev. Muldraugh McLaughlin was called in 1916. Rev. R. M. Pegram was called in 1918 and during his ministry the lot on High Street was sold and the lot on Broadway was purchased from Perry Gorman and the present brick church was erected. Rev. Lowry Bowman served 1923-1927. Rev. Norman Cook came in 1927, followed by Rev. Alton B. Glasure under whose ministry the educational annex was built. Rev. William C. Brown came after Rev. Glasure. He asked to become Assistant pastor in order to do mission work in the mining camps. (See Hull Memorial, Harveyton, etc.) Rev. Leonard Woodward served the Church for two years. Rev. Basil Hicks is the present pastor. After Mr.

Hicks' arrival the former S. H. Powell residence on Baker Hill was purchased to serve as a manse, the residence on Hall Street having been sold after Mr. Woodward's departure. Young ministers who have come from this church are John Pritchard, an educational missionary to the Belgian Congo and Grover Wilson, Jr., assistant pastor of a Presbyterian Church in Pelham, New York.— (Mrs. W. E. Mattingly.)

WALTER A. HULL MEMORIAL PRESBYTERIAN CHURCH

In June, 1946, Rev. Wm. C. Brown of the Hazard Presbyterian Church, assisted by Mildred McCain, a Bible school worker, conducted a Bible School in the Hilton Coal Company Camp. The use of a vacant Baptist Church, owned by the family of the late Sam Napier was secured and one hundred and fifty children enrolled. A Sunday school and Evening services were begun. Rev. Warren Gaw, evangelist, conducted revival services with 32 professions. The Hilton Presbyterian Church was organized November 17, 1946, and Rev. William C. Brown was called as pastor. Elders were N. Smith and Joe Meadows. Deacons were Jack Collins and Henry Stidam. The Hilton Church was moved at a later date after a lot was secured at the mouth of Lotts Creek and a modern brick building was erected. The dedication was held November 13, 1947, and the church was named "Walter A. Hull Memorial Presbyterian Church" in memory of the late Walter A. Hull, whose widow, Mrs. Kate Hull and daughter, Ellen Bane Hull Foreman, had contributed generously to the new building in memory of their late husband and father, a devoted churchman and outstanding civic leader of Hazard. The ladies of the Hazard Presbyterian Church assisted in furnishing the Sunday School rooms. Rev. Brown resigned as pastor of Hull Memorial and Harveyton Churches on July 1, 1952, to become pastor of Glomawr Church which he established in March, 1952. Rev. Lamar Williamson succeeded Rev. Brown as pastor of Hull Memorial and Harveyton.—(Rev. and Mrs. Wm. C. Brown.)

HARVEYTON PRESBYTERIAN CHURCH

Under the leadership of Rev. William C. Brown, pastor of the Hazard Church, an outpost Sunday School was started at Harveyton, Kentucky, November 11, 1944. The use of the old recreation building was granted by the Harvey Coal Company and the interior was repainted and redecorated by members of the Sunday School. An organ rostrum was built and an organ and song books purchased. A revival was held by Rev. Leslie Patterson in the spring of 1945. A Bible school was held in the late summer. Another revival was held by Rev. Bill Lawson in the fall of 1946. A number of people were added to the Church, and services were held each Tuesday night. In August, 1946, Rev. Wm. C. Brown resigned his pastorate of the Hazard Presbyterian Church and with his family moved to Harveyton. The Harveyton Presbyterian Church was organized January 12, 1947, with forty-six members. Rev. Brown was called as pastor. Chester Begley and John Davenport were elected as elders. Murdock Riley and Paul Bellow were elected deacons.—(Rev. and Mrs. Wm. C. Brown.)

PRESBYTERIAN CHURCH EXPANSION

At the present writing, the Rev. Wm. C. Brown has organized and is pastor of the Glomawr Presbyterian Church, is holding services and doing Bible School work at Lothair and neighboring points. A Presbyterian Church has been organized at Tilford, near Leatherwood No. 2 Mine, and a pastor has been called there, the Rev. Charles Sydnor. Active Women of the Church organizations are present at both points.

VICCO PRESBYTERIAN CHURCH

In 1905, or before, Rev. Albert E. Smith came from Hindman to Vicco and began the work of the Presbyterian Church. The first Sunday School was started in a small building next to Martin's Store, and the present church was built, with a manse behind it on a hill. The old Church and school at Sassafras served for material to build a small church at Kodak, which is now served by the pastor of the Vicco Church. Rev. Smith was burned to death in 1930. Rev. Boaz Smith followed him, serving for eight years. Rev. Thomas Pritchard followed Rev. Smith and was at Vicco until 1951. During Rev. Pritchard's ministry a new manse was built and the Church membership substantially increased.—(Mrs. George Wyatt, Rev. Thomas Pritchard.)

THE BUCKHORN CHURCH

The Buckhorn Church, Presbyterian in denomination, has been known in the annals of the Presbyterian Church U.S.A. as having one of the largest memberships of a rural church in Kentucky. Organized by the late Rev. Miles Saunders and his daughter, Louise, the first pastor was the eminent late Harvey S. Murdoch, closely associated with W. O. Guerrant in the Soul Winners' society. The present church building was designed by the late Edward S. Geer, a Brooklyn architect, who caught the spirit of the log buildings on the Buckhorn campus (see Chapter on **Buckhorn** and it is widely known as the "log cathedral." The church roll numbers over 900 members, many non-residents, now, and is at this writing undergoing major renovations due to extensive flood damage. Dr. Elmer E. Gabbard, head of the Buckhorn school, is pastor of the church. Dr. Gabbard is known throughout the state for his work in the mountains, having been at Buckhorn since 1936. He is an outstanding minister of the Gospel and served as Moderator of the Synod of Kentucky, Presbyterian Church U.S.A. during 1951-52.—(Mrs. Rice Kirby.)

FIRST BAPTIST CHURCH
(First Missionary Baptist Church)

In the year of 1897 a pioneer Missionary Baptist minister, Rev. A. S. Petrey, who was at that time teaching in Cumberland College at Williamsburg, Kentucky, and had been assigned to do mission work and to solicit students for Cumberland College, rode into Hazard via Leslie County after closing a very successful meeting there. Soon after his arrival a revival meeting was held in the Courthouse, and seventeen people were converted. An appeal was made by Dr. R. R. Baker and Pearl Combs for Rev. Petrey to return to Hazard to establish a Church. An immediate decision could not be reached. He returned to his home and family in Williamsburg, Ky., and after much thought and prayer resigned his position with the college, sold his home and made arrangements to return with his family to Hazard. After a hazardous drive in a one-horse wagon over snow-covered muddy roads from Jackson, he arrived in Hazard with his wife and two small daughters, Maude and Ruth on February 10, 1898, to begin his new work.

The First Missionary Baptist Church was organized August 27, 1898. The Charter Members were Rev. A. S. Petrey, Sarah Petrey, Dr. R. R. Baker, Elizabeth Baker, Nancy Ann Baker, Allen Deaton, Sarah Deaton, Eli Couch, Polly Couch, Sallie Davidson, John S. Combs, Rebecca Combs, Felix Combs, Sara Combs, Elvira Combs, James Engle, Pearl Combs, Baylas Couch, William Greer, Dan Cornett, Martha Cornett, Kate Johnson, Anna Johnson, John W. Walker, I. D. Johnson, Martha Johnson and Mrs. Powell Logan.

The lot on main house for the church building was secured from Polly Ann Combs and heirs, and with the help of two other men, Rev. Petrey cut the timber and hauled the logs down Messer Branch to the sawmill owned by J. L. Johnson where the lumber was prepared for the building. After a year of hard labor and great financial difficulties a beautiful structure 40 x 60 feet with four gables, high tower, diamond shaped auditorium, and colored windows was dedicated. The Church was very active, its influence was soon felt over a large area. Students from Perry and neighboring counties who attended the Hazard Baptist Institute, the Church School, returned to their homes at the close of school and established Mission Sunday Schools in their communities.

In the year of 1910 during the time when Rev. Petrey was being confronted with difficult financial problems of the Hazard Baptist Institute, the Church Building was destroyed by fire. This great loss was felt very keenly by the entire community. There was no money to build another Church; however, through the cooperation of other Baptists over the state and under the strong leadership of Rev. Petrey, a larger and better building was started. Many disappointments and hardships were encountered, bricks were made from clay across the alley, lumber was obtained from J. L. Johnson, lime, doors, windows and hardware were pushed up the river from Jackson on flat boats. When the flat boats had arrived within seven miles of Hazard, they became frozen in midstream and remained there for two weeks. Wagons were sent over the rough frozen road to the boat for the supplies. The L. & N. R. R. was completed in time to bring the pews by freight. Services were held in the Hazard Baptist Institute auditorium and court house while the Church was being built. The Presbyterian Church donated the use of their Church Building on High Street for the evangelistic Meeting held March-April, 1912. (Hazard Herald March-April, 1912.)

The New Church was dedicated in 1912 and Dr. J. W. Porter of Lexington preached the dedication sermon. Rev. Petrey served this Church as Pastor 1898 to 1918. In this Church his great missionary program started. In his life story he called this Church the "Mother of Missions." He organized seven other Churches during this Pastorate. He was founder of Three Forks Association in 1900. Other Pastors were Rev Ammerson, H. C. Combs, A. R. Abernathy. During Rev. Abernathy's Pastorate a nine room brick parsonage was erected on Cedar Street. Also Junior and Intermediate Departments were added to the basement of the Church. He served from 1920 to 1925. Rev. C. D. Stevens served following five years. During his Pastorate he was elected President of Hazard Baptist Institute and was given leave of absence for one year in behalf of the school. Rev. Lewis Martin served as supply and then was called as Pastor upon resignation of Rev. C. D. Stevens in 1930, a large indebtedness was paid off during his ministry. Rev.

A. B. Pierce followed in 1934, and the Educational Building was begun. Rev. H. G. M. Hatler came in 1936; under his guidance the Educational Building was finished. Rev. Frank Badgett followed and the Blue Grass and other Missions were begun. Under the present pastor, Rev. Winn T. Barr, the County Mission Program was set up, organ chimes were installed, and the Community Kindergarten established in the Educational Building, September, 1952.

J. C. McIntosh, Tom Baker, Nita Owens, and Ragan Helton, declared themselves for Christian Service. Rev. Lester Cornett served as associate pastor from February to September in 1952.—(The late Eli Brashear, J. M. Owens and Rev. Barr.)

BROWNS FORK BAPTIST CHURCH (Colored)

Rev. Birch came into the vicinity of Browns Fork around 1897 and the Browns Fork Baptist Church was organized in the old log school house. Some of the charter members were Angeline Christian, George Olinger and Dan Olinger. A lot was purchased from Bill Combs in 1903 and a Church was built in 1904. Rev. Yates served the Church twenty-three years as Pastor. Under the Pastorate of Rev. Foeman a new Church Building was erected. William Dunson, present Pastor, has served the past sixteen years.— (Nannie Cornett.)

DWARF BAPTIST CHURCH

Rev. A. S. Petrey held a revival meeting at Dwarf in the summer of 1900. Evening services were held in the school house and Richard Gayheart arranged seats in his orchard where services were held in the morning while school was in session. As a result of this meeting the Dwarf Baptist Church was organized. Permission was granted by the First Baptist Church of Hazard for Rev. Petrey, their Pastor, to fill the pulpit of Dwarf one Sunday of each month. Some of the early members were Mr. and Mrs. Silas Ritchie, Elbert Owens, Rachel Owens Brashear, Dr. S. M. Ritchie, Nannie Ritchie, and Flora Owens.

Two Ministers came out of this Church, Silas B. Ritchie,

who succeeded Rev. A. S. Petrey, served as Pastor until his death and Henry C. Combs who later served the First Baptist Church of Hazard for two years. In 1923 or 1924 the Church building was destroyed by fire. Many of the members had moved away and there was no money to rebuild. The lot was deeded to Dwarf graded school with the privilege of worshipping in the new school building. In 1942 Robert and Seba Sloane donated one-quarter acre of ground to the Dwarf Church and plans for building a new church were begun. The congregation moved to Chester Gayheart's store building where services were held until they moved into the new brick church on Highway 15.— (Robert Slone.)

STONY FORK BAPTIST CHURCH

Rev. A. S. Petrey began preaching on Leatherwood in the early 1900's. Leatherwood Church later called Stony Fork Baptist Church was established by Rev. Petrey and Rev. Lewis Lyttle in the Miniard school house in 1909. Allison Miniard stated that Rev. Lewis Lyttle was Pastor. Early members were Mr. and Mrs. George Miniard, Allison Miniard, Mr. and Mrs. Andy Shepherd, Bertha Ison, Della Cornett, Laura Smith, Susan Shepherd, Mr. and Mrs. P. H. Hall, and Mr. and Mrs. Will Hall, Lewis Little, Belle Little, Joe Jackson, A. B. Melton, J. R. Browning, Sallie Holbrook, Mamie Whitaker, Nancy Hibbard, and Dora Ellen Morgan.— (Stella Cornett, Allison Miniard.)

MT. OLIVET BAPTIST CHURCH

A meeting was held by the Rev. A. S. Petrey at the old lower Leatherwood school house below where Mt. Olivet church now stands in 1909. Dalton Logan relates a Sunday School was organized the following summer of 1910 by Dora Cornett, French Cornett, Carrie Cornett, Dalton Logan and by Barney Baker of Hazard who was teaching school in the community at that time. Barney Baker was elected superintendent and the others served as teachers. These young people were students at the Hazard Baptist Institute and were home for summer vacation. The Sunday School disbanded at the end of three months when this group returned to Hazard Baptist Institute in the fall.

Following another meeting held by Rev. Petrey at this school house, the Mt. Olivet Baptist Church was organized in July 23, 1914. Letters were granted from the First Baptist Church in Hazard for the following charter members: French Cornett, Marion Ison, Carrie Cornett, Dora Cornett, E. H. Brashear, Rachel Brashear, Dalton Logan, Millard Halcomb, Susan Cornett Beams, Corbia Brashear, Preston Brashear, and Marion Brashear. Rev. A. S. Petrey was chosen Pastor, Dora Cornett, clerk, Dalton Logan, E. H. Brashear, and Marion Cornett were elected deacons. Mrs. K. W. Cornett states that in the spring of 1915, the Sunday School was reorganized, Dalton Logan elected superintendent, again lasting only a few months since the workers were either students in Hazard Baptist Institute or county teachers. In 1917 D. W. Cornett was elected superintendent of the Sunday School and continued until present date. In February, 1917, a mission Sunday School was established at Jeff by Dalton Logan.

A site for the Church Building was donated by Joe Duff, near the mouth of Little Leatherwood where the present Church Building now stands. In 1947 letters of dismission were granted seven members to organize a Church at Leatherwood. Rev. Petrey served this Church as part time Pastor for twenty-one years.—(Dalton Logan, Mrs. K. W. Cornett.)

YERKES BAPTIST CHURCH

The Yerkes Baptist Church was organized in 1914 by Rev. A. S. Petrey, who had been preaching in this community for many years. Charted Members were Mollie Campbell, William Campbell, Callie Campbell, Peggy Campbell, James Campbell, John C. Campbell, Elizabeth Campbell, J. C. Colwell, G. C. Colwell, Margaret Colwell, Hobart Colwell, Cassie Colwell, Nancy Colwell, Poppy Baker, James Baker, Bett Baker, C. A. Baker, Fannie Baker, Aaron Brock, Orlena Brock and Vina Colwell. Meetings were held in the home of William Campbell who donated the land for the church building. In 1915 while Rev. Petrey was part-time pastor the church house was built. Mollie Campbell was the first Sunday School Superintendent.—(The late Rev. A. S. Petrey and Nancy Colwell.)

MT. ZION BAPTIST CHURCH (Colored)

In the summer of 1913 Sunday School was organized in the home of Rev. Alex Cornett located on Big Bottom Branch, now Liberty Street, where it was held until early fall when it was moved to the hall in the Razor Building. Under the leadership of Rev. James Haywood, the Church was organized October 13, 1914. Rev. Faulkner of Richmond, Kentucky, was chairman of the meeting. Rev. James Haywood was called as Pastor, H. T. Townes, Ben W. Carter, W. M. Smith, and Will Hogg were elected deacons. Charter Members were H. T. Townes, Ben W. Carter, W. M. Smith, Will Hogg, Mary Carter, Rev. James Haywood, Rev. Alex Cornett, Mabel Holt, Mary Sweat, Lucinda Williams.

The name Mt. Zion was given to the Church. A lot on the hill back of Mount Mary Hospital was secured and under the leadership of Rev. James Haywood, a Church building was erected which has been replaced by a new brick building. H. T. Townes, who died February 1, 1953, was superintendent of this Sunday School for 40 years. Pastors who have served this Church were James Haywood, Rev. Foreman, G. D. Miller, M. M. McMillen, D. T. Woods, Claud Taylor, R. J. Madison, R. A. Beal, Arvol Carrol, and J. J. Smith.—(The late H. T. Townes, J. J. Smith.)

MT. OLIVE BAPTIST CHURCH (Colored)

A series of Prayer Meetings were held in the home of Joseph Boyd who was running a boarding house at Four Seam Coal Company. Here the Mt. Olive Baptist Church had its beginning. Through the cooperation of the Four Seam Coal Co., a building was provided for a House of Worship and was dedicated July, 1917, and named Mt. Olive Baptist Church. Rev. A. L. Lee, Henderson James and Charles Lee of Diablock composed the Council. Other present were Rev. White, Rev. Levi, Willie Meadlock, and Sallie

White. The members later moved into town and in 1929 permission was granted from the association to move the Church into the City of Hazard. During Pastorate of Rev. M. L. Jackson, the Church was moved to West Main Street. Following Rev. Jackson's resignation Rev. S. L. Sims was called as Pastor. Other Pastors were Rev. Romes, W. Y. Davis and P. K. Finley, it was during his Pastorate that the Church was moved to the Razor Building on East Main Street, and under his leadership the new stone church was erected on Memorial Drive where the first services were held in June, 1940. Rev. J. A. Taylor served from 1942 to 1948. He was succeeded by the Rev. R. W. Richmond, present Pastor, who came in 1948. Since then a modern brick parsonage has been erected.—(Rev. R. W. Richmond.)

PETREY MEMORIAL CHURCH

Petrey Memorial Church had its beginning when the Second Baptist Church was organized by the late John W. Walker, who had been holding a revival in a tent at Walkertown. In an interview with Mrs. Polly Walker, wife of the late John W. Walker, she states that a group of members from the Second Creek Baptist Church, which was organized by Rev. Petrey in 1915, where Rev. Walker was serving as Pastor came and assisted with the organizational meeting which was held under the shade of large beech trees near the spot where the Church now stands. Rev. Walker became the first Pastor. The first Deacons were Tilman Bartlett and Dan Patrick. Early Members were Ann Walker, Susan Fields, Lona Walker, Polly Walker, Ollie Walker, Anice Turner Luttrell, Cynthia Couch and A. H. Turner. Anice Turner Luttrell states that the Church Services were held in the school building for some time. On June 4, 1921, a lot on the hill where the Church now stands was purchased by The Second Creek Baptist Church from Nancy Messer and given to the people of Walkertown to build a Church. Rev. A. S. Petrey relates in his life story that he was called as Pastor in 1922. There were thirty-five members. A concrete basement had been constructed on the lot. Under the leadership of Rev. Petrey the Church building was soon completed. During a revival more than one hundred professions were made and eighty-six were baptized by Rev. Petrey at one time. Rev. Petrey served this Church eighteen years but due to ill health he was forced to retire at the age of seventy-nine. This was his last Pastorate. Sherman Jones, present clerk, states that Rev. O. C. Anderson was called as Pastor and served three years. During his Ministry a building fund for a new Church was started. Rev. L. M. Bratcher followed and served one year, continued with the building fund. Rev. J. E. Howell became Pastor February 1, 1948. Under his leadership the new Church building was erected and dedicated July 24, 1949 and at that time named "Petrey Memorial Baptist Church" in honor of the Rev. A. S. Petrey. News Story Courier-Journal—July 25, 1949 stated—The Building was opened with a special service honoring Rev. Petrey. The State Board of Missions announced the release of a book on the life of Rev. Petrey, "The Prophet of Little Cane Creek" and tribute was paid to Rev. J. E. Howell, the Pastor, in getting the building completed.

The Big Creek Baptist Church whose building is now under construction was organized by Rev. J. E. Howell and members of the Petrey Memorial Church. Sunday School Mission Points have been established at Allais, Ary, and Hiltonian, Kentucky. Ministers coming out of this Church are J. B. Allen, Elmer Sizemore, and Rex Purvis.—(Mrs. J. W. Walker, Mrs. Anice Turner Luttrell, Sherman Jones, Rev. J. E. Howell.)

LOTHAIR BAPTIST CHURCH

A tent meeting was conducted by the Rev. A. C. Hudson at the back of the depot in summer of 1922, and the Lothair Baptist Church was organized. Services were held in the Old Theater over Lothair Confectionary while the Church was being built. Some of the early members were: W. S. Stallard, W. W. Miller, Logan Johnson, Troy Stacy, John D. Bowling, Nancy Combs, Cynthia Morgan Muncy, Louie Morgan Evans, Cynthia Evans Bowling, M. M. Hampton, Lewie Keith. First deacons elected were W. S. Stallard,

W. W. Miller, Logan Johnson and Troy Stacy. H. G. Sizemore was called as Pastor. The late G. W. Nicholson was the first Sunday School Superintendent.

A lot 100 x 150 feet was donated by the late Jesse Morgan and in 1924, under the leadership of Rev. H. G. Sizemore plans for a church building were begun. Native stone on the hill above where the Church now stands was used. In 1925 the stone Church, now located on Highway 15, was completed. Four Ministers have come out of this Church; Amos Combs, W. W. Miller, M. M. Hampton, and Lewie Keith. Pastors who have served this Church are H. G. Sizemore, Edd Gabbard, L. T. Westberry, M. C. Denny, H. D. Smallwood, Frank Beck, and O. B. Gabbard, present Pastor. —(John D. and Cynthia Evans Bowling.)

LONE PINE BAPTIST CHURCH

Constituted in 1934 after a revival by Rev. L. W. Martin at Viper, Ky., on left fork of Masons Creek in Rogers Branch School House. Church Building was constructed in 1934. Charter Members were Mrs. E. H. Brashear, Mr. and Mrs. Troy P. Brashear, Mrs. Morton Brown, Mr. and Mrs. S. B. Crutcher, Mr. and Mrs. G. C. Whitaker, Mr. and Mrs. M. C. Brashear and Mrs. Carrie Estepp. Rev. M. C. Brashear was chosen as Pastor in 1934 and has continued through the years. First deacons were A. R. Brown and W. M. Pittman. A modern Church Building has been erected and the present membership is approximately sixty.—(Rev. M. C. Brashear.)

BEREAN BAPTIST CHURCH

The original pioneer work in this area was done by Miss Faust, Missionary for many years. Around 1939 Rev. Chas. Robinson came into this area and worked with this Missionary and organized the Macedonian Community Church which met in the school house at Beehive. Later the Blue Diamond Coal Company opened a mine at Toner (now Leatherwood), Kentucky, and seeing the need of a church there Rev. Robinson accepted the challenge and carried on the two works for quite a while. An organizational meeting was called on August 4, 1946, in the school house at Toner for the purpose of founding an Independent Baptist Church. The Charter Members were Mr. and Mrs. Earl Helton, Mr. and Mrs. Milford Minor, Clarence Minor, Mr. and Mrs. C. R. Mooney, Mrs. Goodloe Davidson, and Ora Lee Francis. Rev. C. H. Robinson was called as Pastor. C. R. Mooney was elected Clerk and Earl Helton, Church Treasurer.

In the fall of 1948 The Macedonian Community Church with its twenty some members, (Mrs. Grant Asher, Mrs. Denver Ison, Mrs. Usley (Jack) Shepherd, Missess Stella and Athaline Callahan, Mrs. Blaine Cornett, Polly Verlin, and Vernice Cornett, Mr. and Mrs. A. L. Miniard, Mrs. Charles (Clarice) Hatcher, Mrs. Robert (Bernice) Conrad, Mr. and Mrs. Meb. Roberts, Stella Cornett, Mrs. Jack Shepherd, and others whose record has been moved) joined forces with the Berean Baptist Church at Leatherwood to form one. Soon after this they moved their meeting place to the vacated store building belonging to Mrs. A. L. Miniard, at the mouth of Beehive Creek. Rev. C. H. Robinson concluded his Ministry in February, 1951, to take another Pastorate. In March, 1951, Arman Wright was called as Pastor. A new church building is being erected about one-quarter of a mile from the mouth of Owens Branch.— (Rev. Arman Wright.)

BETHANNA BAPTIST CHURCH

Bethanna Baptist Church is located on Highway No. 7, eighteen miles southeast of Hazard, Kentucky, between Leatherwood Creek and the small village of Cornettsville. This Church was organized in 1943 by Rev. John Greenleaf of Philadelphia, Pennsylvania. He came to this section of Perry County by the efforts of Rev. Charles Robinson who ministered on Leatherwood twelve years. A real need was realized by Rev. John Greenleaf for a Church to serve the people of the north Fork of the Kentucky River from the sections of Blackey to Viper including parts of Leatherwood. In the latter part of 1942 and early 1943 the work first begun in a Junior Lodge Hall, owned by Denver Minniard at the mouth of Leatherwood. Charter Members were Deacon Willard Cecil, Odessa Cecil (Deacon), Geneva Cecil, Mrs. Tom Robinson, Clifford Robinson, Christine and Bobby Medlock, Bobby and Doris Ann Bush, Mrs. Bill Bush, Mrs. Juda Halcomb, and Mrs. Henry Creech. Early in 1944 plans were made to build the Church now known as Bethanna Baptist, (which means House of Grace). Through the help of Mr. Turner Howard, the land was given to the Church. J. C. Codell of Winchester, Kentucky, gave generous donations and other gifts were given by citizens and friends of this locality. In 1945 the Church was opened for Services under the Council and support of Mid-Missions whose headquarters are in Cleveland, Ohio. The Church has Sunday Services and weekly Religious Activities. Rev. John Bullock replaced Rev. Greenleaf as Pastor in 1947 through 1952.— (Mrs. Denver Minniard.)

TYPO BAPTIST CHURCH

The Typo Baptist Church was organized in the school house on August 7, 1950. Rev. A. S. Petrey was elected moderator. Letters from the Combs Baptist Church were granted to the following charter members: Walter Fields, Herman Combs, Mary Combs, Bertha Crawford, Carley Hill, Martha Combs, Alta C. Fields, Zada Engle, Eliza Jane Fields, Lidia Flanery. S. C. Couch was chosen Pastor. Early deacons were Herman Combs and Walter Fields. Walter Fields, clerk, and Herman Combs, treasurer. A new church building is now under construction.—(Sam Combs, Typo, Kentucky.)

JEFF BAPTIST CHURCH

This church was organized July 8, 1951, with twenty charter members. It had been a mission point for many years (see Mt. Olivet) and later taken over by the late G. W. Nicholson and members of the First Baptist Church of Hazard. W. L. Franklin elected Pastor, Maxine Hall, Clerk. Old store building was purchased from Floyd Hall and converted into a church building.—(Maxine Hall.)

"Rev. A. S. Petrey affectionately called "Brother

Petrey" known over the entire Southland as an outstanding educational and religious leader throughout Eastern Kentucky over a period of fifty years."—(Hazard Herald). A loved and honored citizen, died August 28, 1952—funeral held in Petrey Memorial Church—buried on Englewood Cemetery, Hazard, Kentucky.

CATHOLIC CHURCH

In the year 1913, the Consolidated Coal Company of Jenkins, built a Church and Priests' residence in Jenkins for the benefit of their Catholic employees. Father James E. Massa was the first resident priest for this new Catholic Parish, and it wasn't long until he began to look around his new environments, and found that over the mountains there were others of the Catholic faith in and near Hazard. With the permission of the authorities of the coal company, Father Massa came through the mines from Jenkins to Neon, and from there proceeded to Hazard. In Hazard at that time, the known Catholics were the B. F. Nofsinger family and a James A. Roan. Nearby in Diablock, Mr. and Mrs. Lambert and Pat Gallagher were employed by the Diamond Block Coal Company. The Nofsingers lived in the house at the turn on Baker Hill, and it was in their home that the Holy Sacrifice of the Mass was offered for the Catholic People in Hazard.

In 1916, Kathleen Osborne came to Hazard from Cynthiana, and very shortly thereafter was married to James Roan. Also in 1916 the Nofsinger family returned to Louisville. There were numerous Catholics who lived at various mines in and around Hazard, but because there were no roads and the only method of travel was the L. and N. Railroad, it was exceedingly difficult for them to attend the once a month services.

In 1918, Father Earl E. Bauer took over the charge of the Jenkins Parish with the Hazard Mission, and he remained two years. During the period when the Nofsingers left Hazard, services were held in the James Roan Home. In 1918 Rose Osborne came to live in Hazard. In 1920, Father Bauer was succeeded by Father John McCrystal who remained until 1930. Father Henry Hagedorn took care of the tiny flock for four months in 1921.

Early in the Twenties, Father McCrystal decided that the congregation had grown sufficiently to warrant a public place for holding the divine services, so arrangements were made to rent a store-room in the Fulp Building. In 1923, Miss Myrtle Kesheimer came to Hazard, and being an accomplished musician, it wasn't long until a small portable organ was procured, and soon the Mass was being properly accompanied by the newly formed choir. In spite of the fact that there were not enough voices among the members of her own church to have the kind of music she wanted to have in the praise and adoration of her Creator, she trained her friends from other churches in Hazard in the art of singing the Latin propers and Latin songs, so that on special occasions, for example the Midnight Masses on Christmas, the dedication of the Church, these ceremonies were beautifully enhanced with the singing of her choir.

The first Confirmation service was held in the year 1925, with Bishop Francis W. Howard coming into Hazard from Covington, his see city. In 1926, the first piece of real estate to be owned by the Catholic Church in Hazard was acquired from Bailey P. and Clara Wooton. This was a big lot situated on the corner of Cedar and Poplar Streets, and it was the plan of the Bishop that "some day" there would be a hospital built there to help take care of the miners and the other citizens of Hazard. Plans were also laid for a small church nearby which would care for the growing congregation.

Services were still held in the store room in the Fulp Building until the Big Flood of 1927. The flood waters wrecked the store-room chapel, and services were then held in the homes of the parishioners again, in the Broadway School, and wherever else it was possible to have Mass.

On November 21, 1929, Bishop Howard bought the property of Edgar and Lucy Smith, which was situated immediately in the rear of and adjoining to the Wooton property fronting on Poplar Street. It was still Bishop

Howard's intention to build a hospital, but with the depression coming on, the building program was set aside at that time.

Father McCrystal took up his residence in Hazard in 1927, and helped to convert the cottage into a Church and residence for himself. In 1930, Father Aloysius Greisinger succeeded to the pastorate of the Hazard Parish, and at this time, it was officially called the St. Mary Mission. Father Greisinger was succeeded by Father Edmund Priest in May of 1931. Father Priest had seen service in the First World War, and had been ordained late in life at the age of forty, and this was his first appointment.

Because of the depression, in August of 1932, the parish went back to its status of a mission, and Father William Gockel began caring for the parish from Jenkins. He was succeeded in 1935 by Father Paul Spain. During this time, services continued to be held in the little five room cottage, with the entire congregation dispersed throughout the house, while Mass was being offered in the front room. During a visit of Bishop Howard, Father Spain received his permission to start building a Church in Hazard.

Father Spain envisaged a stone church modeled after a chapel he had visited in Italy, and the present Church is an almost exact replica, and the building was accomplished by the united efforts of the entire congregation. Hopes were running high until disaster hit the small parish with the sudden death of their Shepherd, Father Spain, in 1939.

Father George Donnelly was appointed to succeed Father Spain, and he took over the finishing of the Church Building, and immediately he built the present parish rectory. The Church was dedicated under the title of the Mother of Good Counsel in the summer of 1939.

When Father Donnelly left in 1942 to enter the Chaplain's Corp of the U. S. Army, Father Carl Fischer was sent to Hazard to take care of the parish, and he remained until January 15, 1946, when he was succeeded by Father Edmund Priest. Father Priest had many plans to beautify the grounds around the Church, being an able gardener and landscaper, but these plans were set aside on the occasion of the untimely death of Father Priest as a result of an heart attack on December 11, 1946. For the next two months, the parish was in the hands of the Passionist Fathers of Cincinnati, who came to the aid of Bishop William T. Mulloy, one of these was Father Malachy Farrell. On February 16, 1947, Father Anthony Kraff, a priest of the Precious Blood Society was appointed to the Hazard parish.

With the coming of Sister Mary Gabriel, OBS and her staff of Benedictine Sisters in 1947 (see hospital), the new work in the hospital, and always increasing numbers of families, it has been necessary for other priests to come to help with the work. Father Anthony Migoni, C.PP.S., served from June, 1947, to July, 1948. Father Alvin Burns, C.PP.S., assisted in the work from August, 1948, to June, 1951, and Father Richard Reimondo, C.PP.S., is the present assistant.

In September, 1947, the Most Reverend Bishop purchased the Turner property on Cedar Street, which was converted into the Mother of Good Counsel Catechetical Center, and three Benedictine Sisters began the kindergarden program.

Tremendous changes have taken place in these short years. A church, hospital, kindergarten, catechetical center, priests' residence, with two priests in residence, daily Mass at the Church and Hospital Chapel, nine Sisters of the Order of St. Benedict, who care for the sick in the hospital and for the altars in the Church and Chapel—these are the things that all the priests and people have labored for in the years past.—(Father Anthony Kraff, Mrs. Rose Osborne Foreman.)

PENTECOSTAL CHURCH OF GOD

The Church was first established in "Backwoods" section of Hazard, Kentucky, on Laurel Street about 1915, with the late Rev. Wm. Rison as its first Pastor and a small membership. With a body of men composed of A. Y. Bartlett, W. P. Haney, Archie Gross, John Strong and the late Wm. Rison, the Church was moved to its present location at Wabaco about 1920. Since then the Church has grown to a large membership and has progressed spiritually under the leadership of its present Pastor, Rev. Charles Deaton. Elders were L. B. Brashear, G. C. Benton, Allen Stidham, E. L. William, Leonard Hale. Deacons were Clarence Powell, Everett Bartlett, O. L. Yancey, and Henry Yancey.—(Rev. Chas. Deaton.)

CHURCH OF GOD

The Hazard Church of God was organized in 1917 by Rev. W. R. Rembrant in the section of Hazard then known as the backwoods. It was set in order with thirty members and the first Pastor was Rev. Wm. Rison, now deceased. The Church remained there until 1930 and moved to Walkertown under the Pastorate of Rev. R. H. Ball.

In 1932 the building at Walkertown burned and the Church was again moved to Hazard. They rented a building from the Kentucky Blue Grass Mining Company and in 1943, under the leadership of Rev. F. S. Crank, the Church purchased a lot on Maple Street. This same year they exchanged Pastors and continued their building program under the Pastorship of Rev. J. I. Adkins. Rev. Adkins served the Church for three years and Rev. F. W. Black became Pastor of the Church. During his ministry the remaining indebtedness of the Church was paid. In September, 1948, Rev. E. T. Stacy became Pastor of the Hazard Church and under his leadership the modern parsonage, a choir box and a baptistry were built. In September, 1950, Rev. J. R. Lenning came from Crescent Springs, Kentucky, to Pastor the Church and under his Pastorate the Church has purchased new pews and made other necessary improvements. The present pastor is Rev. P. F. Taylor.

Some of the other Churches of God in this locality started as missions from the Hazard Church are Blue Diamond, Combs, Christopher, Tribby and Vicco. — (Mrs. Charles Cook.)

ST. MARK'S EPISCOPAL CHURCH

Around the year of 1910 when the population of Hazard was small, an Episcopal mission had its beginning when

Rev. Alexander Patterson was sent by Bishop Burton to hold services. Rev. A. S. Petrey offered his pulpit and services were conducted at the First Baptist Church. Rev. Patterson walked most of the way from Jackson to Hazard. While here he was a guest at the home of Mr. and Mrs. Lee Daniel.

For several years, Hazard was listed as a Mission Station where occasional services were held. In 1921, it became an organized Mission with the name St. Mark's. In 1933, Mr. Leach, a Canadian, came to Hazard once a week on Sunday evening from his Church in Pikeville to hold Evening Prayer. Similiar efforts were made in 1938 by Rev. Ben Tinsley and in 1944 by Rev. J. E. Merrick, both of whom were ministers to the church in Pikeville. Some of these meetings were held at the First Christian Church but more frequently at the Kentucky and West Virginia Power Company. Mr. Merrick's last visit to hold services was in October, 1945. Most of the families who made up Hazard's Episcopal congregation had moved away, so St. Mark's was listed as inactive until 1950.

On Sunday, December 3, 1950, a meeting was held at the Grand Hotel by a new group of Hazard Episcopalians with Rev. John C. Petrie, Rector of Christ Episcopal Church in Harlan, to discuss reactivation of St. Mark's Mission in Hazard. After December 3, events moved rapidly, with regular services being held, pledges made, a Ladies Auxiliary and Men's Vestry being formed and meeting regularly. The Sunday Services were held first at the radio station, the chapel of the First Christian Church, and the City Hall, then later at the Kentucky and West Virginia Power Company. One service, which was broadcast, was held at the Bowman Methodist Church.

On March 1, 1950. the Right Reverend William R. Moody, Bishop of the Diocese of Lexington, came to Hazard and confirmed eight people in a service held at the home of Dr. and Mrs. A. Karl Tatum. By April of that spring a resident minister was sent to Hazard from Middlesboro, Rev. John Piper. Under his leadership, a Sunday School was started, four children baptized, one marriage performed and a Church lot purchased. In June, 1951, ground was broken for the construction of a Chapel on the lot, which is located on Walnut St., opposite the Bobby Davis Park. This Chapel is placed on the back of the lot, so that construction of a Church in front of it in the future will be possible.

The original congregation which gathered in December, 1950, and through whose efforts St. Mark's has been re-established included Mrs. Duff Arnett, Mr. and Mrs. Arch Collins, Mrs. William Combs, Mr. and Mrs. Frank G. Foreman, Jr., Mr. William Walter Hall, who became one of the Lay-Readers, Mr. and Mrs. J. V. Hines, Jr., and son, Mr. and Mrs. William Holt and daughter, Mr. Eugene Martin, the other Lay-Reader serving St. Mark's, Mrs. Martin and children, Dr. and Mrs. Minor Payne and children, Mrs. Kathleen Smith and sons, Mrs. Eileen Stacy, Mr. and Mrs. Fred Stewart and children, Dr. and Mrs. Karl Tatum and children, Mr. and Mrs. D. E. Watts and children, Mrs. Carl Weiss and children, and Mr. and Mrs. Willie Dawahare and daughter.

The first funeral service to be held at Saint Mark's Church was for the church's first vicar and builder, the Rev. John S. Piper, who died December 30, 1952.—(Mrs. Duff Arnett, Mrs. A. K. Tatum, Jr.)

There are many more interesting church histories in Perry County but lack of time for research prevented including them.

CHAPTER IX
COURTS
Nora McIntosh Campbell

"On Monday, 10th day of June, 1822, County Court commenced and held in the town of Hazard. Magistrates Jeremiah Combs, Jesse Bolin, Robert S. Brashear, William Stamper and Robert Hicks present."

The first business was the appointment of "Nicholas Combs, Richard Smith and Robert Hicks to view the road from Martin Fugit's to the mouth of Trace Fork."

The records show no trials or misdemeanors of any kind at this first term of court, but some lawlessness must have existed as the need for building a jail was recognized by appointing Alexander Patrick, Jesse Bolin, and Nicholas Combs as a committee to plan a jail and sell public lots to finance it. Also to let a contract for building the jail to the lowest bidder.

Elijah Combs, Jesse Bolin, Jeremiah Combs, Robert Hicks and Robert S. Brashear were appointed to lay off lots, streets and alleys for the permanent seat of justice in the county of Perry, to number the lots and give at least twenty days notice at three of the most public places in the county of the time of the "sail."

Other orders were for certain people to report and show why their children were not better supported. Robert S. Brashear was appointed guardian of the children of Mason Combs, deceased. It was ordered that Samuel and Rachel, negroes of Mason Combs, be sold at the October term of court at the best price that could be had with good security.

The election judges were appointed and court was adjourned until the next day. The minutes were signed by Jesse Bolin, and all of the foregoing information was taken from his record of this first term of court in Perry County.

Jails

When the court convened the next day, the committee submitted plans for the new jail. There is no picture of this first jail, but the following is an exact copy of the plans, taken from the First Minute Book of Perry County, 1821-37.

"Outside walls 16 feet feet square, 5 feet thick, to be hewn one foot boards and the inside wall to be one foot thick and the timber to be hewn one foot boards and to be built one foot apart and to be filled up with rocks twixt the walls and the bottom of the floor. And to be dug three feet deep and to be floored with hewn timber one foot thick. The width and breadth to be completely floored. And the lower story to be built 9 feet high and the top to be covered with timber to be hewn one foot boards from side to side. The outside wall to be built four rounds high above the lower story and out of hewn one foot boards and said jail to be covered with shingles and sufficient door to be built made in the side of the jail and one door above in the center of the upper story." (1)

The location of this first jail is not known. In 1837 the court ordered a stray pen to be built at the back of the jail, so the jail would form one side of the pen.

At the November term of court in 1860, it was ordered that a new jail would be built on the same plan as the old one except that where the old jail had rock filled walls, the new one was to be built of logs and fitted in between the walls with square timbers set end on end. R. C. Combs contracted to build the jail. (2) It was located on the street now known as Broadway, near the site where the Presbyterian Church now stands.

Ironically, the jail built in 1860 by R. C. Combs was burned in 1885, while he was jailer, as may be confirmed by the following entry found in the Perry County Minute Book No. 5, dated February 2, 1885, page 350:

"Ordered by the court upon satisfactory information that the jail house of Perry County, which was recently burned, was fired by incendiaries. Said court offers a reward of one hundred dollars for the apprehension or information leading to the conviction of the guilty parties."

The following description of the burning of the jail was given by several eye-witnesses to the fire. When the jail burned, it contained one prisoner Ap Eversole who had been sentenced to hang for the shooting and killing of Mrs. Bill Baker. He had been granted a new trial, because it had been brought to the attention of the Circuit Judge that the jury had not not stayed together while making their decision. It was generally assumed that some friends or relatives of Mrs. Baker either set fire to the jail or hired someone to do it, because they were afraid that the accused might be acquitted. However, this was never proved and no one was ever arrested for the crime.

According to a description of the jail, there was only one outside door on the second floor which was reached by an outside wooden stairway. Also, there was only one small window. The fire was started by throwing kerosene on the stairway and igniting it. The screaming of the prisoner spread the alarm, but it was too late to reach the door to the jail when the rescuers arrived. They could not remove the bars from the window, so they tried chopping through the wall, but as fast as they made a hole, the timbers between the walls fell through and filled it. Although the imprisoned boy stood by the window while efforts were made to rescue him, he was suffocated before the flames reached him. The jail was rebuilt at once.

In 1899 the first brick jail was built at a cost of $5,800.00. It was a small square building located on the corner of Main and Fleet Streets in the corner of the courthouse lawn. (See picture.)

The present county jail was built about 1914 during the administration of Judge J. G. Campbell. It is located on the corner of Main and Jail Streets. The front is on Main Street and is the jailer's residence. The section for the prisoners is behind the residence and is only visible from Jail Street.

Court Orders

At the March term of court, 1823, Mary Webb bound her daughter, Arminda Webb, to Robert Cornett to "teach her the art, trade and mystery of spinning and weaving and find her good and sufficient meat, drink, aparrel and lodging fit for an apprentice. Also teach her, or cause her to be taught to read and write. At the expiration of her apprenticeship (10 years) to pay her 3 pounds, 10 shillings and a decent suit of clothes."

In April, 1824, the court ordered James Collins to "mark

stock a crop in the left ear and a slit in the right." This was what might be called the registration of his mark, for the purpose of identification.

In November, 1831, Leonard Pigman petitioned for a pension for Revolutionary War services. He was allowed a claim of $12.00 to $50.00 as a pauper of Perry County in 1833. Andrew Burns, Roger Turner and Dewey Bush, old Revolutionary soldiers, applied to the June term of court, 1833, for pensions and David May, also a veteran, produced and made oath to his pension declaration in 1834.

The magistrates present at the November term of court in 1833 were Jesse Bolin, Robert Hicks, Jeremiah Combs, Joseph Cockeral, Samuel Hurley, Abel Pennington, James Turner, Daniel Duff, Robert S. Brashear and Elijah Combs. They reported fines collected, and defined the boundaries of all magisterial districts.

Court Houses

The records do not mention where the first June term of court was held; however, the second term was held in Elijah Combs' residence, September, 1822. Court continued to meet there until August, 1823. The next term of court met in the "Courthouse," but there are indications that the Combs house was referred to in that manner, and there is no record of a courthouse being built. However, in Minute Book 1, January Term, 1833, P. 296, "ordered that court adjourn to the dwelling house of Elijah Combs." The first definite record of the existence of a courthouse shows up in March, 1836, when it was ordered "that A. F. Caldwell and Elijah Combs be appointed commissioners to the jail and courthouse and report what repair think is necessary to be done to each at the next term of court." The building, moving and repairing of the jail is mentioned each year.

At the November term of court, 1836, Elijah Combs, Jesse Combs and A. F. Caldwell, who had been previously appointed, reported the following plans for a brick courthouse:

"Plans for a new courthouse of brick—wall 48 feet long and in the clear and 24 feet wide on a stone foundation 2½ feet above the surface of the earth, brick floor lined with the foundation and the brick wall 10 feet high: 2 chimneys in each end and two rooms in each end, 12 feet square, with fire places, and one window to each room; the clerk's room of sixteen lights, Leaving a room in the center 24 feet square with 4 windows, Two on each side; one door to one of the small rooms designated for a clerk's office, and two smaller windows on each side of the door into the large room, both in the front side and door through the partition into the other small rooms leading from the large room, the Judge's platform two feet high opposite the door; a good jury bench at the foot of the same, and a neat bar in the form of a half moon and all the inside wall plastered in a neat and substantial manner, the wall to be brick, 2½ feet thick and all finished off in a neat and workmanlike stile, and furnished with a good and lasting stove placed in the large room between the jury bench and the bar, at one end of the bar, convenient to the clerk and the whole house; —rooms and all to be finished off with choice mill cedar underneath and everything to be neat, substantial and convenient according to plans, and plastered on the inside and a roof, the jury rooms painted partition of brick, one brick thick, the large rooms plastered and the Clerk's office." (3)

The plans were accepted and A. F. Caldwell, William Mattingly and Jesse Combs were appointed commissioners to let out the building contract to the lowest bidder.

George S. Martin was the successful bidder for the sum of $2,220. He had to fill a bond for double the amount of his bid that he would fulfill his contract according to the above specifications. Elijah Combs signed his bond for $4,440.

At the June term of court, 1866, it was decided to rebuild the court house. It was to be a two story framed, weather-boarded and ceiled building, built on the foundation of the old one. Harve Henley, the successful bidder, was to use the brick from the old courthouse to build the chimneys for the new one. Elijah Cornett was appointed to sell the remaining bricks as a whole or in lots, in whatever way he could get the best price, according to Perry County Minute Book 4, page 652.

The courthouse built in 1866 must have burned about 1885 or 1886, though old settlers argue that it was 1890. There is no record of the burning, but it is recorded that the contract was awarded to Col. L. H. N. Salyers to build a new brick courthouse on the same plan as the courthouse at Beattyville. All the old settlers agree that Col. Salyers rebuilt the old frame courthouse, and that the brick one built by him burned in 1911. An order noted in Perry County Minute Book 5 changed the roof on the courthouse built by Col. Salyers from a gable roof to a hip roof.

In 1912, a new brick courthouse was dedicated in Hazard. Following is a description of the new courthouse from **The Story of Hazard** by Louis Pilcher, (page 20).

"On arriving in Hazard, the most noticeable thing is the new fifty thousand dollar courthouse, a model of architecture with electric lights, water works, fire-proof vaults, modern fixtures, clock and water tower for sewerage, toilets, and fire protection. Delegates and committees from other places are visiting it with a view of replacing their old courthouses with similiar buildings. This new courthouse is a credit to the intelligence of the County Judge and his Justices of the Peace."

This building was designed and built by B. F. Smith, architect, of Washington, D. C.

During Judge A. M. Gross' term of office 1934-38 there were two stone wings added to the rear of the courthouse. This addition was built by the W.P.A. and furnished much needed office space.

MARRIAGES

The first marriages, as recorded in Marriage Book A, dating from 1821-37, rarely gave anything except the fact of the marriage, the groom's name and who performed the ceremony. For example, the first entry reads:

"B Grigsby .... I do certify that within couple is married by me. ....
       Paid   Jeremiah Combs"

The third entry reads:

"Jesse Combs—I do hereby certify that the within couple is joined together by me, on the 11th day of June 1821—
                                  Jesse Bolin"

While Jesse Combs was County Court Clerk he quaintly

recorded the births and deaths of his family in the back of the first marriage license book, such as:

"Louisa Combs was born on Wednesday the 27th day of November, 1831 at day brake.

John D. Combs was born on Thursday the 10th day of May 1838 about 4 ours after midnight.

Elijah Combs Jr. escaped on the 13th day of April 1847 about an hour in the nite or a little upwards of an hour."

The record also states that "Jesse Combs deceased this life on the 6th day of January 1874 at about day light."

In the second marriage book, the marriage bond is signed by both the bride and groom. The marriage certificate is not filled out until December, 1899, in Marriage Book G. The first marriage books are lettered A through T. E is missing, probably lost when the courthouse burned. After T, the marriage books are numbered 1 through 93, to date.

DEEDS

The first deed recorded in Perry County was in Deed Book A, by Jesse Combs, the first County Court Clerk, on April 17, 1821. This deed, however, is not the deed with the earliest date in Deed Book A. Following is an exact copy of a deed dated August 1, 1820, from Deed Book A, page 9:
"Joshua Mullins
101 Deed/ Fee Paid
Archible Gibson

This indenture made this eight day of August one thousand eight hundred and twenty between Joshua Mullins of Floyd County and state of Ky. of the one part and Archible Gibson of same county and state on the other part.

Witnesseth that the said Joshua Mullins for and in consideration of one hundred and fifty dollars to him in hand paid the receipt whereof is hereby acknowledged hath granted, bargained sold conferred and by these present to grant bargain and sell and confer unto the aforesaid Archible Gibson his heirs and c forever one certain tract of parcel of land lying and being in the County aforesaid containing one hundred acres by survey and bounded as follows court: Beginning at a sycamore standing in a bend of Carr's Fork of Kentucky River N.75 E 68 poles to a beech tree and sugar tree N 30 E 80 poles to a sugar tree thence N 20 poles to a sugar tree N 25 E 29 poles to a sycamore tree, S 45 E 12 poles to a stake, N 30 E 80 poles to a chestnut, N 21 E 14 poles to a white oak E 11 poles to 2 maples. S 8 E 22 poles to an elm and beech, S 75 E 2 poles to a beech, E 196 poles to two sycamores, N 63 E 44 poles crossing the said fork to a poplar, S 13 W 34 poles to a stake S 34 W 5 poles to a stake N 87 W 175 poles to a stake, S 60 W 213 poles to the beginning, which said hundred acres of land all and singular the benefits therewith belonging or in any wise appertaining the said Joshua Mullins do warrant and defend to and against all other persons claiming under my little bit against no other claims whatever.

In witness whereof I have hereunto set my hand and affixed my seal the day and year first above written. Signed, sealed and delivered in the presence of us.

                              Joshua Mullins (seal)

Test:—
John Adams
Spencer Adams
James (x) Davis
    mark
State of Kentucky
Perry County Set.

I, Jesse Combs, clerk of the County Court of Perry County do certify that the foregoing deed was this day proven by the oaths of the two subscribing witnesses on the 29th day of August 1821 to the act and deed and seal of the said for the purpose therein certified and the same duly admitted to record in my office.

Given under my hand this 29th day of August, 1821
                              Jesse Combs, C.P.C.C."

WILLS

No court record would be complete without mentioning wills. The earliest will on record is that of Simon Stacy, filed on October 14, 1822, and recorded in Deed Book A. All wills were formerly recorded in the deed books.

Elijah Combs, Sr., was the first settler in Hazard, and a summary of his will illustrates the typical early estate settlement:
Elijah Combs, Sr.
To Will
"Jackson G. Combs, Jesse Combs, Sr., Josiah Combs, Jesse Combs, Jr., John Combs."

"I Elijah Sr. of Perry County and State of Kentucky being weak in body but of sound mind and disposing memory do hereby make my last will and testament in manner and form following. That is to say that I give to my son, Jesse Combs, my negro man, Lewis. Also the land in the following boundary lying and being in Perry County." (There follows a minute description of a large boundary of land.) "I desire that my son Jesse Combs shall have the use of the above mentioned land and negro man Lewis during his natural life. But they shall not be sold to pay his debts and shall be used only for the use of his family and at his, my son Jesse's death, I give the above mentioned negro Lewis and all of the above land to my three grandsons to wit: Josiah H. Combs, Jesse Combs and John Combs to be equally divided amongst them. I also give to my son Jesse Combs two cows, one horse and ten head of common sized hogs, also two feather beds. I give to my son Jackson G. Combs, two negro women, Nancy and Mary. Also, all the balance of my property on my farm. Also, all the balance of my house furniture, beds, etc., also all the land I hold in the following boundary." (Here follows another description of land.) "I heretofore have given to the balance of my children their part of my estate all that I intended to give them, and lastly I do hereby constitute my grandson Josiah H. Combs executor of this, my last will and testament hereby revoking all other or former wills and testaments by me heretofore made. In witness whereof I hereunto set my hand and hereunto affixed my seal this 17th day of August in the year 1855. Signed, sealed and delivered as for the last will and testament of the above named."

his
Elijah X Combs
mark
Elijah Combs in the presence of

	: copied
John G. Lacey	: and given
Henry C. Hargis	: to
Hezekiah Combs	: John Duff

"Proved in open court by John G. Lacey and Hezekiah Combs, two of the subscribing wittnesses thereto 8th day of November 1855 before John Hyden Probate Judge of Perry County, the Commonwealth of Kentucky, Perry County Court." (4)

The administrator of Nicholas Combs, Sr., deceased, came in the court and made the following report, concerning the sale on the 12th of January, 1854, of the following property:

Jesse Combs, coal picks	$ 1.40
coal shovel	.75
1 gig	.30
Moses Combs, for rent, 1 field	6.00
Peggy Combs, for rent, 1 field	1.00
R. C. Combs, iron	1.75
R. C. Combs, raft of logs	7.55
R. C. Combs, hire of a slave	56.00

On the 6th of February, 1854
R. C. Combs, adm.

The June term of court, 1850, set tavern prices as follows:

"For French Brandy—per ½ pint.........9 e
For Rum—per ½ pint ....9 e
For Gin—per ½ pint ....9 e
For Wine—per ½ pint ....9 e
For Whiskey—per ½ pint ....9 e
For Peach Brandy—per ½ pint 1¼
For Apple Do—per ½ pint 1¼
For Diet ....5 cents
For Bedding ....5 cents
Horse and C per night
fed night and morning 25
Single feed for horse ....9 e
For pastridge 12 hours ....9 e
It is ordered that tavern keepers fill their ½
pints slap full and be shure and keep ½ pints."

The above is an exact copy from the record. As "cents" is written in full twice, it seems reasonable to presume that the "e" is an abbreviation for cents.

All the early records were written by hand, making them sometimes difficult to read and understand, since the script was formed in the old-fashioned manner, as in the early type, which is marked by the similiarity of "s" and "f". Also, it is assumed that the "pastridge" means just what it sounds like—"pasturage."

Courts no longer set the tavern prices. It is now set by the tavern keepers, a step forward in the development of free enterprise.

The Old Order Changes

The coming of the railroad in 1912 in Perry County maked the passing of circuit-riding judges, the last of their tribe in America.

The following is a description of the circuit riders as told to the Kentucky State Bar Association in July, 1933, by the late Hon. Bailey P. Wooton, Attorney General of Kentucky.

"In December, 1897, when Judge W. F. Hall closed his last court at the expiration of his term of office as Circuit Judge of the old 26th District at Hazard, Kentucky, there was not a foot of railroad nor a mile of improved dirt road in all that vast territory embraced by Harlan, Leslie, Clay, Owsley, Perry, Knott, Letcher, Pike, Floyd, Magoffin and Jackson counties, a territory of 150 miles across from railroad to railroad. It embraced the headwaters of the Big Sandy, the Cumberland and the three forks of the Kentucky River. The largest county seat within it had fewer than 500 people.

The time of this story is the early part of the twentieth century; the place may be anywhere within this great circuit; the scene, a courthouse; time, three o'clock, p. m. Darkness comes early in the mountains in these December days. The jury is dismissed, the sheriff adjourns court until court in course. The gavel falls and the judge, Commonwealth's attorney, and visiting lawyers are in a commotion to get started to the next place of holding court, anxious to cover a part of the forty or fifty miles before pitch dark, that the rest of the journey may be more easily negotiated on the next day, Sunday, following. Prancing, pawing horses, eager to be gone, and frisking from a week or ten days' stay in the stable, are brought up before boarding houses and hotels in the little county seat; leggings and spurs are donned, saddle bags are adjusted; an easy swing into the saddle, a wave of good-bye to the friends and hosts waiting to see the start, and the judge, accompanied by his Commonwealth's attorney and the visiting lawyers, riders of the circuit, are off. Three or four hours of hard riding brings the cavalcade to what might be a half dozen regular stopping places; Jim Hays', on Long Fork of Buckhorn; Smokey Allen or Anse Hays' on Troublesome; John Spencer or Lige Duff's on Grapevine; Jim Lewis' on Coon of Cutskin, but most likely to Pud Breeding or Spencer Combs' on

Carrs Fork. It is dark, cold and raining, a cheerful firelight can be seen. 'Hello' comes from one of the crowd, answered by a rush of the prospective host, the barking of half a dozen dogs, and a cordial, 'Get down and come in,' for the court and his retinue of lawyers were genuinely welcomed on these three-times-a-year trips. Each rider, the possible exception of the judge, looks after the care of his own horse, for the hard riders of the hills keep the best blooded horses the Blue Grass affords in the pink of condition, for they, as their masters, must have stamina to withstand the hardships of forced marches over the mountain trails. Saddle bags and slickers, leggings and spurs are piled in one corner of the room, about which the firelight throws a soft glow, and all join in answering a stream of questions from the host who has not, perhaps, had an opportunity for the news in a month. The squawk of chickens and the rattle of dishes whet the appetites, if any whetting is needed, and warn us of approaching supper. The host produces from somewhere something white and clear from a brown jug, with cornshuck stopper, and having the kick of a mule. Keen appetites are soon appeased by fried chicken, cornbread, and hot coffee. During the meal discussions range from law to theology; from 'Who wrote Shakespeare?' to the price of poplar trees. The most intricate points of law and procedure were regularly and sometimes hotly debated. These were veritable law schools, and those entering into discussions showed a knowledge of the law as laid down by Coke & Blackstone, Greenleaf and Chitty that might well be emulated by the law student of today. Reference by these lawyers to sections of the Code, Statutes and leading texts were regarded by one another as commonplace. They arrived at their conclusions by process of reasoning, by sound logic, and by a knowledge of fundamental principles of justice, and not from a line of cases. These were not case lawyers. The doctrine of **stare decisis** had no lodgment in their minds, for there was not, at that time, a complete set of even the Kentucky Reports within the vast territory mentioned; but if one cared to examine the contents of the saddle bags in the corner of the room, he would most likely find a volume of Blackstone or Greenleaf, or the latest works on land titles and criminal law. He was sure to find Montesquieu's **Spirit of Laws**.

Bedtime comes early in the mountains, but a few drinks have set Captain James B. Fitzpatrick, a gallant Confederate soldier, to reciting 'Tam O'Shanter' and 'Twa Dogs.' The more drinks he gets the more dramatic he becomes, and more real the ghost at the Kirk. He carried a dog-eared copy of Bobby Burns in his pocket and knew by heart every poem in it from 'Cotter's Saturday Night' to his favorite, 'The Deil Awa' with the Exciseman.' He probably had in mind the 'Revenuers.' Sleep came often to his droning of 'Annie Laurie' or the 'Lass that made the bed to me.' Morning came all too soon, the time to get up being announced by the vigorous ringing of a farm bell fastened to the end of a pole. A bounteous breakfast is eaten in comparative silence, the convivial spirits of some of the party the night before having become somewhat dampened, giving Crit Bach a chance for a dissertation on the relative merits of Solomon's Proverbs and Paul's Epistles, while Ed Hogg, a Shakespearean scholar of no mean ability, regales the court and host at the other end of the table with good advice from **Hamlet**, and, with twinkling glance toward the hostess, **The Taming of the Shrew**, a play he sincerely enjoyed.

Again the call for the horses; a smiling, glad-hearted host, entreating an early return, and all ride out into the mist of early dawn, clattering down the creek beds over stones and through mush ice, a happy throng. Early dusk brings us to the next county seat, where the concourse is met with glad 'How-de-dos' from the populace, all of whom, it seems, have turned out to see the arrival of the court, and to extend to the judge and circuit riders a royal welcome.

Monday morning the court room is packed, hitching space along the horse racks, erected on three sides of the court house, is at a premium, for every able-bodied man in the county came to the opening of circuit court in those days. The assemblage in the court house is tense as the judge opens his court, empanels his juries and instructs the Grand Jury. These instructions were eagerly listened to by the people, and were an event in their lives and in their conversations thereafter. Many of them were profoundly eloquent, filled with sound advice, and were of lasting good. There was decorum in the court room. The jailer and the high sheriff stood at attention with "45s" for ready reference, and, if a feud trial or a hotly contested election case was on, they searched each person who entered the door for deadly weapons; but they experienced their greatest difficulty, as a rule, in keeping the laity from monopolizing the space reserved for lawyers."

From these excerpts of Perry County records it is evident that the smallest detail of caring for the interests of the locality was not overlooked from the building of a stray pen to care for lost animals to the looking after of the interests of orphan children.

CHAPTER X

TRANSPORTATION

Sally Lathram Hines

Highways

The history of transportation in Perry County is little different from that of any other Eastern Kentucky County.

First, there were the narrow winding forest trails made by buffalo and other wild animals of the regions through gaps up and down rivers and creeks; these trails were followed by Indians and the first white inhabitants of the section, and later widened for ox and mule team and used as trade routes over which a limited amount of merchandise was brought in for the few settlers. Small push boats began to ply the North Fork of the Kentucky River. As this timber industry began to grow, logging down the river became a major occupation, and while this timber industry was at its peak the railroad was built in Perry County. The next step of importance was the coming of the highway, and county roads were built which served as outlets for the inhabitants to different parts of the county. The airplane has made its presence known in the mountains and may be the chief means of transportation in future years.

When the county was organized in 1820, there were no means of travel except by foot. The people were self-sufficient in their own seclusion from the outside world, and there was little need for travel.

The early settlers began to make their first plans for an outlet into regions beyond the mountainous section when they felt the need and desire for certain commodities and household goods. There were a few salt wells in Perry County but not enough to supply their own needs, so the first trade routes were the trails used by the people who brought salt into the country from the Garrett Salt Works in Clay County.[1]

The citizens of Perry County, which then included a large area of land, soon realized it was necessary to establish a road to the county seat at Hazard. It was planned to have the new road run along the North Fork of the Kentucky River, and it was to be known as the Irvine-Pound Gap Road. It would require funds to survey and build the road. Money was scarce and there was but little taxable property. It was found that the "Seminary Lands" (See chapter on Schools) could be turned into a source of revenue for that purpose. January 1, 1831, Perry County Court was ordered to sell the Perry County "Seminary Lands" and apply the proceeds of the sale (450 lots were sold) in opening a road from Estill County to the Perry County Courthouse, and hence to the Virginia Line. Land warrants of 10,000 acres to be located in the county were also to be appropriated and used for the building of the road. This was a good start but little was done toward the building of the road for many years, as this route up the North Fork of the Kentucky River was ninety-five years being completed, and was the last of the four main roads to receive State aid, and the last to be improved. (2)

The grade of this road was not to exceed five degrees, although it would reach ten degrees in some places on account of the narrow gaps through which the road must pass. The width would be eighteen feet on level ground and sixteen feet on hillsides. As funds were inadequate to improve the entire road, it was recommended that the work begin on the lower section immediately above Irvine, from which point there would be a wagon road connection with Central Kentucky. The tributaries of the road likewise were to receive scant aid from the state. Most of the improvements were made on the upper section of the road extending from Hazard. Several of these improvements were made probably because of the salt works on the North Fork, and a branch road near Manchester was granted small appropriations. (3)

The first term of court was held at the log residence of Elijah Combs because there was no Courthouse, and the first act of the new court on June 11, 1822, was for Nicholas Combs, Richard Smith and Robert Hicks to view the road from Martin Fugit's to the mouth of Trace Fork. The September term of court, 1825, ordered that a road be opened along Rockhouse Creek to connect with the road to Floyd County Courthouse.

Records in the Perry County Courthouse show that at most every term of court in the early and middle nineteenth century land warrants were made and court orders issued for the building and improvement of roads, but only small sections were benefited. At the March term of Perry County Court 1832 (O.B. No. 27) the following orders were entered.

"That E. Combs, Joseph Hammons, John W. Bates, B. Webb, view the road from Perry Courthouse to the Virginia line and made report to Court; that Elijah Combs, B. Begley, and Patrick B. Webb appoint to view the road from Estill County line to Perry Courthouse and report to Court." At the March term of court, 1833, we find the following order: "Met at the Virginia line on top of Cumberland Mountain where it proposed the said road begin and viewed the grounds. The road is to run about fifty miles from where the said road is to commence, to Perry Courthouse, and great convenience will result to the Public as well as to the individuals if said road is established and because there is no Public road between Virginia line and the Perry County Courthouse and the citizens of the county labour under great inconvenience for the want of a road and there will be no private inconvenience if any person of the said road should be established and the said proposed road will run through the land of Benjamin Bentley, Thomas Bentley, John Holbrook, Lewis Bentley, Joseph Hammons, John W. Bates, Benjamin Adams, Ephraiam Hammons, John Johnson, Biram Combs, Elijah Combs, John Caudill, James Collins, Abraham Burgey, Thomas Francis, John Mullins, Delphia Johnson, William Adams, Nancy Maden, John Cornett, John Combs, Jeremiah Combs, Jepey Stacy, Lydia Combs, the clerk is ordered to issue a sps vs. the above persons returnable to the next term of court."

The above orders were convincing evidence that Perry County in 1832 extended from Estill County to the Virginia line on top of Pine Mountain at Pound Gap.

The act of February 24, 1834, granted $500 in land warrants to the road from Perry County Courthouse, (Hazard) extending in the direction of Floyd County Courthouse (Prestonsburg). Insignificant improvements also were made on a briddle path which extended from Hazard across the divides to the Middle Fork of the Kentucky River, and up another stream to headquarters, crossing Pine Mountain at War Gap and reaching Harlan on the Cumberland River. The road from the mouth of Troublesome to Sounding Gap became the established mail route, and in years 1836 and 1837 a conditional grant of $3,000 for improvements was made. Prior to this time this road was little more than a trail or bridle path. (4)

"Passing from Mr. Maguire's near the Middle Fork over the hills to the mouth of Troublesome Creek—the country is very thinly settled as there is little land adapted to tillage and it's considered impassable for wagons. Bridle paths are the only roads and there is no means of transporting the products of the country to market except by flatboats at high tide or on pack horses." (House Journal—Kentucky.—1838-1839— p 252)

During the French-Eversole feud soldiers from the 1st Regiment of the State Militia were called to Perry County to act as guards. The trip from Louisville was made by train to London—the nearest town in this mountainous section that was reached by railroad—then by wagon for the remaining seventy-five miles to Hazard. In his report Captain Sohan said:

"The road is simply indescribable, being so rough that most of the command preferred walking to riding. We marched for hours in water, the natural bed of the creeks being the only available way through the hills, and this was generally the best part of the road; at other times it took all hands to help the teams up the hills, or to keep them from falling over the precipices." (Military History of Kentucky p 269—More about this trip in Executive Journal No. 2 1890-1891 p 180)

After the train came to Jackson in 1891 the mail came from there to Hazard daily. W. O. Davis was the contractor for this mail route. The cost of the road for this established mail route was estimated at $200 per mile along the river and creeks and through the bottom lands, and at $2,000 per mile for about eight miles which had to be cut in the sides of the mountains. The sums of money appropriated for the improvement of the road, and improvement of the connecting roads, were very inadequate and but little could be done on the whole length of the road. Usually the main bulk of money appropriated was spent on improving a very small section of the road. The road was to be placed in charge of Perry County Court for working and repairs, but the court was not to have any power to alter or discontinue the road. (Proof of this found in Perry County Court Records.)

Older settlers tell how the first dirt roads of the county were laid off in sections along the creek beds. Each section was three to five miles long and an overseer was appointed by the County Judge. The roads were made fifteen feet wide and the tree branches had to be cut fifteen feet overhead.[5] Every male between the ages of 16 to 60 had to work on the road two days a year—usually on Friday and Saturday—the time and place appointed by the overseer. The man received notice to meet the overseer on a certain day and to bring his working tools—a mattock, hoe, and shovel. If it were impossible for him to report on that day he could hire a substitute from another section, and if he refused to work, he was fined $20.00 for the offense. A day's work consisted of ten hours hard labor for which he received fifty cents. Most of the work was done in the fall of the year, after the crops were laid by, or the harvest gathered. These roads were passable in summer, but after the fall rains, and the winter freezes and thaws, the roads became quite muddy and were filled with chugholes, which made it impossible for sleds and wagons to pass over them.

"Court ordered Jackson Combs to build a good strong bridge across the mouth of Laurel branch sufficient for wagons to cross with safety and so high as not to be injured by high water, and out of good lasting timber and to build a road around the bend of the river from General Elijah Combs' fence to the mouth of Laurel branch." (Book A—p 379)

For a time, until about 1830, the mountain roads, although steeper and more subject to frequent washouts, were not much inferior to those in Central Kentucky, where dirt roads prevailed. Indeed, in some cases they were somewhat better, for the waste from the coal-measure when composed of sandstone and slate was superior for road purposes, to the miry clay of the lowlands. The contrast in the road between the two sections of the state became steadily greater, and it was during this period that the rugged mountain region, left henceforth to shift for itself in the matter of highways, became isolated to such a marked degree. The following extracts show the appropriations made to the different roads in Kentucky over a certain period of time.

"Owingsville and Big Sandy,
    1837-1847 ....$168,783.83
Mt. Sterling to Virginia line,
    1836-1845 .... 23,243.40
Pikeville and Sounding Gap,
    1836-1847 .... 6,324.00
Irvine to mouth of Troublesome, 1839   448.50
Mouth of Troublesome to Sounding
    Gap, 1836 .... 731.50
Wilderness and Cumberland Gap,
    1836-1843 .... 6,655.75 [6]

An overland route was blazed from Norton, Virginia to Hazard by a man named Coffer, who carried such goods as he could on saddles strapped to oxen. When the trail had been widened, he brought the first wagon to Perry County. This was in 1880. Mr. Lee Daniel, a native of Hazard, tells of this event. The wagon was drawn by oxen and ladened with goods, and was a great improvement over the pack saddle method. Coffer found a ready sale for all the wagons he brought in, and they became known as "Coffer Wagons." Mr. Daniel also relates that John Bill Baker bought up all the old, poor horses he could find in the surrounding country and drove them to North Carolina where he exchanged them for mules, which were less clumsy than oxen and made better speed in transporting goods. Mules were also bought at the Mount Sterling Market and driven into this country. Until the railroad reached Jackson in 1891, the nearest railroad was at London, Kentucky, and from there merchandise was brought into this country by means of ox and mule teams. This was a distance of seventy-five miles and it took ten days to make the round-trip with ox teams and seven days with mule teams. The usual load was 1500 to 2000 pounds, and the usual team consisted of four mules or seven oxen.

Mr. Calaway Colwell, a salesman for the Gene Baker Motor Company, relates the following incident that happened on his father's farm near Yerkes. A stationary boiler was being moved from the Big Creek in Perry County to Trace Branch in Leslie County. It was all a team of twelve oxen could do to pull it, and when they came to a bend in the road on an ascending grade, the oxen were unable to pull the load, as they were pulling against themselves on the curve. It was necessary to tear down a number of panels of fence so the team could have a straight pull, and in that way they were able to get the heavy load up the steep grade.

After the coming of the railroad in 1912, the rich coal deposits were opened, mostly with outside capital. Mining towns sprang up all over the country. Hazard, the County Seat, began to build and grow rapidly. People came from every section of the country. They could not bring their automobiles with them—there were no roads over which they could be driven. Wagon roads consisted, mainly, of creek beds unsuitable for heavy loads. Their roadways were, for most part, the waterways, or as Emerson Hough once put it in making reference to the roads of the people of the mountains, "their viaducts are their aqueducts." This condition had existed from pioneer days, and little had been done in road building over a period of a century and a half. The small population, most of whom had come across the mountains of Virginia from North Carolina and from Tennessee, were not content to remain in seclusion. Foremost in the minds and the hearts of these settlers was the plan for a road to serve as an outlet to Virginia, branching off into Tennessee, hence into North Carolina. As has been said, the struggle to obtain this road began as early as 1831, and it was almost a century before State Highway No. 15 was completed across Kentucky, and the dream was realized. The story of the untiring effort to build this highway, as told by J. A. Smith, is typical of much of the road-building in Kentucky.

In 1922 Smith, the "Boy Judge," became County Judge of Perry County. The slogan of his campaign was—"Better Roads for Perry County." He at once set to work to make this slogan come true. He realized that money for highway construction must come from taxation, supplemented with aid from the newly organized State Highway Commission. State Highway No. 15 would run through Perry County and Judge Smith worked diligently with the cooperation of the people, the civic organizations, and the local newspapers, to get the road built. The Commission worked out a plan with the judge for the letting of the first contract in Perry County for a two mile section of the road from Hazard to Christopher. The Commandri Construction Company did the work. It was hard to get bidders as the state had but little funds for road-building. Then, too, the bidders were hesitant about taking the contract as building material, especially limestone, was hard to get. The contractor got coal from Coal Seam No. 4, which mixed fairly well with asphalt.

Perry County did not have sufficient funds to meet its part of the cost of construction, but the demand and the necessity for roads were so great by this time that the County Judge called upon the people to vote for a $500,000 road bond issue to provide the necessary funds to meet the requirements of the State Highway Department. The people voted overwhelmingly for the issue of these bonds. Although the county was now in position to meet its financial requirements, much work had to be done. Locations had to be made, and the right-of-ways secured.

The following year, 1923, the project was continued to Jeff, and from Hazard to Lott's Creek in the opposite direction. This was a distance of approximately seven miles and within that distance it was necessary to build four bridges across the river at an approximate cost of $300,000. This was a costly project. The Highway Commission's funds were limited at this time, but after much argument, the Commission yielded and a second contract was soon awarded to the Williams Construction Company. This put the county through its most costly part of construction on what was later to be known as Highway 15.

This project was from Christopher to the mouth of Carr's Fork, and from Hazard to the mouth of Lott's Creek. These roads were at first only graded, drained, and graveled —later they were black-topped. During 1924-25 the road was extended from Jeff up Carr's Fork to the Knott County line, and from Lott's Creek to the Breathitt County line on Troublesome Creek.

In 1920 the Legislature of Kentucky designated by law a state-wide system of highways which was to connect every county seat in the state, and was known as the primary system. This gave rise to many "Good Road Associations" throughout the state on the idea of getting through highways instead of just patchwork in various counties. On July 14, 1922, at Jackson, Kentucky, under the direction of W. H. Holiday of that city, the Kentucky-Virginia Association was formed and he became its president. This association was organized for the purpose of promulgating the building of a highway from Lexington, Kentucky, to Pound Gap, Virginia. The road beginning in Lexington was to go through Winchester, Stanton, Campton, Jackson, Hazard, Whitesburg, Jenkins, and on to Pound Gap, Virginia.

Meetings were held at the various county seats along this route to bring to the attention of the people the importance of this highway in giving them an outlet. The response was unanimous all along the route and one of the most important meetings was held at Winchester. Delegates came from every county. From Perry County Judge Smith and the entire Fiscal Court were present. With them went Jesse Morgan, Dr. A. M. Gross and others. The members of the State Highway Commission, with Green Garrett, its chairman, and Joe S. Boggs, the State Highway Engineer were there. Many interesting talks were made by various leaders from the different counties setting out the great importance of this highway and the readiness of the county officials in each county to participate in its construction. Jesse Morgan got somewhat oratorical when he exclaimed, "Proud Mother Virginia, the descendants of your pioneers that came and settled this fine section of Kentucky will soon be coming to visit you—not over trails that our fathers came on horseback and afoot will they come to you, but they will come on white ribbons of concrete in shining limousines." This prophecy has come to pass for almost simultaneously contracts were let along the Kentucky-Virginia route in the other counties and it was not a long period of time until the road was really open from Lexington to Pound Gap—Perry County coming to the front along with the rest of the counties—and now, State Highway No. 15, The Red River Trail, goes from historic Winchester in the rolling bluegrass region, through Cumberland National forest, into the green covered Appalachian Mountains. Two miles out of Whitesburg, Route No. 15 joins with U. S. 119, passing Jenkins and Pikeville to the West Virginia line. At Jenkins Highway No. 15 also joins into the Mayo Trail U. S. No. 23, and runs to Pound Gap, Virginia, at the Virginia State line. Thus, bringing to pass the dream first conceived in the minds and hearts of the pioneers of Eastern Kentucky, and traveling over this road one sees some of the most beautiful scenery in our country, and many historic places of interest.

The Red River Trail (Highway 15), is also a part of the Appalachian Way Association organized in 1924 for the purpose of sponsoring the building of a highway from Chicago to Charleston, South Carolina.

The state kept up incessant fight for other roads, as a result State Highway 80 was built. The highway runs from the Brakes of the Big Sandy River on the Virginia line, to Columbus, Kentucky, on the Mississippi River, and is called, "The Frontier Road." A small section of this road is in Perry County—the road between Hindman in Knott County, and Hyden, in Leslie County. The route is through the most primitive region of the rugged grandeur of Kentucky, and is joined with the state roads from the Virginia line to the Tennessee State line. Kentucky's final section of the highway, a 3.1 mile stretch, has been completed joining the Virginia road at the border of Pike County, Kentucky, and Buchanan County, Virginia. (COURIER-JOURNAL, June 2, 1951.)

During these years of road construction work was not

confined alone to the building of the main highways. The people from every section of the county made pleas for their roads to be removed from the creek beds. Their pleas were answered. Work started in nearly every section of the county and the people who lived on the various streams from Leatherwood, in the upper part of the county, to Squabble Creek in the lower end of the county, soon enjoyed a dry-land road which served them well during the milder seasons of the year. To accomplish all this was no easy task and would have taken many years but for the fine cooperative spirit of the people who lived on these roads. They set back fences, felled trees, split the stones, and raked the dirt. These roads were at first only graded, drained, and graveled, later many have been blacktopped. Many of the roads maintained by the county alone, are yet passable only in dry seasons, but some can be traveled the year round. There are about one hundred miles of these dirt roads leading off from the main highways.

The great number of motor vehicles used on our roads, highways and streets is shown by the number of licenses isssued in the county, and when we consider the through traffic and tourists that pass through our county, we get some conception of what the roads of Perry County, and other Eastern Kentucky Counties, means to the people of this section. Much of the coal of the mountains of Eastern Kentucky is hauled out by truck and loaded into coal cars to be shipped by rail. Through transportation of all portables is rapidly being taken over by truck since we have good roads over which they can travel. In 1952, there were 5,249 car licenses, 2,112 truck licenses, and 45 motorcycle licenses issued in Perry County.

Mr. T. E. Moore, Jr., a lawyer and prominent man of the city, states that when he came to Hazard in 1896, the only streets were Main Street, Court and Fleet Streets, and the County Road, now High Street and that nothing was done to improve these streets until nearly a century after they were laid off. There were no sidewalks except a few boardwalks on Main Street opposite the courthouse square, going back to the old Combs Hotel, now the Grand Hotel.

Mrs. Bess Zoellers had the honor of being the first woman to walk across the new bridge. The old wooden bridge across Town Branch leading to Baker Hill was built by Barney Baker in 1927. When Baker Avenue was being constructed the material for it had to be hauled up the rough haulway of Town Branch. The material for most of the houses built on Oakhurst, Cornell, Lyttle Boulevard, Laurel, Craig, and Cedar Streets had to be hauled in the same way. When the City of Hazard was being built, Town Branch was Nature's gift—it bore the traffic. When the city had grown until the narrow Main Street had become so congested that a new street had to be built, it was only befitting that Old Town Branch should be the location chosen as the street—to relieve the traffic—and the name "Memorial Drive" was rightfully given it.

It allows through traffic to by-pass the main part of Hazard. Main Street and High Street had been carrying an approximate 6,800 cars and trucks daily, according to count of the Kentucky Department of Highways.

Plans for the project were approved early in 1949 by the U. S. Bureau of Public Roads. The contract was awarded to Nally and Ballard, Bardstown contractors. The contract included the grade, drain, and base surfacing. It also included the three overhead bridges, (two new ones and repairs on the wooden bridge off Broadway.) The concrete surfacing was awarded to Foster-Creighton Company of Nashville, Tennessee. The total cost of the project, including the right-of-way, in which the city of Hazard shared, was $555,000.

The street is one-half mile long, 40 feet wide with a four and one-half foot sidewalk on each side. Roadside improvement was under the direction of Charles A. Hall, assistant to District Engineer C. T. Warwick, assisted by the Perry County Garden Club.

The new Relief Route was dedicated July 12, 1951, when Governor Lawrence W. Wetherby officially opened the road, and the ribbon was cut by Dewey Daniel, regional vice-president of the Kentucky Chamber of Commerce. Ceremonies were conducted at a special constructed speakers

He said, "Progress along these streets was hazardous at any time. The hogs took over every mudhole and made of it a hogwallow, cattle roamed over the town at will."

Harold E. Dye in his book, "THE PROPHET OF LITTLE CANE CREEK," writes this story concerning the early streets of Hazard:

"One day the wife of one of the leading business men of the town came tripping down the street in her pretty dress, she knew all eyes were upon her as she made her way along the boardwalk. She clutched at her rustling skirt now and then to keep it from dragging in the mud. Suddenly a big shoat came from under the walk. He was dripping with mud. Just as the fair lady tried to step by, the hog shook himself violently and the mud flew. She screamed, but her nice dress was ruined."

Older citizens of the town say that in winter and in rainy seasons the mud would be belly deep to mules, traffic would mire in the mud and have to be dug out. Cobblestones were placed end-wise at cross sections for the people to step on and if they happened to slip off the stones they would lose their boots in the mud. Broadway was unimproved. It had large ledges of sandstone, making it very rough in places for wagons.

There were no bridges until 1912 when the bridge from Main Street to the L&N Station was built by the Hazard Bridge Company, which bridge was washed away in the 1927 flood. This bridge, however, was immediately rebuilt. Duke Payne, who later came to Hazard as minister of the Christian Church, worked with his father on the construction of the new bridge. There was no bridge over Town Branch to what is now Lyttle Boulevard and Laurel Street. Persons going from Broadway to the section known as "The Backwoods" reached what is now Lyttle Boulevard by going down a long series of steps on the Broadway side and up ascending steps on the opposite side.

Town Branch rendered a great service to the City of Hazard prior to the improvement of Broadway and the building of the bridge across the branch in 1917. The steel structure of this bridge is still being used, although the wooden floor has been repaired and replaced many times.

stand on the side of the highway. Many state, district, county, and city officials were on the platform and took part in the dedication. Fred B. Bullard, publisher of the HAZARD HERALD, acted as master of ceremonies and Mayor M. K. Eblem delivered the welcoming address. William P. Curlin, Commissioner of Highways, and Henry A. Spalding, Hazard City Engineer, each gave a short talk, as did most of the guests on the platform as they were introduced by Bullard. Among the noted guests was Simeon S. Willis, former governor of Kentucky, under whose administration the project was started.

Davis Street is one of the latest streets to be improved by the city. It goes past the new Memorial Gymnasium and the Bobby Davis Park, and when completed will be landscaped and beautified in keeping with the Park. It will cross Memorial Drive and be extended past the highway to intersect with High Street.

Aviation

The Government, in establishing airports in Kentucky, made a number of surveys in Perry County, but found only one location with enough level space for the landing and taking-off of planes, and that only for the accommodation of small planes. The location was about three miles out of Hazard on Route 15. The land was a part of the old Crawford place, and was then owned by an heir, Jennie Crawford Combs. She agreed to sell the land for an airport, but reserved about four acres on which to build a home for herself.

In 1944, Clyde Baumgardner, and the late F. L. Cisco, became interested in the project of establishing an airport on the above mentioned location, and through the co-operation of the Chamber of Commerce, and other interested citizens, purchased the land, about eighty-four acres, and re-sold it to the county.

There was but little done to improve the airport for a number of years. It was used by privately owned planes of E. J. Davis, John F. Gilbert, Clyde Baumgardner, Bud Igo, and others, for their own use and convenience. Often on special days and on Sundays crowds would gather to watch the airplanes take-off and land. Passengers, for a small fee, would be taken for a short ride over the city and county. The planes were also used for advertising purposes.

In 1948, the Perry County Airport Corporation, a $240,000 project (including the cost of the land), started the development of the airport. The cost of the construction is to be shared alike by the County, State, and Federal Government. The airport, itself, is now in perfect condition with a runway of 2,100 feet. Small planes for 7 and 8 passengers can be accommodated, and when the airport is completed, will have feeder service to make connection with other airports.

The Kentucky River lies between the airport and the highway, so the only way it can now be reached is by boat, or by crossing on a swinging bridge. However, a $60,000 bridge is to be built and a $24,000 Administration Building has been completed. Air transportation in Perry County will never be extensively used, as the mountains limit the size of the airport and planes, but will serve as a great help and convenience in getting to and from the mountains of this section in case of emergencies.

River

The river was the only means for transporting logs out of Perry County after logging became the chief money-making industry. The logs were dragged to the river's edge, and loaded onto rafts made the proper lengths to take the bends of the river, and these rafts were piloted by experienced river men who knew the channels.

These hardy men who worked on the river had many interesting experiences. Many of the voyages were pleasant with favorable weather during the entire trip, while others were made in cold and frigid weather when the ice would freeze on the rafts, making the trip even more hazardous. At times the river would freeze so solid that it would be necessary for the men to anchor their rafts and abandon them until the freeze was over. Occasionally the thaw came with floods caused by torrential rains in the mountains. The ice would break up in huge blocks which would rush down the river, tearing the rafts apart. The scattered logs would be carried down the mighty river like helpless human beings, some to go to the different terminals where they would be caught in booms built for that purpose, while others would be caught in drifts along the river where they would remain until dislodged by some future flood. The task of separating these logs was a tedious one. Each timber owner had his mark on his logs and would claim his timber when it was separated at the booms, which were simply logs chained together and stretched diagonally across the river.

The North Fork of the Kentucky River was improved and freed of incumbrance to the mouth of Leatherwood Creek in Perry County where salt works had been opened and were in successful operation in the 1820's. However, fish and mill dams and such obstructions were numerous. In the bends of the North Fork were masses of detached rocks 100 to 315 cubic yards above low water, which during a boating stage caused swift currents. The lightest canoe could not navigate sections of the stream.

Expenditures by the board of Internal Improvement for open channel work on the North Fork for the years 1837-1841 was $3,497. The state undertook no further work upon the river except within the area of the newly developing coal fields. An act of March 1, 1869, authorized the expenditure of $5,000 on the North Fork between its mouth and Brashear's Salt Works at the mouth of Leatherwood Creek.[7] By 1870 these various amounts had been spent in clearing the stream for the benefit of the coal and lumber industries which were now of greater significance to the state than the salt works. The river at that time was 125 feet wide at Hazard, and deep enough for flatboats and rafts to operate.

In 1880, the Federal Government took over the work of the Kentucky River that the state had been forced to abandon. The dams were to be repaired and operated free of toll and the slack-water extended into the mountains to Hazard, or to Leatherwood Creek as had been originally planned. The expense was greater than the engineers had estimated. No further expenditure was made for the maintenance of dams after 1893 when the engineers rcommended its abandonment on the grounds that they were a detriment to the logging industry. In accordance with the river and harbor act of February 27, 1911, an examination of the North Fork of the Kentucky River was made and the engineers reported against removing obstructions because of the recent extension of the railroad in the valley.[8] By this time, too, roads throughout the county were beginning to be improved, and the river was gradually becoming less useful as a means of transportation in Perry County.

As the population in the mountains grew the need for merchandise increased, and push boats on the North Fork of the Kentucky River became an important means of transporting goods from Jackson. Early settlers say that these boats were propelled by men with push poles, usually three on each side of the boat, and a seventh man to "hold." The six men would place their poles at the bottom of the river at the front of the boat and walk to the stern pushing it the length of itself. The man who was to "hold" placed his pole against the river bed and held the boat until the other men could walk to the front again and repeat their performance. Many boat loads of merchandise were lost by capsizing. The following news was taken from the HAZARD HERALD of March 12, 1912:

"On last Saturday night, between the hours of eleven o'clock and daylight, a boat operated in the interest of Uncle Ira Combs of Jeff, sank at the bottom of Pigeon Roost, ten miles below Hazard. The boat with the entire cargo, we are informed, was for Mr. Combs store at Jeff, and the remainder was for Mr. L. E. Petrey's new store at Hazard. The boat was tied up for the night's lodging. The heavy rains of the day before, and the subsequent rise of the river, caused the boat to press against the limb of a large tree, causing it to tilt and sink."

Mark Stanifer relates an interesting voyage he made with a raft of logs from Hazard to Madison, Indiana. This trip required several weeks and was very pleasant and uneventful until they neared Carrollton, Kentucky, where the Kentucky River flows into the Ohio River. There the current came practically to a standstill. They were unable to proceed until a passing steamer tied onto their rafts and towed them into the Ohio, from which point they made the trip without further trouble. He relates that he and his crew came home via London, riding the train to that point, and walking from there to Hazard, a distance of seventy-five miles.

Commerce was carried on almost exclusively by means of the Kentucky River and its forks. Agricultural products, together with the timber, made up a considerable part of the river cargoes. (Kentucky River Navigation—Verhoeff —p 142) The North Fork of the Kentucky River was also used near the end of the logging season to transport goods on flat boats. Freight and household goods being sent to Hazard would be sent by rail to Winchester or Mount Sterling, where they were transferred to sleds and wagons and hauled to Irvine and Beattyville, where they would be loaded onto flatboats and sent on to their destination. After the railroad reached Jackson in 1891, goods were shipped by rail to that point, and sent on by boat to Hazard.

Mrs. Boyd Combs tells of her first trip to Hazard, when she came here in September, 1911, to teach in the graded school. She was then Mary Gaines and lived on a farm near Frankfort. She came as far as Jackson by train where she was told she could get the mail hack to Hazard the following morning. She and the driver Pole Napier, left Jackson at six o'clock and got to Hazard at five that evening. She said when they would come to a steep up-grade in the road the driver would walk by the side of the wagon and drive the team. After leaving the mail at the post office, he drove her on to the Davis Hotel which was run by W. O. Davis and his wife "Aunt Bink." The following morning she found room and board in a private home for $13.00 a month. (Her salary for teaching was $50.00 a month.) In April, when the school year had ended, she and the principal and his wife, Mr. and Mrs. Steiner, started out in a gasoline boat to go to Whick where they meant to take the train, as the rail had been completed that far, but on their arrival at Whick they were told that a slide along the track would delay the train for some time. It was then night and they had to stay in the depot until morning. She said there were no seats or chairs in the depot, and they took covers from their trunks and made beds on the floor where they slept until morning. They took another boat to Jackson where they got the train and continued the trip to their homes.

Mrs. Combs said when she came to Hazard the following September to resume her teaching the L. & N. had completed the railroad beyond the town, and she made the entire trip by train.

Perry County had no navigable water courses for steam boats but did have over seventy-five miles navigable for push boats carrying as much as 30,000 pounds. Forest products floated down the stream from Eastern Kentucky ranked first in quantity of shipments. Coal ranked next. The first coal to be sent out of Perry County was taken out in barges in very small quantities. It was so slow and expensive a process that the service was discontinued with the coming of the railroad.

The river, in a way, brought about its own decline as a thing of usefulness and beauty. The very timber it floated to market held back the soil, and after it was cut, erosion began. The soil from the uplands was washed down the river by the rain, slowly but surely filling it up. At present it is a mere trinkle, and only after great rains does it show any semblance of its former self. With the coming of the railroad in 1912, and the building of the roads and highways in Perry County, the river gave up its claim of being the principal means of transportation.

Railroads

The history of transportation by rail dates back many years. In fact the moving of coal and timber from Perry and other eastern counties may have had its conception in the incorporation of the Kentucky Union Railroad Company March 10, 1854, under the special act of the Kentucky Legislature. It organized to build a railroad from L.&E. Junction in Clark County, through Powell, Wolfe, Breathitt, Perry, and Letcher Counties, to Big Stone Gap, Virginia;

hence through the Cumberlands to Abingdon, Virginia, to connect with what is now a line of the Norfork & Western Railroad. This ambitious project was never realized in its entirety. In fact, until the year 1873 this company contented itself with acquiring timber and coal-lands in Breathitt, Perry, and Letcher Counties, and making a number of surveys trying to select a route cheap to construct, economical to operate, and yet reaching a maximum number of coal fields.

Actual pick-and-shovel work did not start until sometime in the year 1886, during which year the line was built from L. & E. Junction to Clay City, a distance of 14.7 miles. Once this work started, it moved along fairly rapidly, and by December, 1890, it had been extended to Elkatawa, Kentucky. It was completed to Jackson, a distance of 3.7 miles, on July 15, 1891. At Nada, Kentucky, the foothills were encountered. It is quite possible that the added cost of construction due to mountainous terrain forced the Kentucky Union to establish Jackson as its last outpost.

The L. & N. became interested in the development of the coal fields and the extension of their lines as early as March, 1903, and went into the matter with thoroughness. After an extensive investigation it was decided that the time was not yet ripe for the undertaking of the huge engineering project. However, early in 1910, after additional research, it was decided to make the venture. The L. & N. purchased the entire stock of the Lexington and Eastern Railroad which had previously acquired the property from the Kentucky Union, and which had Jackson as its eastern terminal. Then they began to plan to reach the timber and coal fields of the mountainous section.

The fact that a railroad was to be built into Eastern Kentucky was great news. The newspapers throughout the section received it with much enthusiasm. THE MOUNTAIN EAGLE, of Whitesburg, heralded it with these words:

"Railroad matter settled, within two years the Lexington and Eastern (The line continued under this name until 1915) is to be completed from Jackson to the mouth of Boone in Letcher County, coming by way of Hazard, and Whitesburg. Biggest and richest coal and timber lands in the world will be developed. Contract will be let on or before October 15, and dirt will be flying by January 1, 1911. Millions will be spent in construction of the line, and when finished the mountain counties will become the richest in the entire south."

The first step toward such penetration was the locating and purchasing of the right-of-way, which began August 29, 1910. The task of locating the line was entrusted to Mr. J. E. Willoughby, the L. & N. engineer of construction, and that of purchasing the right-of-way to Mr. E. S. Jouett, chief attorney for the L. & E., and who later became the L. & N. Vice-President and General Counsel. (Now retired.)

Mr. Willoughby selected the route generally along the North Fork of the Kentucky River, which had been the River route of transportation. The problem of locating the line was more difficult than it might have been in other sections due to mountainous topography and narrowness of the valley. It was necessary to survey through the most valuable land with little regard for homes, barns, and gardens. Then, too, the natives had had very little contact with people from the outside. In many cases the surveyors were absolutely forbidden to step upon the land. These arbitrary edicts against the march of progress were enforced by some of the owners who sat on their rail fences with shotguns and rifles in hand. However, Mr. Jouett appointed right-of-way agents who were generally prominent, well known men of the counties in which they were to work, and, with a great amount of diplomacy and tact, these agents were able to allay the fears and suspicions of the land owners and to convince them of their good intentions.

When the right-of-way was secured, the purchasing of the line began almost simultaneously. The right-of-way agents took option on the land that might be needed by the railroad. Five dollars was the amount required to clinch the option. An old survey known as the "Walker Survey" was used as a basis for the option. It provided for a route on both sides of the North Fork, and later one of the optional routes was to be selected. The company exercised the claims and took deeds to the properties involved. Purchasing the land for the right-of-way was not too difficult even though there seemed to have been distrust among some of the citizens. This, no doubt, was due to the wisdom of employing local men as agents. Condemnation suits were necessary in only a few cases, and many of the citizens who were interested in progress and future prosperity even donated their property. Records show that 112.34 acres were donated.

The following extract is a copy of a letter written by Mr. Jouett in connection with his work of securing the right-of-way.

"The general feeling among the citizens was somewhat hostile, the opinion prevailing that we simply were trying to tie up the available right-of-way to prevent the building of a railroad by another company. I argued this with the leading citizens and finally convinced them of our faith by agreeing to a reverter of the parcel involved upon failure to build a railroad in four years. I made a thorough organization under Jesse Morgan and B. P. Wootton our efficient attorneys, and several other lawyers whom I employed to help temporarily. I held a town meeting, and after enlisting all the officials, squads were sent out covering the entire line through the country, and soon closed all the contracts."

By January 1, 1911, the right-of-way was secured, and the contractors were able to begin the building of the line. The successful conclusion of the work of securing the right-of-way was aided in no small way by the assistance of C. Bascom Slemp, who later became secretary to President Coolidge, and by John C. Mayo, who was a manager of the Northern Coal and Coke Company in Eastern Kentucky. Both of these men have been active in the development of the Eastern Kentucky Coal Fields.

The grade and construction work was a huge undertaking. When it is considered that there was to be built seven steel river bridges and seven tunnels, beside the numerous smaller girder bridges and concrete underpasses in Breathitt and Perry Counties, one can to some extent visualize the magnitude of such an engineering project.

The grade work was done by hand, or at least without steam shovels, bulldozers, or any motorized machinery whatsoever. Except where tunnels were being driven there were no air compressors for drilling and practically all the drilling was done by hammer and chisel. At Lennut was located a power plant to furnish power for a compressor for drilling and blasting a tunnel. The dirt was moved by mule-drawn wheel scrapers, aided by small hand scrapers. About six mules were required to draw one wheel scraper. Even wheelbarrows were used to haul dirt. Practically all laborers were foreigners brought in by the contractors on free transportation. However, many men along the line worked and hired out their teams. The contractors furnished crude sleeping and living quarters which were thrown up temporarily. It was probably due to the low cost of labor that the building of the line was possible.

Most of the machinery used for the building of the railroad was moved up the North Fork of the Kentucky River in push boats to places where it was to be needed. The steel for constructing the bridges was brought to Jackson by train where it was unloaded to be used later. The track was laid to the first crossing of the river, then the steel for that particular bridge would be reloaded at Jackson and hauled over the newly laid track to where the bridge was to be built; track would again be laid to the next river crossing and steel for that bridge would likewise be hauled. This procedure continued until all the seven steel railroad bridges were completed. The building of the bridges was under contract to the Virginia Bridge and Iron Company. (Steel needed for bridges south of Viper was brought in by that company as needed and was not stored at Jackson.) The bridges were put up and merely pinned together until it was safe for light engines to move over, and were riveted later. This was done so the track-laying could proceed as rapidly as possible. Some of the steel girders, because of the length, required three flat cars to haul them.

Mr. A. B. Combs (Bige) gives interesting information concerning the moving of machinery, building materials, supplies, and timber up the river on flat boats for use in the construction of the line. He was in charge of buying the timber needed, some of which was brought from Quicksand in Breathitt County, while some was bought along the right-of-way near where it was to be used. He was also placed in charge of building the flat boats needed for this transportation. Mr. Combs states that he and his brother Johnny were the first to stick a pick in the ground to start grading for the road south of Hazard Tunnel after the tunnel had been bored through. This tunnel was blasted through March 21, 1912, and the HAZARD HERALD headlined this event with these words:

"Hazard tunnel punched through March 21. Track laying at rate of a mile and a half a day on the home stretch."

Mr. Dewey Daniel was the fourth man to walk through this tunnel, being preceded only by those in charge of the work.

The grade work was under the supervision of J. O. Willoughby who has been previously mentioned as the L. & N.'s engineer of construction, but later it was placed in the hands of Mr. W. E. Smith who later became Vice President and general manager of the L. & N. system. In May, 1912, the work was placed in the hands of Mr. J. C. Nickerson who completed the laying of the track from Krypton to McRoberts, November 16, 1912. Mr. Nickerson remained with the construction work until December 31, 1913, ballasting and strengthening fills, and doing such other work as was required for the new railroad. He returned in later years to become superintendent of the Eastern Kentucky Division of the L. & N. (The name given the new line October 1, 1915.) He is still active in that capacity.

The laying of the track was an interesting procedure. A train made up of flat cars was pushed with the engine. First came the rail-laying, or pioneer car, followed by the rail car, next were the cars loaded with cross ties, then came a material car loaded with spikes, splices, bolts and other things needed for the laying of the railroad. The rails were on supports on each side of the cars. There was a small narrow gauge track which ran down the middle of the flat cars. Ties were moved out over this on a dolly car and dumped over the end of the rail-laying, or pioneer car; the rail was moved out over these cars on a set of rollers which were between the rails of the narrow gauge track, and dumped over the end of the pioneer car. Two steel rails would be unloaded, placed on the ties that had been previously laid and bolted together by means of track splices with a bolt and four bridal bars. These bridal bars acted as spikes and could be applied immediately. The rails were partially spiked to the ties with just enough spikes to assure the safety of the engine and cars with light equipment to pass over it. The train would move up the length of the rails and the same procedure would be repeated. Much time was saved by permanently spiking the rails to the track after the train had passed over the track. Rails were laid at the rate of from one to one and a half miles a day.

The Hazard Herald of May 30, 1912, came out with the following headline:

"HURRAH! THE STEAM CARS ARE IN HAZARD. COMMERCIAL SERVICE THE 25TH."

June 17, 1912, went down in Hazard as a red letter day, the day the first train entered the town. The Hazard Herald carried these headlines June 20:

"LARGE CROWD GREETS ENGINE NO. 324 AS SHE CROSSES TRESTLE IN TOWN ACROSS THE RIVER. BAND PLAYS 'GLORY HALLELUJAH!'"

When the track had been laid across the trestle at Messer Branch a number of young women mounted the engine and track-laying car and decorated both of them with flowers, bunting, and flags. A barrel of cider was opened and everybody drunk to the future of the town, its people and the railroad. It was at this celebration that Mr. J. A. McDowell, general manager of the L. & N. announced that regular passenger service would be inaugurated between Hazard and Jackson on the 25th of June. The great day came at last, and the HAZARD HERALD'S story of the event said:

"First train was well patronized. Nearly everybody went to Jackson or some other point on the line. Orderly crowd. Everybody smiling— The train consisting of a combination coach and baggage car, and a partitioned car for colored people and smoker, and a first class coach, pulled out of Hazard at 7:00 a. m. Tuesday morning, June 25, 1912, Jackson bound." The late John A. McIntosh said that he was issued Ticket No. 1 on the first passenger train from Jackson.

This mode of travel marked a new era for the citizens of Perry County in transportation, and it is said that this was the first time one had made a round-trip to Jackson in one day. The occasion of the running of the first train was celebrated by all the citizens. The station was crowded with people, many to view their first passenger train, and the same situation prevailed at all the smaller platforms along the line that were to be used as stations. People from their homes along the road witnessed this strange sight, and for years crowds collected at the stations only to see the trains go by, while many rode this train on its maiden trip just for the thrill of their first train ride. The service was immediately utilized by traveling salesmen and other business people who covered more territory than had been possible with the older mode of travel. These passenger trains connected with other trains at Jackson which went to Winchester, Lexington, Louisville, Cincinnati, and other cities. All this made it possible to connect Perry County with the outside world.

With the coming of the railroad, industry began to flourish and territory served by it began to expand with leaps and bounds. It was possible to get the needed supplies, materials, and provisions into this section with reasonable speed and dispatch. With the growth in population, additional service was needed, and it was added as rapidly as was consistent with a new railroad. With the completion of the new line to McRoberts, November 23, 1912, both passenger and local freight services were extended to that point. However it took about twelve hours to make the run from Lexington to McRoberts, due to the unsettled condition of the roadbed. There were two through runs each way every day. When the patronage built up to where it was profitable the L. & N. added to the equipment modern pullman cars on their night runs, and a comfortable parlor car to their day runs. Even though the run was rather slow the trips were made comfortable for those who cared to take advantage of these added conveniences. Courteous attention by the uniformed crew made the trip pleasing to the most exacting traveler.

Lunch periods were arranged at various places along the line, and Hazard was one of the places where the train stopped for meals. There was built and operated the Crescent News Lunch Room and Restaurant near the depot. This place of business was in charge of Mr. Pat Maran, who later became mayor of Hazard (now deceased.) This place of business was extensively patronized by passengers.

As the population continued to grow in Perry, and other Eastern Kentucky Counties, the need for additional service was felt, and an extra train was placed into service between Lexington and McRoberts. The night train was made more or less a fast train, making stops only at the larger towns. Hazard was one of these stops. Passengers availing themselves of the sleeping cars were permitted to remain in the pullman until seven o'clock a. m., likewise, they were given the privilege to enter the cars at nine p. m. and retire for the night, even though the train was not scheduled to leave until ten, thus making the home trip more pleasant. As the territory throughout the country continued to develop, the coal industry grew accordingly and a number of short branch lines were completed between 1916 and 1922. These trains carried both freight and passengers and were affectionately known to railroad men as "shorty dogs" or "dinky trains."

Both passenger and local freight business flourished on the railroad until the highways began to find their way up through the mountain section, and with the coming of the roads in the early 1920's, both passenger and local freight business began to decrease until it reached the point where it was no longer profitable to the company or useful to the citizens, so services on these branch lines were discontinued, the railroad company gracefully bowing to progress in transportation, and the citizens availing themselves of the use of much quicker bus and taxi service, and to the more convenient truck service for freight. However, the L. & N. offers freight service to these points by trucking the freight that arrives in Hazard by rail to different business houses through the county. The work is done by **Harry H. Greer**—by contract with the L. & N.

Through passenger and local service began to decline with the coming of the county and state roads. As the building progressed it became necessary to discontinue the use of the pullman cars and the parlor cars on the passenger trains, and even the discontinuances of one of the through passenger trains each way. The railroad company however, continued to furnish through passenger service each way twice daily for the use of those who did not own their own automobiles, or lived at points where access to busses was not available. The trains were run at a loss during the lean years of the "Depression" which followed World War II, for only a few rode the trains in those days.

The L. & N. Railroad suffered inestimable loss and damage in the 1927 flood. Every bridge in Letcher and Perry Counties that crossed the Kentucky River that had been built by the highway department, except three, was washed out. All the swinging bridges, as well as the bridge in Hazard, connecting the town with the depot, were completely washed away. The railroad lost no steel bridges in Perry County, on its main line, but one bridge was washed away at Blacky on its Rockhouse Branch line. Cars of coal were placed on the bridges at Lothair, and Jeff to weight them down, which no doubt, saved them.

Every depot between Jackson and Hazard was under water; in some the water was as high as ten feet in the offices, many records were destroyed, and much freight damaged in the warehouses. The telephone equipment was ruined, and lines washed out due to the poles being torn down by the swift water, and by drifts. In Hazard yard the water was well up in all the company buildings, and at Crawford yard the water was entirely over the 266 cars of coal that were stored there, leaving logs and drifts deposited on the cars, after the water receded. Every journal box on the cars of oil had to be cleaned and repacked before the cars could be moved. Nearly 9,000 gallons of car oil, and 53,000 pounds of packing were required for these cars alone, with a cost of $5,656.63, and when we consider the hundreds of other cars all up and down the line, that required this treatment, it can be seen that the cost of this item alone was tremendous.

Fills all along the line were washed out, some even up to the rail, while others were weakened. Ballast was washed from the track, and mud was left deposited, which had to be removed, and many miles reballasted. Restoring the lines of communication was of first importance, and many miles, of water-proof wire were used by stringing it along on the ground, miles of it being as much as three feet under water. (This wire was dropped from the rear end of a moving train.) Men from all departments of the railroad went to work at whatever needed to be done, and soon the trains were moving again.

Superintendent J. D. Haden paid high tribute to the citizens all along the line, in a letter written for the L. & N. Magazine of July, 1927, in which he writes:

"The Superintendent of a highway steam shovel outfit stopped his work, and put the shovel to work loading gravel for ballast... Superintendent of mines, on their own initiative put gangs of their own men to work on the track, and in one instance, organized a gang of line men from their electrical forces, and used their own material for building several miles of telephone line."

Information concerning the 1927 flood was given by T. H. Hines, engineer on the Eastern Kentucky Division of the L. & N. He also gives an interesting experience of his own during this flood. H was running a freight train from Ravenna to Hazard, when he encountered the high waters at Chavies, where he and his crew were tied up for three days on account of the flood. They arrived there about nine o'clock Monday morning, May 31. The water was over the track by the time they arrived there, and was continuing to rise, the train could proceed no further. As the water got deeper and deeper over the tracks he would back his train up grade a short distance, backing up still farther, as the water continued to rise, until the rear of the train was near Line Tunnel. It was impossible to back farther, as the train was at the highest point it could reach. The river reached its crest about midnight, and the water was up to the top of the car wheels of the entire train.

This crew witnessed the strange sight of seeing the river flow around the mountain at Line Tunnel from the opposite direction of the natural flow of the river, and went back into the river again. The water was about three feet deep in the tunnel.

Passenger train No. 1, enroute to Neon, was also tied up at Chavies, and the engineer pulled his train onto the tracks of the Conova Coal Company. There was a short incline going into this track, which placed this train out of the high water, except the rear coach, which was a sleeping car, and it was in water up to the steps.

There were many passengers aboard this train, and the problem of getting food for them arose. Upon investigation of the crew, it was found that the freight train carried several cars of meat, and that the passenger train had a great amount of bread, and many cans of milk, being shipped as express. There was a crew of civil engineers located there with camp cars. A Negro cook was in charge of the cars, so their problem seemed to be solved. As the crews were being held there for an indefinite time, and the food was likely to spoil on the road, sufficient food from the train was confiscated to feed the passengers. The Negro cook at the camp cars, and the porters off the passenger train were put to work preparing the food for both the passengers and the crews, and sumptuous meals they were—with no ration books.

The passengers were well pleased with the treatment accorded them. After they resigned themselves to the predicament in which they had been placed—by this act of Providence, there was a common contentment among them until the train could be sent along its way.

World War II brought a new need for passenger service through the country, as automobiles and gasoline were rationed to the extent that riding in one's own car, even if he were fortunate enough to have one, was out of the question. Therefore, the main line passenger trains were again scheduled to make two trips each way between Lexington and Neon. These trains were crowded to capacity on every run with service men and women on furloughs, and with war workers from distant plants coming home to their families over the week-ends. Thus, the railroad did its part—along with everything else—in helping win the war. These trains were not as comfortable during the war and for a few years after, as it was necessary to use old and outmoded equipment such as oil lamps, and seats covered with split rattan instead of the usual plush covering. The traveling public was very understanding concerning the uncomfortable coaches, as it was known that the better equipment was necessary on the trough trains so that all possible comfort could be provided those compelled to travel long distances.

Soon after the end of the war when people could again purchase automobiles and gasoline was more plentiful, travel on passenger trains began to decrease, and it was not long until they were again running at a loss. In March, 1949, the railroad obtained permission to discontinue one of the runs each way. Thus, the railroad has bowed again to the march of progress, and to the more satisfactory way of travel by private automobile and bus, and to the more convenient manner of obtaining their freight by truck.

It must be remembered that the paramount purpose of building the line into the coal fields was that of transporting coal, but for the first few years, while the passenger service was flourishing, the amount of coal mined and transported was meager. However, by 1915 the development was rapid, and with World War I, the movement of coal became something of grave importance. It was hard for the railroads to keep up with the rapidly increasing production of coal. The movement of coal down the line was limited, due to the unsettled condition of the roadbed, and to the track's not being sufficiently ballasted to permit any great speed. Small engines were required because of these same track conditions. There were no double tracks, no block system, and many of the old wooden cars were still in service. Numerous delays were caused by couplers being pulled out, and other unavoidable conditions common to a new railroad operation. Even with the light equipment and slow speed, there were many derailments of loaded coal cars, and frequently the road would be tied up by these derailments that would require two or more days to clear up. One day the workers left the terminal at Ravenna to go to a wreck up the road, and before this wreck was cleared up there was another one, then others, and members of the crew say it was thirty days before the wrecker was able to return to the home terminal. However, there were but few of the train crew who were injured or killed because of these derailments.

Great improvements have been made in the railroad since those days, and now instead of the smallest freight engines pulling thirty cars of coal, the L. & N. uses the largest and most modern locomotives, hauling as many as one hundred and thirty loaded coal cars down the river, and as many as one hundred sixty empty cars up the river to the coal fields. The company has recently installed a block system from Winchester through Hazard, and as far up the line as Blacky, which increases the efficiency to the maximum and insures safety in the operation of the trains. This most modern block system is known as the "Central Control System."

During all these years the road has been modernized in other ways by adding double track at strategic points, lengthening sidings where needed, and by eliminating stops at various places. Thus, they were in much better position to handle the increased coal business during World War II than when the first war was in progress, and more than double the amount of coal was moved from this mountainous section. The L. & N. officials again handled their transportation of coal heroically, this time under the supervision of such men as J. C. Nickerson, J. T. Alexander, B. R. McClanahan, C. W. Watson, V. L. Rogers, and A. G. Spoonamore, and others who contributed to the work of helping to transport coal for defense purposes.

Additional lines are now being built to other new coal operations—the most important one is up Leatherwood Creek, a distance of approximately eighteen miles southeast of Hazard. The work of locating and surveying this line was intrusted to Mr. A. A. Spitzer resident engineer, and the contract for grading it was awarded to the J. C. Codell Construction Company of Winchester, Kentucky. One line branches off from the main line near Cornettsville and extends south to the mouth of Beech Fork, while still another line goes west to Toner, and a third line extends east to the operations of Jewel Ridge Coal Company, and to the operation owned by the Fourseam Coal Company. (Later sold to Blue Diamond Coal Company.) The L. & N. EMPLOYEE MAGAZINE of June, 1944, headlined an article with these words:

"CONSTRUCTION OF LEATHERWOOD CREEK BRANCH IS PROCEEDING RAPIDLY THROUGH THE RUGGED TERRAIN OF EASTERN KENTUCKY."

The article went on to say: "Some day soon long trains of coal will rumble through the valleys of Leatherwood Creek and Clover Fork, deep in the heart of the hills of Eastern Kentucky. They'll be coming 'round the mountain over the Old Reliable's newly-built 10.32 mile Leatherwood Creek Branch."

The task of locating and surveying the line was one of requiring a vast amount of planning, and Mr. Spitzer stated that he and his crew literally sweated blood on the Leatherwood job, because of the narrow valleys hemmed in by towering mountains. Considerations necessary for grade and curvature were complicated by creeks which travel all over the valleys; there were private or family graveyards that had to be gotten around, also a number of private roadways that had to be rerouted; then there was the task of building a roadway for the purpose of moving construction machinery to the places where it was needed. In spite of these obstacles Mr. Spitzer finally located a line with the maximum grade of 2.5 degrees and a maximum rate of curvature of only 9 degrees.

The grading and building of the right-of-way, as has been previously stated, was done by the J. C. Codell Construction Company. They had on hands for the work the following machinery: 42 trucks, 13 air compressors, 5 cranes, 2 diesel compressors, 24 jack hammers, 2 diesel locomotives, 13 bulldozers, 4 steam shovels and an electric power station, and in addition there were 4 LaTurneau scrapers. With all this machinery the construction crew was able to literally move mountains. It was a far cry from the machinery used less than forty years prior when the main line of the North Fork was under construction.

Permission was given by the Interstate Commerce Commission to build Blair's Fork Branch February 5, 1948. Even though a locating party had been in the field since March, 1946, and a construction party since December 1, 1947, actual work could not start until the go-ahead signal was given by the Interstate Commerce Commission. Resident engineer on the project was Logan D. Thomas who was associated with Resident A. A. Spitzer on the Leatherwood and Rockhouse jobs. The J. C. Codell Construction Company began actual work March 15, 1948, and completed the job in an unbelievably short time. Coal began to move from this branch in January, 1949. A description of this work on Leatherwood and Clover Fork Branch so coinsides with that of Blair's Fork that further description is not necessary.

When the branch lines up Leatherwood and Blair's Fork were completed the L. & N. could visualize a bottleneck at Hazard in the movement of coal due to the increase of business from these lines, and the new line built to Rockhouse Creek in Letcher County. Hence, the solution was to build a new assembly yard at Dent which is at the mouth of Leatherwood Creek, eighteen miles east of Hazard. The construction of Dent Yard, so named for John K. Dent, vice-president of the railroad who was coal-traffic manager for years, began early in 1949. The construction required removal of 78,000 cubic feet of rock and 110,000 cubic feet of earth. Embankments required 34,000 cubic yards of rock and 3,000 cubic yards of earth. Incidental to the building was the straightening of the North Fork of the Kentucky River for 1,200 feet. It was necessary to build 7,850 feet of new track, and shift 6,593 feet of old track. (Courier-Journal April 29, 1951.) (The article also stated that the cost of construction was $1,000,000.) The new rail facility can handle about six miles of gondola and hopper cars. In addition to the tracks it has a car-repair track, an inspection pit, a 105-foot turn-table, a water station, a coaling and sanding station capable of holding 100 tons and 5 tons respectively, a cinder conveyor, a yard office for the yard force, and a track for storage of cabooses.

The yard can handle 810 cars and each of its six tracks can take care of from 130 to 145 cars. Trains from the new yard move directly to the DeCoursey Yard 234 miles away on the Ohio River opposite Cincinnati. Dent Yard is currently handling 600 cars of coal a day, a little more than half its top capacity. It was officially opened April 9, 1951. Approximately fifty employees have been assigned to the yard in addition to train crews moving through it. Yard master of the new layout is George Steele. Joe Brakefield and James Parris are foremen of the mechanical department.

This brings the history of the railroad in Perry County up to date, and now as the war clouds are hanging heavy with the United Nations in open conflict in North Korea, and with the Reds in China, we know not what the outcome will be, but if World War III is inevitable the Louisville and Nashville Railroad is in position to make a great contribution to our country.

CHAPTER XI

EARLY PERRY COUNTY FAMILIES

By Eunice Tolbert Johnson
(Unless otherwise acknowledged)

BAKER

John Baker and his family came from Bakersfield, North Carolina, in 1811 and settled on Cutshin Creek, then Clay County later Perry County, but now Leslie. As they reached the mouth of Second Creek, they hurriedly pitched tent and that night a son, Isaac, was born. Their other children were Wilson, John, Betsey, Rebecca, Rachal and Sally. Wilson was 18 years of age when he came with his father into Perry County. He married Sallie Fields and they had eleven children. His son, Roderick Baker, who was an early registered doctor in Perry County, married Betty Johnston. Another son, Bill, an early preacher, married Susan Johnson.

John, the second son, was the father of Henderson and Whining Bill Baker. Betsey Baker married Bill Campbell, Rebecca married Adam Campbell and Rachel married Jim Campbell. Sally married William Begley, Jr., and Isaac, the youngest, married Elizabeth Griffith of Floyd County. They settled in Hazard and built a log house where the Hurst Hotel now stands. It became the first boarding house in Hazard, according to family tradition. Their first child, John, was born there in 1843. John married Katherine Dehart. Other children of Isaac were Dave, who married Emoline Combs, W. W. (Bill), whose first wife was Josephine Martin, second wife, Nan Vermillion. Henry married Sarilda Johnson, Louanna married Clinton Combs, Margaret married Robin Baker, Martha married Dr. Fletcher, Minerva married Dr. John Marcus Daniel and Cynthia married Harrison Combs.

Isaac Baker lived to be 98 years old, and he is buried in the Baker Cemetery in Hazard. John Baker and his wife, Cloey McIntosh are buried on Cutshin. He was killed just before the Civil War by two of his slaves.—(Lee Daniel, J. D. Smith, the late Luther Johnson, Mrs. Grace B. Combs.)

BEGLEY

William (Bill) Begley, of Irish descent, was born in North Carolina between 1770 and 1780. He married Winnie Sizemore and came to Kentucky around 1800, settling about one mile up Cutshin Creek, later Perry County but now Leslie. He served as Justice in the Perry County Courts from 1824 through 1829, and died around 1830.

His children were Hiram, who married Cynthia Allen, Pleasant, who married Ann York, Edward (Ned) who married Betsy Lusk first, then Nancy Bowling; Ned was killed during the Civil War by a guerilla band. Other children were Russell, whose first wife was a Roberts, second wife a Ritchie; William Begley, Jr., who was born about 1810 married Sally Baker, sister to Isaac Baker. Mahala married John Huff and Rebecca married William Asher.

Hiram, the oldest son of William (Bill) Begley was born about 1802. Family tradition says that he was an active man both physically and politically and was something of a prize-fighter. He was continually in office and served in Perry County as Magistrate, High Sheriff and was a member of the House of Representatives in the Kentucky Legislature.

When the first census of Perry County was taken in 1830, the schedules were signed by Hiram Begley, who designated himself "Assistant to the Marshall of the District of Kentucky." Hiram and Cynthia had 19 children, 12 of whom reached maturity. His oldest son, Felix T., married Sarah May the first time, then Fanny Martin. Felix T. also served as Sheriff of Perry County and was a successful herb doctor. Hiram Begley died in 1867.—(Jackson Allen Begley, Mrs. Opal Begley Britton.)

BOLING

Jesse Boling was born in Wilkes County, North Carolina, in 1759. He married Polly Greene in 1776. In 1780 he enlisted in the Revolutionary War and was made a Sergeant. After the War, Jesse and his wife came to Kentucky and settled in Perry County.

His son John E. married Susan Sizemore and their daughter Polly married Jesse Combs, the first County Clerk of Perry County. They were married by Jesse Boling.

He applied for pension in October, 1832, while living in Clay County. In 1840 he was 82 years old and living in Breathitt County where he died and was buried.—(Mrs. John E. Campbell.)

REVEREND JESSE BOWLING (BOLLING) (BOLING)

Reverend Jesse Bowling, of English ancestry, was born at Hillsboro, N. C., in 1759. He was in the battle of Cowpens during the American Revolution. He married Mary Pennington of Lee County, Virginia, and came to Clay County, Kentucky, in 1810, settling on the Middle Fork of the Kentucky River. This section was later Perry County, now Leslie. The Perry County records show that Jesse and his sons were prominent in the early government of the county. His children are as follows: Hannah, Justice, John, Jesse, Jr., William, Elijah, George, Polly (Mary), Elizabeth (Betsey), Rachel, Nancy, and Patsy. Hannah married first a Huff; second, Nelse Guy. Justice married Hannah Reed. John married Polly Lewis. Jesse, Jr., married a Lewis for his second wife. William married Deborah Duff, daughter of Daniel Duff. Elijah, born in 1798 in Lee County, Virginia, was 12 years of age when his father came to Kentucky. Elijah married a Roberts; George, a minister, married a Lewis; Polly (Mary) married Abram Barger; Betsy married Abel Pennington; one daughter married Joseph Spencer; another married a Maggard and one died single.

Reverend Jesse Bowling's father was Major John Bowling of the American Revolution. He had nineteen children. Major John's father, John Bowling, married Mary Kenson and they had one son and five daughters. He was a son of Colonel Robert Bowling of the King's Army before the Revolution. Colonel Robert married Jayne Rolfe and her father, Thomas Rolfe, who married Jayne Praythress, was a son of John Rolfe.—(Mrs. William Everett Bach, Lexington, Kentucky—the late Luther Johnson, Buckhorn, Kentucky.)

BRASHEAR

Benois (Benjamin) Brashear and his brother, Robert, both Huguenot refugees, landed in Virginia in 1653. Due to conditions prevailing among the colonists, who were to a great extent English and not in sympathy with the French, they found their surroundings unpleasant so they moved to Maryland in 1658. The brothers were descendants of the House deBrassier, members of which are still living in and near Carpentros, France.

A short time after the Revolution, Samuel Brashear, a great-great-grandson of Benjamin and Mary Brashear migrated to what is now Sullivan County, Tennessee. He married Margaret Eakin, a native of Ireland. Their children were Margaret, Sampson, Isaac, John, James, Ezekiel, Robert S., Phoebe, Peggy and Ellen.

After Samuel Brashear's death, his family moved to Perry County around 1818. Isaac and John moved to Missouri; James married Elizabeth Young and operated a mill on the Kentucky River in Perry County and Robert S. married Polly, daughter of Mary Everage, second wife of William Cornett. Robert S. Brashear operated a salt work at the mouth of Little Leatherwood and he was also a probate judge of Perry County in 1855. Ezekial married Minerva Combs, daughter of Jesse Combs, of Hazard. He was a Circuit Court Clerk of Letcher County for many years. Sampson married Margaret Bright of Tennessee.

Dr. Walter Brashear, the noted Kentucky surgeon, was the first surgeon in the United States successfully to perform an amputation at the hip joint. The operation was performed in 1806 on a mulatto slave at St. Joseph's Hospital in Bardstown. Dr. Brashear was also a descendant of the immigrant Benois Brassier.—(The late Eli Brashear.)

CAMPBELL

The first family of Campbells came into this section from North Carolina before Perry County was formed. William, Caleb and Lewis Campbell each had land grants on Troublesome Creek in 1822. They were of Scotch descent. Caleb Campbell's children were Andy, who married a Napier, Lewis, who married Rachel Allen, a daughter of Sam Allen, and settled around what is now the community of Rowdy. William (Buck) married Polly Allen, John D. married Sallie Holladay and settled on Troublesome Creek. Mary married Jim Napier and moved to Lost Creek, Zack married a Noble and settled in Wolf County. Others in the Campbell family settled on Big Creek and the original farm is still owned by the Campbell family.

John Campbell and his wife, Polly Couch, came to this section around 1809 and settled in Campbell Bend. He lived to be 104 years of age. Their children were Hiram, Steven, Jack, James, Elijah, Bill, Pike, Frank and two daughters.

Dan, the son of Bill, married his first cousin, Rebecca, the daughter of Elijah. Their daughter, Sallie Campbell, married Roderick McIntosh, son of John McIntosh, a native of Scotland who had come to America with the British Army. John and Roderick settled on McIntosh Creek in Clay County around 1810, later Perry, now Leslie County. — (Walter Campbell, the late Sherrill Napier, Mrs. J. E. Campbell and Sam Begley.)

JOHN COMBS FAMILY

John Combs, ancestor of the Perry County Combs family came from London, England, to Jamestown, Virginia, May 20, 1619, on the **Marigold**. His son, Mason Combs, lived in Virginia but died in Surrey County, North Carolina in 1785: Mason was the father of Nicholas (Danger) Combs and John Combs, who with their sons came to Perry County in the 1790's to locate home sites.

The Combs family is of English descent; John Combs and his eight sons became known in Perry County as the "Nine". They came by way of Pound Gap, and John and his wife, Nancy, settled on Carrs Fork. Their eight sons were Mason, William, Nicholas, Henry Harrison, George, Elijah, Biram and John, Jr. Their only daughter died young.

Mason, the oldest, married Jenny Richardson and settled on the Kentucky River at the mouth of Carr Creek.

Mason's Creek was named for him. He named some of his sons for British generals, though he was not known to be a Tory. His children were Clinton, Washington, Boneparte, Tarleton, Preston, Mart, Nancy, Willie, Tabitha and two others. Mason died in Perry County in 1822.

George, the second son, married Lydia Herald and settled on Cedar Point in Lothair. His children were Matilda, Lydia, Claibourne, Biram and Elizabeth.

Nicholas, who settled in Breathitt County, died in lower Perry County after 1850. His only son, Nicholas, Jr., lived in Breathitt.

Henry Harrison married Rachel, daughter of Benjamin Clements, the first time, then married Phoebe Francis and settled in "Old Big Bottom" now East Hazard. He was a river man, building and running flatboats from the mouth of Troublesome Creek as far as New Orleans. His children were, Matthew, Henry, Jr., George, James, Francis, Stephen, Polly, Winnie and Elizabeth who married Old Jerry Combs. In 1812 he moved to Troublesome Creek where he died.

Elijah married Sally, daughter of Michael Roark of Virginia, and settled on the site of present Hazard, near the end of the bridge. His children were Polly, who married John A. Duff, the first surveyor of Hazard and son of Rev. Daniel Duff, Lucinda, who married Shade (Shadrach) Duff, brother of John A., Elijah, Jr., who married Polly Ann Combs, daughter of Long Jerry Combs (who was the son of John Combs, Jr.), Jesse, who married Polly Boling, granddaughter of Jesse Boling. Jesse's son, Jesse Combs, Jr., was the first doctor in Hazard. A Dr. Roberts of Virginia came here and taught him medicine. Elijah's other two children were Jackson, who married Patsy Ann Combs, and Louisa, who married Robert Bustard Cornett, son of William Cornett.

Biram, who settled briefly in Perry County, took up residence in Wayne County in 1804 and later moved to Johnson County, Indiana. He had one son named Biram, Jr., and probably two others, Robert and Harrison.

William, who settled at the mouth of White Oak, just below Vicco, lived on the old John J. Godsey place. He soon left for Breathitt, lived there as late as 1825, then moved on to Fayette County. He had no children.

John Combs, Jr., was born February 7, 1761. He served two years and four months as Private with the Virginia Troops under Captains Jonathan Langdon and Benjamin Casey and Colonel James Wood. He enlisted January 1, 1777, at Shennandoah County, Virginia. In 1825 he was pensioned on Certificate No. 19554. In his application for pension he stated that his wife, Margaret, was about 55 years of age and referred to the following children: John, age not stated, Sally, a widow, 27 years old, Margaret, 18 years old and her child, Hezekiah, one year old. Other children by his first wife were Jeremiah, (Long Jerry), Shadrach, Mason, Millie and William.

John, Jr., first settled on Line Fork, now in Letcher County. He resided in Perry County in 1825 when he applied for pension, where he was still living in 1837.

John Combs, the father of these eight sons was born in Westmoreland (at present King George) County, Virginia around 1735. He died in Perry County late in 1819 and was buried at White Oak, just below Vicco. The Combs descendants are numerous, and they have intermarried with practically all the early settlers of Perry County.—(National Archives, Washington, D. C., Dr. Josiah H. Combs, John Fitzpatrick.)

NICHOLAS (DANGER) COMBS FAMILY

"Danger" Nick Combs, Sr., (brother of John Combs, Sr.) married Nancy, daughter of Thomas Grigsby, in Virginia. Danger came to Perry County in the 1790's, probably at the same time as his brother John. He came through Pound Gap, from around Holston where he had been living for some time and settled on the North Fork of the Kentucky River, near what is now Combs, Ky. He was one of the largest land owners in Perry County at that time. He received his first land grant in 1810 when this was Clay County and he had other grants on Ball Creek, Lotts Creek, Combs Mill and Trace Creek.

He remained a Tory and tradition says that because of

this he became unpopular with the other Combs. His children were Rebecca, Alicia, Jeremiah C., Nicholas, Jr., and Samuel. Alicia married Richard Smith, a Primitive Baptist preacher and settled on Lotts Creek. Their first son, William, was born in what was later Perry County around 1795 (for other children, see Richard Smith biography). Jeremiah C., "Chunky Jerry", first married Nancy Summers, then Sally Grigsby. "Chunky Jerry" was around 16 years old when his father came to Perry County. He settled around the mouth of Walker's Branch, and was one of the first Justices of Perry County. He died in 1853 and was buried in Walkertown, now North Hazard. Nicholas, Jr. ("Bird-eye"), married Eliza Combs, a daughter of John Combs of Boyle County. The log house built by "Bird-eye" above Combs is still standing and is owned by Will Brewer. "Bird-eye" was born in 1793 and died around 1886. Samuel married Nancy, a daughter of William Cornett, the Revolutionary War veteran. They lived first on Second Creek, moved to a site near Buckhorn School, and finally settled in Owsley County. Their children were Robert C., who married Eliza Godsey, William, married first to Mary Begley, then to Mrs. Mary Herndon Burke, Wiley married Elizabeth Jane, daughter of Boneparte Combs, Daniel Garrett married Rachel Turner, Andrew J. married Elizabeth, step-daughter of William Burke, Nicholas married a Bolen, Rachel married Levi Pennington, Nancy married Jack Edwards, Mary married Elijah R. Begley, and Lucy married a Cole. "Danger" Nick's other daughter, Rebecca, married John Williams.

"Danger" Nick died in Perry County near 1838. He is buried in the Old Combs Cemetery on Meadow Branch near Combs Bend.—(Dr. Josiah H. Combs, John Fitzpatrick.)

COPE

James D. Cope and his wife Betsy Hammond Cope came to Kentucky with Daniel Boone and his party and settled near Mt. Sterling before 1798. He was of English descent.

There was a great drought in the Blue Grass around 1800, so James Cope moved into the mountains and settled on upper Quicksand. Around 1860 he sold out to the Bachs and moved on the Kentucky River above the Mouth of Howard's Creek near Haddix.

Some of his children were Thomas T., Wiley and William Jackson. This area was then Montgomery County. James D. Cope was Justice of the Peace in Perry County in 1883 and Wiley Cope's name is found on the first Minute Book of Perry County many times. William Jackson Cope made salt on his father's farm during the Civil War.—(Fred Cope.)

CORNETT
(By Georgia Cornett Combs)

About 1740 seven Cornett brothers came to America from England and settled in different parts of the country. William Cornett, Revolutionary soldier, was the son of John Cornett. William was born in Henrico County, Virginia, in 1761. While a resident of Buckingham County, Virginia, in 1779, he enlisted in the Revolutionary War and served six months in Captain Anthony Winston's Company, Col. Scripp's Virginia Regiment. In 1780 he re-enlisted as a private and served six months in Capt. Saunders Company, Col. Patterson's Virginia Regiment.

He first married Rhoda Gilliam and to them were born four children, John, Arch, Lucy and Elizabeth. John married Rachel Smith and settled on Carrs Fork. Arch, born in 1789, married Judy McDaniel and settled on Clover Fork of Big Leatherwood. Lucy married Woleary Eversole, son of Jacob Eversole, and Elizabeth married William Campbell. After the death of his first wife, William Cornett married Mary Everage in 1796. Soon after their marriage they came to Kentucky and settled near the mouth of Bull Creek, in what was later Perry County, and there they lived for the remainder of their lives.

Mary Everage had two daughters by her first marriage; Sally married Thomas McDaniel and Polly married Robert S. Brashear of Little Leatherwood, Perry County.

To William Cornett and Mary Everage were born seven children, Robert Bustard, born 1798, married Louisa Combs, daughter of Elijah Combs, Roger, born 1805, married Polly Lewis, Nancy married Samuel Combs, son of "Danger"

Nick Combs, Rachel married John A. Caudill, Samuel married Polly Adams, Nathaniel Woleary married Lydia Caudill and Joseph E. married Sally Brown. His youngest son, Joseph E. helped to lay out the town of Whitesburg and later became County Judge.

William Cornett made his first visit to Kentucky about 1796, with Gideon Ison. They came from Virginia on a hunting expedition, as game had become scarce in that part of the country. They had heard that deer, bear and other game were plentiful in Kentucky. Though fearful of Indians, they gathered their equipment and started, with pack horses, to the "Happy Hunting Ground." They crossed Big Black Mountain and after two or three days travel, came to the mouth of Beech Fork on Big Leatherwood. Here they saw 20 or 30 acres of level land covered with extraordinarily fine timber. There were also signs of plenty of game and they established their first camp at this spot. Their only question was whether or not Virginia crops would mature in the new country. They decided to cut down a beech tree and return in June. If the bark on the tree had bursted from the effects of the sun that would be a sure sign that crops would mature. No records tells of their return to Beech Fork, but it is known that they returned to Kentucky soon afterwards.

William Cornett died November 26, 1836, and Mary Everage, his second wife, died January 28, 1852. They are buried in the Cornett graveyard near the site of their old home. His reason for wanting to be buried at this particular place was that he dreamed of driving his wagon and team to a large sassafras tree on top of the hill and he could never drive them from under it. He requested that he be buried under the tree.

He had 102 grandchildren, a large number of great-grandchildren and hundreds of descendants in Eastern Kentucky.—(J. D. Cornett, Genealogy of William Cornett.)

DAVIDSON

Daniel Davidson came from North Carolina before Perry County was formed and settled on Grapevine Creek.

He married Sarah Duff, daughter of John A. Duff and his wife Polly Combs, daughter of Elijah Combs. Their children were: John A., Elijah Combs, Henry, Dock, Bob, Dulcie, Mahala, Arminia, Nancy, Shadrack (Shade) and Eleanor. John A. married Mary Ann Combs. Elijah married Mary Spencer. Henry married, first, Linda Hensley and, second, a Deaton. Dock's first wife was Lettie Duff and his second wife was Dorcas Hensley. Bob married a Spencer. Dulcie married Lou Crawford and settled near the site of the airport. Mahala married Farris Jones of Lost Creek. Arminia married Matt Napier. Nancy married William Combs first, then Jim Grigsby. Shade left and went to Missouri and Eleanor died when young. Daniel and his wife were buried on Grapevine.—(Mrs. Nancy Ann Grigsby Davidson; Mrs. Opsie Oliver.)

DUFF

Daniel Duff, a Baptist minister, was born in Guilford, N. C., in 1772. His ancestors had come to America from Dubftown, Scotland. The name had been spelled "Dubf" in Scotland. Daniel's Bible, a small English book and his arithmetic, are now owned by his great grandson, Claude Duff of Owsley County. Ira Duff owns the Bible belonging to Daniel's son, John A. Duff.

Daniel married Nancy Ann Allison and moved to Lee County, Va. They came to this section of Kentucky around 1818 and it was at the suggestion of Reverend Jesse Bowling that they settled on Grapevine.

Daniel had the following children: Rachel (Betty), Mary, Martha, Deborah, Margaret, Colson, Alexander, Matilda, Drucillia, John A. and Shadrack. Rachel married Joshua Oliver, Mary married a Shepherd and moved to Missouri. Martha married William Bowman and moved to Iowa. Deborah married William Bowling, son of Rev. Jesse Bowling. Margaret married John Hays. Colson married Elizabeth Gilbert. Alexander married Catherine Noble; Matilda married John Lewis; Drucillia married William Gilbert and moved to Carter County, Ky.; John A. married Polly Combs, daughter of Elijah Combs; and Shadrack

(Shade) married Lucinda Combs, also a daughter of Elijah. Shadrack was killed while a young man in a powder blast that blew up a tavern belonging to Elijah Combs. He was one of the first to be buried in the Combs graveyard on Broadway.

After the death of Daniel's wife in 1849, he went to live with his daughter, Drucilla, in Carter County. A short time later he married Ellen Noe, a widow. He died on August 15, 1855, and was buried near Olive Hill, Ky.

Daniel's father was Shadrack Duff and his mother was Deborah Dixon. Shadrack was a Revolutionary soldier and was killed at the battle of Guilford Court House on March 15, 1781. (Mr. and Mrs. S. E. Duff; J. C. Hurst, Lexington, Ky.)

EVERSOLE

Jost (Joseph) Ebersohl (Eversole), ancestor of the Kentucky Eversoles, landed in Philadelphia on September 3, 1739, from Holland on the ship **Robert and Alice.** His son, Jacob Eversole, of Swiss-German ancestry, was born in 1760 in Pennsylvania.

Jacob and his wife, Mary Kessler, joined a company of pioneers who were following Daniel Boone to the Blue Grass region of Kentucky. When they arrived, they found many settlers ahead of them so they came to the mountains of Eastern Kentucky and bought a farm near what is now Krypton. Jacob built a one room cabin near the mouth of Lick Branch around 1789; in 1800 he built a large two-story house on this site. When Jacob died, his son, Woolery continued to live in this house until the time of his death. Then it passed to Woolery's son, Major John C. Eversole, who was killed by guerillas just after the Civil War. This house still stands and is now owned by the heirs of the late Sarah Eversole Bogg, who was a great-great-great-granddaughter of Jacob. (See picture.)

Jacob, who was a Baptist minister, was also a miller and had one of the first water mills in this part of the country. Jacob and Mary's children were John, born in 1785, Peter (1790), Joseph, Abraham and Woolery, (1797). John, the oldest, settled in Harlan County. His children were Roland,

Polly (Mary), Susan, Absalom, Hiram, Abraham, and Elizabeth.

Peter Eversole married Annie Phipps and settled in Clay County on Goose Creek. Their children were Orphus, John and Sally. Orphus married Louisa Couch and John married Mary Hubbard. Joseph settled in Clay County; his children were Hence, Elihu and Billy.

Abraham married a Miss Williams and settled in Clay County. Their children were William, John, Joe, James. Lewis, Elijah and Woolery. Woolery moved out West.

Woolery, the youngest son of Jacob Eversole, married Lucy Cornett, daughter of Revolutionary War veteran William Cornett. Their children were Joseph (1817), John C. (1828), William (1814), and Rachel (1820) (Elizabeth). Joseph married Sarah Bolin and settled near Chavies. John C., who became a Major in the Civil War, married Nancy Duff and lived on Grapevine. William married Barbara Chappell and Rachel (Elizabeth) married A. Boling.

Woolery applied for his first land grant in 1807, for 19 acres on the North Fork of the Kentucky River, then in Clay County. It was signed by Governor Isaac Shelby in 1815. In 1824 he bought 150 acres of land from George Cotton in consideration of 400 bushels of coal, at the price of one shilling per bushel. This land was on the North Fork of the Kentucky River, and was a part of the 23,190 acre survey of Pickett and Marshall, who received it as a Virginia Grant. Both of these old documents are now in possession of his descendant Farmer Eversole, Jr. Woolery died in 1871.

His parents, Jacob and Mary Eversole, lived to be nearly 100 years old.—(**Ebersohl Families in America, 1729-1937**, Roy G. Eversole, Mrs. F. J. Eversole, Jr.)

FRANCIS

Thomas Francis was born in 1778, married Jane Hammonds, daughter of John Hammonds, a son of Ambrose Hammonds. They lived first in North Carolina, moved to Virginia, and around 1816 settled on Carr's Fork, later

Perry County now in Knott County. They were of French descent.

Their children were Rebecca, who married Ambrose Amburgey. Sarah, who married George Washington Johnson. Samuel, who married Leodicia Hogg. Simeon, who married Cassie B. Smith, daughter of William B. Smith. Elizabeth, who married Wilburn Amburgey, son of John Amburgey and two daughters, Mrs. Thompson Combs and Mrs. Fielding Combs, who remained in Virginia.

After the death of his first wife, Thomas Francis married Mrs. Lourania Hagan, widow of John Hagan. Their children were Lourania, who married Thomas Smith, Anne Francis who married Hiram Stamper, Elizabeth, who married James Stamper and Marjorie, who married John Stamper.—(The late H. H. Smith.)

FUGATE

Martin and Jonathan Fugate were early settlers in this section. Jonathan owned land on Quicksand; Martin had land grants on both Troublesome and Buckhorn in 1821. Martin came from France when a child and was reared by a fisherman in the colonies. He came to Kentucky and settled on Troublesome Creek before this section was Perry County.

He married Elizabeth Smith, daughter of Richard Smith, of Ary. Some of their children were Martin, Jr., Prewitt, Hannah, who married James Ritchie, son of Crockett Ritchie, settled on Buckhorn Creek, and Zachariah, who married Polly Smith, daughter of Richard Smith. Zachariah and Polly's children were Minerva, Mary, Zack, L. D., Dan, Martin and Martha.

Jonathan's Fugate's daughter married Lorenzo Smith, son of Richard.

Martin Fugate, Sr., lived in what was later Breathitt County and is buried there. Some of his descendants say that he was a Revolutionary soldier.—(Mrs. Nancy Francis, Jason Ritchie.)

GRIGSBY

John Grigsby and his brother Thomas came from North

Carolina by way of Virginia before 1821 and settled near the head of Lotts Creek. John married Martha Campbell and had children, as follows: Samuel, Thomas, Sally, Nancy, Martha, Cynthia, Bill, John and Luke. Samuel married Eliza Jane Napier, daughter of McCager Napier and settled on Ten Mile Creek. Thomas married Lourania Jones and settled on Lost Creek. Sally married Chunky Jerry Combs, son of "Danger" Nick Combs. Nancy married Luke Feltner Martha married a Combs. Cynthia married Elijah Cornett, son of Robert Bustard Cornett and his wife Louisa Combs and settled above Hazard. Bill and John both settled on Lotts Creek. Luke left Perry County and was not heard from again. John Grigsby and his wife are buried on Lotts Creek.—(Mrs. Nancy Ann Grigsby Davidson.)

GROSS

Simon Gross came from North Carolina about 1816, and settled in what is now Breathitt County, near Buckhorn. He married Dorcas Becknell and they had three girls and seven boys. Richard married a daughter of Kinkead Terry, Tod married Sally McIntosh, daughter of Old Levi. Bill married a Stamper, John married a daughter of Henley McIntosh on Quicksand, Ned married a daughter of Bangor Bill McIntosh, Jennie married Peter McIntosh on Turkey. Polly married Jerry Roberts, Lize married a Thorpe, Peter marred Dorcas Smith and there is no record of Henry.

Peter and Dorcas had seven children. Lucinda married John W. York, Jerry (Jack) married Peg Ingram first and Mary Deaton the second time. Mary married Billie Sandlin, Lize, married Jim Sandlin, Nance married Price Ingram, Elizabeth died while young and John married Ella Riley.

Four generations of the Gross family have lived on the same farm, and have been largely instrumental in the development of Buckhorn community. The older members of the Gross family were members of the Primitive Baptist Church and were Democrats. The name Gross is English.— (The late Luther Johnson.)

HALL
Sarah Millar Amick

The Hall family of Kentucky is of English descent. The first Hall arrived on the Yadkin River about 1765. A son was born on the ocean en route whom the family knows as John Hall, Sr.; John, Jr., was born July 15, 1776 and his mother was Polly Hash. In 1805 the family moved to Ashe County, North Carolina and later to Powell Valley, Lee County, Virginia, where John Hall, Sr., died in 1826. John, Jr., married Elizabeth Whisman, who was born June 20, 1800. This John, Jr., and Elizabeth were the parents of P. W. Hall who came to Perry County. Previous to his coming, a cousin, Ezekial Hall, had moved from Lee County, Virginia, to Harlan County, Kentucky, and from there to Perry County, where P. W. visited him. When P. W. returned to Virginia, he was known to be outspoken in his dislike of Kentucky. In the meantime, John Hall, Jr., had died and his widow, with her children, one of whom was P. W., moved to Harlan County, and later (about 1838) into Perry County.

Here P. W. Hall acquired his first land in a "swap." His family records show that he traded a "rifle gun" for 400 acres of land on Mason's Creek. Later he bought land on the Middle Fork of Mason's Creek closer to the mouth of Carr Creek. The old log house built by P. W. Hall three miles up Mason's Creek still stands, the floors for which were whip sawed. P. W. Hall became a prominent citizen of Perry County; he was a surveyor, an early lawyer, and he dealt in large tracts of land and timber. Many of the Court records in the Perry County Court House are in his hand writing.

P. W. Hall was born May 27, 1823, in Lee County, Virginia. He married Elizabeth Branson, daughter of Leonard Branson, Revolutionary veteran.—(John Hall.)

HOLLIDAY

John H. Holliday came to Kentucky from Virginia and settled on McKinley and Tom's Branches of Troublesome Creek before Perry County was formed. He married Allie Justice of Floyd County and their children were Bill, who married a Sizemore, Green, who was lost during the Civil War, Sallie, who married John D. Campbell, Amy, who married Joshua Smith of Pigeon Roost, Walter, who married a Noble, and Tolbert, a Primitive Baptist preacher who married Rachel Napier. Tolbert's son, Elisha H. Holliday was born near the Troublesome Post Office on that Creek in Perry County on February 15, 1845. He married Harriet Godsey, daughter of Robert Godsey of Lott's Creek.

John H. Holliday served as an early County Judge of Perry County and in 1887 his grandson Elisha served as Sheriff. Most of the Perry County Hollidays are descendants of the old Tolbert Holliday family. They are buried in the Holliday Cemetery on Troublesome Creek. Walter Campbell says that his grandmother Allie Justice Holliday told him that the frst person to be buried in this cemetery was a child of John Hales. Nearly 80 years later, according to Walter Campbell, the old poplar casket was accidently disturbed when a new grave was being dug and it was found to still be in good condition.

The old John H. Holliday homeplace is now owned by the heirs of Squire Whitaker.—(Walter Campbell.)

ISON

Irene Ison Minniard

Gideon Ison I was born in Shropshire, England. He moved to Ireland where he became an Irish Lord, and later returned to England where he served in the English Parliament. According to the U. S. Census of 1790 John Ison and his wife landed on American soil and settled in North Carolina, about the same time his brother, Gideon II, settled in Amherst County (some say Scott County), Virginia (sons of Gideon Ison I).

There is an account near the end of the eighteenth century when the fifth governor of Tryon County, North Carolina, granted a 300 acre tract to John Ison, Jr., (grandson of Gideon I). The latter is regarded as the real pioneer Ison on American soil.

About 1796, George Gideon Ison and his friend William Cornett came from Virginia to hunt game and explore the vast hills behind the Cumberland Mountains. In 1804 William Cornett returned to settle at the mouth of Bull Creek near Cornettsville, Perry County.

In 1804 George Gideon and Annie Ingram Ison settled at the mouth of Big Branch, which later was Perry County, now Letcher County. Their children were Gideon, George, Polly, Cynthia and Elizabeth.

This robust, muscular Ison brought a fighting record with him from Virginia; he was never defeated in a fair fist fight. After he moved to Kentucky, he was challenged by a man from some distance away to a fight. It was a hot summer day, when a stranger came ridng by a field that Ison was plowing and asked,

"Where can I find George Gideon Ison?"

"Right here, feller, you won't have to go any further ... I am the man."

Since Ison was clad only in a long flannel shirt and was barefooted, his opponent demanded,

"Get dressed, Sir. I've come a long way to give you the licking of your life!"

George didn't do any dressing, but in the twinkle of an eye, the visitor was knocked from his horse and whipped before he could get started. The story is climaxed by the feeding of the man and his horse before their departure.

According to the Genealogy of Carlice Breeding, of Whitesburg, Kentucky, most of the next generations of Isons lived near Millstone, Rockhouse, Blackey, Linefork, Big Sandy and Whitesburg. Jonah Ison (fifth generation) son of Gideon Ison IV, was born near Defeated Creek on Linefork, Letcher County, Kentucky. He married Matilda Cornett, lived and reared a family of fourteen children on Leatherwood Creek at Puncheon Camp Branch, Perry County, Kentucky. His tract of land consisted of 1,800 acres on which he and his family toiled until his death in 1911.

JOHNSON

Thomas Johnson, his wife Adelphia Carter Johnson, and his two brothers Patrick and William, came to Kentucky around 1816 by the way of Pound Gap, from the Yadkin River.

They were searching for home sites, and Patrick settled on Rockhouse, now in Letcher County. Thomas and Adelphia (Delphia) settled near the mouth of Breedings Creek on Carrs Fork in what was then Floyd, afterwards Perry, then Letcher, and now Knott County. The old log house is still standing, and a descendant, Patrick Johnson, son of Fielding, and grandson of George Washington Johnson still lives there. For many years this old home was used as a tavern.

Delphia Carter Johnson was the only teacher in that section of the country. Their children were George Washington, William, Artie and Fanny. George Washington married Sarah Francis, daughter of Thomas Francis. They settled on the Big Sandy River. Their children were Fielding (called Babe), George, Leslie, Simeon, Sarah, Susan, Thomas and Adelphia. Susan married George Eversole, Thomas married Lucy Eversole, and Adelphia married Washington Combs, son of Jerry, and grandson of Long Jerry.

Artie Johnson married Nicholas Smith, son of Richard Smith of Ary. They had a son, Sim. Fanny married Humphery Amburgey, son of John, brother of Ambrose. William married Nancy Ashley, daughter of Rev. Jordan Ashley.

Thomas Johnson died at his home on Carr Creek in Perry County in 1828. After his death, his widow, Delphia, married Simeon Justice who weighed 400 pounds. He had a chair made for himself large enought to hold two people, which was used as a courting chair by some of his descendants. It is now owned by Jethro Amburgey of Hindman.

Thomas Johnson, son of George Washington Johnson and grandson of the first Thomas Johnson built the first brick house in Perry County around 1879 near Chavies. The bricks were made from clay on the site where the house now stands. The Johnsons are of Scotch-English descent.— (Edward B. Johnson, the late H. H. Smith, the late J. E. Johnson.)

LUSK

Samuel Lusk came to Kentucky in 1806 from Bluff, North Carolina, and settled opposite the mouth of Linefork Creek on the North Fork of the Kentucky River, now in Letcher County. He married Polly Davis. Their children were: Sally, William V. (Bill), John W., and Betty. Betty (Betsy) married Ned Begley from Leslie County; Sally and Bill never married. Bill Lusk became a surveyor and many of the old land patents and survey of Perry and Letcher Counties bear his name. John W. married Louisa Brashear, daughter of Samuel Brashear and they settled one mile up the river from the mouth of Linefork, where he farmed and operated a grist mill.—(Harvey Lusk.)

MORGAN

Zachariah Morgan came from North Carolina and settled on Poor Fork in Harlan County, when it was still a part of Lincoln County. He was a member of the Baptist Church on Oven Fork, on which site a Church still stands. Of this first church, Zachariah Morgan was a trustee until his death.

His son, Jesse, was born in Harlan County but moved to the Middle Fork, then Perry, now Leslie County. He lived to the age of 96 years.

Jesse's son, Zachariah, was born in 1825, six miles above Hyden. Both Jesse and Zachariah served as Sheriff of Perry County. Zachariah also served as a member of the State Assembly. He served in the Civil War on the Union side and participated in the Battle of Shiloh and General Sherman's march to the sea. Zachariah married Louisa Combs, daughter of Elijah C. Combs, and granddaughter of the Elijah Combs who built the first house in Hazard. They settled on land that had belonged to the Combs family where the golf course is today, and there he lived until his death in 1878. His son Bud was the last of the children to live at the old home-place.—(Biography of Jesse Morgan, Judge Charles Kerr, **History of Kentucky,** Vol IV, 649.)

NAPIER

The Napier family is descended from the Earl of Lennox. A second son, Donald, performed valiant service for the King of Scotland in 1296. The King, after the battle during which the service was rendered, called the soldiers together and said, "Ye have all done valiantly, but there is one amongst ye who hath Na-peer (no equal)," and, calling Donald to him commended him for for his worthy service and in commemoration of this, changed his name from Lennox to Napier.

Sir William Francis Patrick Napier was born near Dublin, Ireland, in 1785. During his young manhood he came to the United States, first living in Virginia but later migrating to what is now Perry County, Kentucky, where he died in 1866.

Stephen, William and McCager Napier, sons of John Napier and grandsons of Sir William Napier, are the ancestors of most of the Perry County Napiers. McCager Napier married Leanna Lewis and had the following children: Jerome, Mack, Jim Paddy, Steve, Eliza Jane, and Edward. Jerome married an Allen. Mack and Paddy married Campbells. Eliza Jane married Samuel Grigsby and Edward married Polly Campbell. There are many descendants of this family in Perry County today.—(Judge Charles Kerr, **History of Kentucky, Vol. V, p. 641**; Mrs. Nancy Ann Davidson.)

NOBLE

Nathan and William Noble and their wives, and brother Enoch, came from Virginia to Eastern Kentucky during the 1780's. William settled at the mouth of Buckhorn Creek (Perry-Breathitt line). Nathan and Ethan Noble settled near a large "deer lick" on Lost Creek (later Perry County, now Breathitt).

Most of the Nobles in this section are descendants of Nathan Noble and his wife Virginia Neace Noble. They had fifteen children. Some of their sons were Lawson, Jack, Nathan, Jr., William, James who married Delilah Fugate and the youngest Henry (b. 1810) who married Isobel Aikman. One daughter married a Combs, one a Harvey, another a Fields, one a Sizemore and two Millers.

Others who came with the Nobles into the Troublesome Creek section were their sisters, Millie, Patsy, Mary and Mollie; their husbands; Samuel Allen, and his Wife; Austin Neace and his wife; Malinda Neace, a sister to Samuel. All were related and they lived together in the community as one big family.

Lawson Noble taught school in the settlement just before the Civil War and Henry Noble was a Baptist preacher.

Virginia Neace Noble was over a hundred years of age when she died in 1880. She had lived to see five generations of her family. Nathan and Virginia were buried on Lost Fork near their old home.

The Nobles intermarried with the Allens, Neaces, Sizemores, Millers, Fugates, Combs, Fields, Harveys, Watts, Campbells, Stacys, McIntoshes and Deatons.

The Noble family are of Scotch descent.—(C. A. Noble.)

RITCHIE

James Ritchie came with his five brothers from England in 1768 and settled in Virginia. After the Revolutionary War he moved to North Carolina where he lived for some time before coming to Kentucky. He settled on Carr's Fork in Perry County (now Knott) around 1815. After his death, all the family returned of Virginia except one son, Crockett Ritchie.

Crockett married Susan Grigsby and settled near the mouth of Clear Creek (now Knott County). He is said to have built the first cabin in Hammond's Gap, on the present Gabe Hudson farm.

His grandson, Austin Ritchie, married Rachel Everidge, daughter of Solomon Everidge, who gave land and was instrumental in founding the Hindman Settlement School, near the Soloman Everidge home.

Most of the Ritchies belonged to the Old Regular Baptist Church. The Troublesome Creek area has many Ritchies families—nearly all of them descendants of Crockett and Susan Grigsby Ritchie.

Their children were Nicholas, who married a Patrick and settled on Ball Fork, Gabe who married Nancy Campbell, daughter of Jack Campbell of Buckhorn Creek. Jack Campbell served in the War of 1812 and is buried on Buckhorn Creek. James married Hannah Fugate, daughter of Martin Fugate, a Frenchman who settled on Buckhorn Creek. John married a Sizemore and settled on Clear Creek in present Knott County. Alex taught school in Dwarf and married Mary Fugate, a granddaughter of Martin Fugate. Polly married a Sizemore, Betty married William Smith, son of Thomas Smith of Ary, Nancy married a Harvey and moved to West Virginia, Arry married Reece Young and lived on Lotts Creek, and Omah married Arch Cornett. Hiram and Isom settled on Troublesome Creek, and Thomas married Kizzie Smith, daughter of Richard Smith.

Nick, Hiram, Isom, Polly, Omah and their families moved to Arkansas around 1850 and never returned to Kentucky.—(Bayliss Ritchie, Dr. S. B. Ritchie, Jason Ritchie.)

SMITH

Richard Smith, son of William Smith of Eastern Virginia, came to Perry County by way of Pound Gap around 1792. He married Alicia Combs, daughter of (Danger) Nick Combs in 1794. They settled on Lotts Creek, just above what is now the Perry County line (now Knott County). It is known as the "Old John Smith Place" but when John moved there it was called "Richard Smith's Place."

There were born to Richard and Alicia Combs Smith at their home on Lotts Creek 14 children, William, Thomas, Samuel, Nicholas, James, Lorenzo Dow, Joshua, Isaac, Patsy, Polly, Elizabeth, Cynthia, Nancy and Kizzie.

William, born in 1795, married Millie Combs, daughter of "Soldier John" Combs, Jr., of the Revolution. William and Millie lived on Irishman Creek off Carr's Fork. Their children were Alex, who married Mary Ashley, William (Med) who married Martha Ashley, twin to Mary. John, who married Willie Combs, daughter of Long Jerry, Thomas, who married Lourania, daughter of Thomas Francis, Richard, who married Polly Kelly, was a Union soldier.

While home on furlough he was slain by mistake by his own men. Jeremiah (Jake) married Elizabeth Stacy. Sarah, married G. W. Kelly and Matilda, married Jehu Cody.

Thomas married a Clemons, of the Quicksand and Knott county families, and had these children, Richard, William, Lute, Aggie and Matilda. His son Richard was a country doctor who lived on the Middle Fork of Quicksand.

Samuel married a Jones of Troublesome Creek-Lotts Creek families and their children were Bill, Dan, Ike, Sam Jr., John, Newt, Minerva, Emmaline, Arminda and Sceatti. Bill, Dan, Ike and John were Confederate soldiers, the latter two being killed in the war.

Nicholas married Artie Johnson, daughter of Thomas Johnson. They lived on Ball's Fork and later moved to Carter County. They had one son, Sim.

James married Rhoda Owens, and they moved to Lee County. Their children were Frankie, Louise, Rebecca, Bill, Elhaney, Ike and Nicholas. Bill, a Confederate soldier, was killed at the mouth of Ball Creek by guerillas while home on furlough.

Lorenzo Dow, called Anze, (he was named for a popular Methodist Circuit rider touring the mountains at that time) first married a daughter of Jonathan Fugate, and his second wife was Frankie Stacy. His children were Zachariah and Pollie.

Joshua married Amy Holliday of Troublesome Creek and their children were John, Richard, Larkin, Hay, Allie, Jermima, Prudence and Emmaline.

Isaac married Cynthia Stacy, sister to "Smoker Bill", and they had 11 children, Catherine, Eliza, Sam, Rachel, Sally, Polly, Tolbert, Jim, Felix, Elizabeth and Shade who married Polly Ann, daughter of Tolbert Holliday, the primitive Baptist preacher.

The daughters of Richard married the following, Patsy (Dinah) married J. C. (Jack) Campbell, of Troublesome Creek, Polly (Mary) married Zachariah Fugate, of Troublesome and Ball Creek families, Elizabeth (Betsy) married Martin Fugate, Cynthia married John Stacy, brother to "Smoker Bill", Nancy first married J. P. Artin and then

George Combs, and Kizzie, married Thomas Ritchie of Clear Creek and Ball Creek families.

Richard Smith was buried in the Smith family graveyard at Ary in 1835. He was a Primitive Baptist minister for 45 years. Sam Smith, of Ary, has his old Bible, which is still in good condition. It has entries of Smith births and deaths dating back to 1816.—(The late H. H. Smith, Sam Smith and Judge J. A. Smith.)

STAMPER

William Stamper was born in 1774 in North Carolina, and married Emily (Millie) Polly, daughter of Edward Polly, Revolutionary soldier. Edward Polly migrated from North Carolina to Kentucky and settled near Mayking on the Kentucky River in old Perry County (now Letcher) where he died in 1845. The name Stamper is of English origin and was derived from an occupation, probably a stamper of coins.

About 1800 William Stamper came from Grassy Creek, North Carolina and settled on Rock House near the mouth of Colly Creek. William Stamper was one of the Justices present at the June term of court in Perry County in 1822. He was Sheriff of Perry County in 1829 and his son, Hiram H. was his deputy. Hiram H. was born in 1806 on Rockhouse. He married Matilda Hogg, daughter of James and Elizabeth (Kelly) Hogg in 1827. Hiram served as Constable in 1826 and his bond was signed by Benjamin Webb and William Stamper. He also served as election judge of Rockhouse in 1835. He later moved to Morgan County, where he died.

Other Children of William Stamper were James B., Sarah, Martha, Rachel, John Whit, Elizabeth, William Buckner, Polly and twins, Nancy and Isaac D., born in 1816. Isaac married Polly Adams and they lived at the old homestead at Colly where they are both buried.

William Stamper and his wife both moved to Morgan County in later years, where he died in 1852. Both are buried in the Stamper Cemetery.—(Descendants of James Stamper 1750-1826, by Oliver Stamper, Mrs. Ila Caton.)

WEBB

Georgia Cornett Combs

The history of the Webb family begins with James Webb, an Englishman who came to America before the Revolution. He was in the War for Independence as an Aide-de-camp to General Washington at the battle of White Plains. He was shot through the body and was left for dead, but he recovered from his wound, and subsquently followed his son Benjamin to Kentucky. James Webb married a sister to Daniel Boone's mother. One of the characteristics of the Webb family is long life. James lived to be 106, and it will be noted that others of this family attained an age close to the century mark.

Benjamin Webb, son of James, was born in 1701, probably on the east coast of Maryland. He posessed an adventuresome spirit, that led him into various occupations. As a Young man, he was for a time a slave trader. From Maryland he moved to Buncombe County, North Carolina, where seven familes who had heard of Kentucky and had "Western fever" started to follow the Boone trail through Powell Valley and over the mountains to the head of the Kentucky River. They located on the Kentucky River near the mouth of Boone's Fork in 1796 or 1797. Later they moved to what is now the coal town of Mayking, then known as Bottom Fork, where Benjamin lived the remainder of his life. He was one of the first Justices of Perry County, which then composed a large portion of Eastern Kentucky, and also was Sheriff of Perry County in 1831. It was his custom to walk to the state capital each year to make settlements of his accounts.

His wife was Jennie Adams, who came to Kentucky with the Webb family from North Carolina when a young woman. She died at the age of 97 and is buried at the Webb family cemetery at Mayking.

One of Benjamin's grandsons was the late Col. N. M. Webb of Whitesburg, for many years owner and editor of the Mountain Eagle.

LIST OF ILLUSTRATIONS

	Page
Old Grist Mill	235
Memorial Gymnasium	236
Main Street (1912)	237
Main Street (1913)	238
Main Street (1913)	239
Main Street (1914)	240
Broadway Street (1912)	241
Flood (1927)	242
Old Tunnel Mill	243
Isaac Eversole Home	244
Bobby Davis Memorial Library	245
Old County Jail	246
First Coal Tipple	247
Old Combs House	248
Ox Team Bringing in Supplies	249
Push Boat on North Fork Kentucky River	250
Court House (1911)	251
First Train (1912)	252
Elijah C. Cornett	253
Hazard Relief Route (By-Pass)	254

Courtesy of L. O. Davis *Copied by Hal Cooner*

Alvin Evans grist mill at Dam on the road to Lothair.

Memorial Gymnasium (1951).

Photo by Hal Cooner

Courtesy of L. O. Davis *Cop-ed by Hal Cooner*

Main Street, 1912—D. Y. Combs Store (corner Main and Fleet Sts.), Nofsirger Drug Store, Fitzpatrick residence, Tin Bldg. (pool room and restaurant), Aunt Sallie Davidson's home and D. Y. Combs' barn, (now Virginia Theater). Right to left—Eversole Store (now Fuller Bldg.), W. O. Davis' Store (now I.G.A.).

Courtesy of L. O Davis *Copied by Hal Cooner*

Main Street in 1913, showing Lexington Boosters arriving. Reading from right to left—The Johnson Bldg., (Engle Hardware Co., The Baltimore Store); Perry County State Bank; R. O. Davis Store; W. O. Davis Hotel; D. Y. Combs Hotel.

Courtesy of L. O. Davis   *Copied by Hal Cooner*

Main Street in 1913, showing Lexington Boosters arriving. Left to right—Dr. Gross-Dr. Hurst's Office (now Sterling Hdwe.), D. Y. Combs Hotel (now Grand Hotel), W. O. Davis' Hotel and store (now Don's Drug Store and I.G.A.) Perry County State Bank (now Fuller Bldg.), Johnson Bldg., Wootton and Morgan Bldg. (now Hazard Drug Store) and First Baptist Church.

Photo by J. R. Kinner

Main Street—1914. Perry County State Bank, Johnson Bldg., Wootton and Morgan Bldg. (G. B. Eversole Co.), First National Bank Bldg. (now Peoples Bank), Jones Bldg., First Baptist Church, Aunt Leah Farler's home, Beaumont Hotel (Main and Court Sts. now Hurst Hotel), and D. Y. Combs Store on corner of Main and Fleet Sts.

Courtesy of L. O. Davis   *Copied by Hal Cooner*

Broadway St., 1912. Right to left—P. T. Wheeler residence (far right corner), Kelly Watts residence (C. E. Brown now), John Watts residence (Geo. Combs Apt. Bldg.), Robin Baker barn, and below, D. Y. Combs' residence, Rockaway St.

Photo by Howard Johnson, Sr.
1927 Flood, corner of East Main and High St.
Hazard, Kentucky

Photo by Howard Johnson, Jr.
Old Tunnel Mill, Dwarf, Kentucky.

Courtesy of Mrs. John F. Gilbert *Photo by Hal Cooner*
Isaac Eversole Home. Oldest house in Perry County—built around 1802.

Courtesy of L. O. Davis

Photo by Hal Cooner

Bobby Davis Memorial Library.

Courtesy of L. O. Davis *Copied by Hal Cooner*

County Jail, corner of Main and Fleet Sts. (still standing around 1915), R. C. Baker Restaurant, and Dr. H. B. Maggard residence in rear, facing High Street.

Courtesy of L. O. Davis   *Copied by Hal Cooner*

Hazard Coal Co., Perry Gorman, Sup't. (now Blue Grass Coal Co.), the first coal tipple in Perry County, then located above the Home Lumber Co. (J. L. and J. E. Johnson land).

Photo by Mrs. H. M. Gallaher

Built by Nicholas (Bird-eye) Combs, Jr., the second oldest house still standing in Perry County.

Push Boat bringing supplies from Jackson—before the railroad was built in 1912. North Fork of Kentucky River—near Hazard.

Main St., Perry County State Bank. Oxen-team bringing in Supplies — Morge Cornett, Matt Cornett and John (Flat) Williams on last ox.

Court House (burned in 1911).

First train to arrive in Hazard, July, 1912.

Courtesy of Mrs. A. N. Peters   Copied by Warner Studio
Elijah C. Cornett. One of the last men to ship coal in push boats.

By-Pass—The Hazard Relief Route, Completed in 1950. Official traffic count indicated that 9,000 vehicles per day traveled Hazard's one-way Main Street prior to completion of this route.

APPENDIX

FOOTNOTES — FORMATION

1. Judge Samuel Wilson's papers, University of Kentucky Library, quoting Kentucky *Senate Journal* 1820-21, 24.
2. *Ibid.*, 1819-20, 175.
3. Hazard, a family name of his paternal grandfather.
4. Willard Rouse Jillson, *Kentucky Land Grants*, 13.
5. R. H. Collins, *History of Kentucky;* II, 631 (Sketch of Montgomery County).
6. *Acts*, Kentucky General Assembly, 1820-21, Section 3,152.
7. Deed Book B (Perry County Court) The five trustees were Elijah Combs, Jeremiah Combs, Jesse Boling, R. S. Brashear, John A. Duff.
8. Judge Samuel Wilson's papers, University of Kentucky Library.
9. Deed Book A (Perry County Court), 204.
10. Deed Book J (Perry County Court), 439.
11. First Minute Book (Perry County Court) 1820-1837, 442.
12. *Acts*, Kentucky General Assembly 1884, Ch. 1141, p.632.

FOOTNOTES — SETTLEMENT

1. Mary Verhoeff, *Kentucky Mountains*, 70.
2. *Ibid.*, 71.
3. Judge Samuel Wilson's papers, University of Kentucky Library.
4. Willard Rouse Jillson, *Kentucky Land Grants*, p.9.
5. *Ibid.*, 291.
6. *Ibid.*, 163, 174, 279, 291, 374, 482.
7. William Littell, *Kentucky Acts*, 1820-21, Sec. 8 (forming Perry County).

FOOTNOTES — SOCIAL GROWTH

1. County Agent's Report, 1949-50.
2. Agricultural Report, 1924, Kentucky Historical Society.
3. Alfred Fenton, *Oliver Hazard Perry.*
4. *Military History of Kentucky*, American Guide Series, p.330.
5. *Ibid.*, p.341.
6. Perry County Court Clerk's office.
7. R. H. Collins, *History of Kentucky*, Vol. I, p.638.
8. Chavies, Dwarf, Gay's Creek, Saltcreek, Stacy, Troublesome, Viper, Jesse, Second Creek, Grapevine, Forked Mouth, Little Leatherwood, Mason, Buckeye Creek, Big Creek and Hazard.
9. Edward O. Guerrant, *The Galex Gatherers*, p. 195.
10. R. F. Johnson, Administrative Director of Perry County Health Department.

FOOTNOTES — SALT

1. Mary Verhoeff, *Kentucky River Navigation*, p.151.
2. *Ibid.*, 151.
3. *Ibid.*, 151.
4. *Ibid.*, 151.

FOOTNOTES — LUMBERING

1. Judge Samuel Wilson's papers, Unversity of Kentucky Library, quoting Twelfth Biennial Report of Bureau of Agriculture, Labor and Statistics Survey.
2. Judge Samuel Wilson's papers, University of Kentucky Library, quoting Report to Labor Department, 1899, by J. E. Johnson, C.C.C. of Perry County.
3. *Ibid.*

FOOTNOTES — COAL

1. Howard N. Eavenson, *The First Century and A Quarter of American Coal Industry*, p.8.
2. Kentucky Geological Survey, November 28, 1910, Series 3, Bulletin 11, p.14-119.
3. Report of Kentucky State Inspector of Mines, 1894, p.200.
4. *Ibid.*, 1889, p.6.
5. *Ibid.*, 1900, p. 286.
6. *Ibid.*, 1902, p.15, and 1905, p.248.

FOOTNOTES — BUCKHORN

1. Asbury Johnson, "A Brief History of Various Families Around Buckhorn, Ky." (notes on the Smith family). A paper prepared in 1927 for a course the writer was taking at Peabody College in Nashville. Illness and subsequent death kept him from completion of this work which he had planned to submit for a doctor's thesis, or dissertation. The notes were given to Mrs. Rice Kirby, Hazard, by Luther Johnson before his death in 1950, with permission to use them.
2. *Ibid.*
3. *Ibid.*
4. Louise Sanders Murdoch, *Almetta of Gabriel's Run*, p.1.
5. *Ibid.*
6. Asbury Johnson, *Op. Cit.*, notes on the Gay family.
7. Elmer E. Gabbard, *Buckhorn: The Story of a Christian Enterprise on Squabble Creek in the Mountains of Kentucky*, p.7.
8. McAllister J. Grey and Grace Owings Guerrant, *Edward O. Guerrant*, (Ch. XIII reprinted for Elmer E. Gabbard with permission of the authors), p. 150.
9. *Ibid.*, p.151.
10. *Ibid.*, p.150-151.
11. G. Gordon Mahy, Jr. *Murdoch of Buckhorn*, p.8.
12. McAllister and Guerrant, *Op. Cit.*, p.152.
13. *Ibid.*, p.155.
14. Edward O. Guerrant, *The Galax Gatherers*, p.195.
15. McAllister and Guerrant, *Op. Cit.*, p.156.
16. Elmer E. Gabbard, *Op. Cit.*, p.24.
17. McAllister and Guerrant, *Op. Cit.*, p.157.

FOOTNOTES — GROWTH OF HAZARD

1. Mutzenburg, Charles G., *Famous Feuds and Tragedies of Kentucky*, p.89.
2. Map drawn by T. S. Ward, who moved to Hazard in 1891.
3. Dye, Harold E, *Prophet of Little Cane Creek*, p.59.
4. Kerr, Charles, History of Kentucky. Biographical sketch of Dr. E. H. Kelley of Hazard. Vol 5, p.505.
5. Allan Trout, *Courier-Journal Magazine*, July 17, 1949.

FOOTNOTES — EDUCATION

1. Judge Samuel Wilson, *History of Kentucky*, II, p.238.
2. Martin Luther Ambrose, *County Academy System in Kentucky*, p.546.
3. *Ibid.*, p.276.
4. *Ibid.*, p.200.
5. Barksdale Hamlett, *History of Education in Kentucky*, **p.4**.
6. *Ibid.*, p.8, 9.
7. *Ibid.*, p.2.
8. *Ibid.*, p.11.
9. Minute Book VI (Perry County Court), p.36.
10. R. H. Collins, *History of Kentucky*, I, p.505.
11. Barksdale Hamlett, *Op. Cit.*, p.146.
12. Louis Pilcher, *Pearl of the Mountains*, p.44.
13. Harold E. Dye, *Prophet of Little Cane Creek*, p.77.
14. Barksdale Hamlett, *Op. Cit.*, p.137.

FOOTNOTES — COURTS

1. Minute Book A, Perry County Courts, 1822-37, p.4, 5.
2. Minute Book 3, Perry County Court, p.64.
3. Minute Book A, *Op. Cit.*, 1822-37, p.431.
4. Deed Book C, Perry County Court, p.401.

FOOTNOTES — TRANSPORTATION

1. William Littrell, *The Statute Laws of Kentucky*, Vol. V., **p.472**.
2. Mary Verhoeff, *Kentucky Mountains*, p.161.
3. *Ibid.*, p.165, 166.
4. *Ibid.*, p.167, 162.
5. *Ibid.*, pp.163-165.
6. *Ibid.*, p.168, 170.
7. Mary Verhoeff, *Kentucky River Navigation*, pp.25-26.
8. *Ibid.*, pp.30-39.

BIBLIOGRAPHY

Ambrose, Luther M., *The County Academy System in Kentucky*, Ph.D. Thesis, University of Kentucky, 1939.

Collins, R. H., *History of Kentucky*, Covington, 1874.

Collins, Lewis, *History of Kentucky*, Covington, 1882.

Dye, Harold E., *Prophet of Little Cane Creek*, Southern Baptist Home Mission Board, Atlanta, 1949.

Eavenson, Howard N., *The First Century and A Quarter of American Coal Industry*, Pittsburgh, 1942.

Fenton, Alfred, *Oliver Hazard Perry*, New York, 1944.

Gabbard, Elmer E., *The Christian Enterprise*, Berea College Press, Berea, 1937.

Guerrant, Edward O., *The Galax Gatherers*, Richmond, 1911.

Hamlett, Barksdale, *History of Education in Kentucky*, Frankfort, 1914.

Jillson, Willard Rouse, *Kentucky Land Grants*, Filson Club Publication, Louisville, 1925.

Kerr, Charles E., *History of Kentucky*, New York, 1922.

Littell, William, *The Statute Laws of Kentucky*, 5 Vol., Frankfort, 1809-1819.

Mahy, Gordon, Jr., *Murdoch of Buckhorn*, Nashville, 1946.

Mather, William, *Kentucky Geological Survey*, Frankfort, 1939.

McAllister, J. Grey and Guerrant, Grace Owings, *Edward O. Guerrant*, Richmond, 1950.

Murdoch, Louise Sanders, *Almetta of Gabriel's Run*, Meridan Press, New York, 1917.

Pilcher, Louis, *Pearl of the Mountains*, Lexington, 1913.
Rafinsque, C. F., *Annals of Kentucky*, Frankfort, 1824.
Tapp, Hambleton, *A Sesqui-Centennial History of Kentucky*, Louisville, 1945.

Verhoeff, Mary, *The Kentucky Mountains*, Filson Club Publication, No. 26, Louisville, 1911.

Verhoeff, Mary, *The Kentucky River Navigation*, Filson Club Publication, No. 28, Louisville, 1917.

Wilson, Judge Samuel, *History of Kentucky*, Chicago, 1929.

OTHER SOURCES

Acts, Kentucky General Assembly, 1792-1820.
Acts, Kentucky General Assembly, 1883-1884.
Perry County Court Records 1820-1950.
Asbury Johnson's manuscript, *Families Around Buckhorn*.
Judge Samuel Wilson's papers, University of Kentucky Library.
Military History of Kentucky, American Guide Series, Frankfort, 1939.
Charles E. Ebersol, *The Ebersol Families in America*, 1729-1937, Lansing, Mich., 1937.

NEWSPAPER SOURCES

Hazard Herald—March, 1912.
Hazard Herald—March, 1927.
Louisville Courier-Journal, April, 1951.
Louisville Courier-Journal, June, 1951.

MAGAZINE SOURCES

Kentucky Progress Magazine, 1928.
L.&N. Magazine, July, 1927.
L.&N. Magazine, June, 1944.

CENSUS, 1830-1950

Year	Total Pop.	White	Indian	Free Colored	Slave
1830	3,330	3,150		25	155
1840	3,089	2,923		23	143
1850	3,092	2,972		3	117
1860	3,950	3,863		14	73
1870	4,274	4,173	5	96	
1880	5,607				
1890	6,331				
1900	8,276				
1910	11,255				
1920	26,042				
1930	42,186				
1940	47,828				
1950	46,439				

CENSUS OF HAZARD

1910	537
1920	4,348
1930	7,021
1940	7,397
1950	6,850

1950 DISTRICT CENSUS

Bureau of the Census — Pikeville, Kentucky

	1950	1940
Perry County	46,439	47,828
Dist. I—Bowling	1,853	2,315
Dist. II—Campbell	2,867	2,882
Chavies, Unincorporated	294	*
Krypton, Unincorporated	215	*
Dist. III—Troublesome	2,213	2,301
Dist. IV—Hazard	23,652	25,841
Blue Diamond, Harveyton, Unincorporated	2,334	*
Bonnyman, Clemons, Unincorporated	915	*

Bulan, Unincorporated	1,452	*
Christopher, Fourseam, Unincorporated	1,275	*
Glomawr, Unincorporated	750	*
Hardburly, Tribbey, Unincorporated	987	*
Hazard	6,840	7,397
Lothair, Unincorporated	1,309	*
Dist. V—Mason's Creek	7,775	8,207
Allock, Vicco, Unincorporated	1,613	*
Jeff, Unincorporated	682	*
Dist. VI—Lost Creek	1,321	1,434
Dist. VII—Leatherwood	4,070	2,245
Dist. VIII—Forked Mouth	2,688	2,603

*—1940 census figures not available.

DONATIONS

To the donors listed below, we express our thanks for their part in meeting the expenses of publishing this book:

Mr. and Mrs. L. H. Stiles
Home Lumber Co.
Mrs. Rachel Tye Baker
Hazard Coco-Cola Bottling Works, Inc.
Hazard Furniture Co.
Mr. and Mrs. Victor Spurlock
Shelton Barber Shop
Mr. and Mrs. E. J. Davis
Peoples Bank
Mr. and Mrs. M. K. Eblen
Garnett Insurance Agency
Mr. and Mrs. William Engle
Mr. and Mrs. Galley Collins
Johnson Funeral Home
Buchanan Coal Co.
Gene Baker Motor Co.
Mine Service Co.
W.K.I.C.
Mr. and Mrs. Dudley Goodlette
Herald Publishing Co.
Citizens State Bank
Sterling Hardware Co.
Dr. J. C. Coldiron
Fouts Drug Company
Grand Hotel
Smith's Department Store
Mr. R. C. Martin
The late Troy Couch
Hazard Drug Co.
Hazard Dry Cleaning and Laundry Co.
Hazard Insurance Agency
Mr. and Mrs. L. O. Davis
Mr. and Mrs. W. E. Mattingly
Lee F. Lykins (I.G.A.)
Mr. and Mrs. Prentiss Baker
Ajax Coal Co.
Dr. and Mrs. W. F. O'Donnell
Judge J. A. Smith
Mr. and Mrs. F. V. Adams

Miss Carolyn Reading, Lexington, Ky.
Dr. and Mrs. E. E. Gabbard
Mr. and Mrs. Denver Minniard
Douglas Sales and Service
Mrs. A. M. Gross
Mr. and Mrs. Charles Whitehead
Mr. and Mrs. H. M. Gallaher
Mr. and Mrs. Howard Johnson
Mr. and Mrs. John Fitzhugh Gilbert
Mr. and Mrs. L. T. Tayloe
Mr. and Mrs. T. H. Hines
Mr. and Mrs. A. N. Peters
Mrs. O. S. Warren
Mr. and Mrs. Dewey Daniel
Kentucky and West Virginia Power Co.
Mr. and Mrs. Perry Gorman

COUNTY OFFICERS

Nora McIntosh Campbell

CIRCUIT JUDGES

1834-41	Joseph Eve
1841-44	Tunstal Quarles
1844-46	George R. McKee
1846-49	B. Kincaid
1850	James R. Rice
1851	Edwin Trimble
1851-56	Green Adams
1856-58	G. P. Pearl
1868-80	William Randall
1880-86	W. F. Finley
1886-93	H. C. Lilly
1893-97	W. F. Hall
1897-06	M. J. Moss
1906-07	G. T. Lewis
1907-15	L. D. Lewis
1915-21	J. C. Eversole
1922-34	R. B. Roberts
1934-40	S. M. Ward
1940-46	Roy Helm
1946-52	S. M. Ward
1952	Courtney Wells

COMMONWEALTH ATTORNEYS

1825	Daniel P. Mosley
1831	Henry Harris
1832	John Hargis
1832	Andrew Colwell
1849	Green Noble
1881	F. B. French
1893-96	Henry L. Howard
1904-16	Ira Fields
1916-22	R. B. Roberts
1922-28	C. W. Napier
1928-34	John Asher
1934-40	J. A. Smith
1940-46	William Dixon
1946-52	Augustus Cornett
1952	Emmett Fields

CIRCUIT COURT CLERKS**

1874-91	Ira Davidson
1891-97	B. F. Fields
1897	I. D. Fields
1904	F. B. Feltner
1904-16	Lee Daniel
1916-22	W. C. Combs
1922-28	Zack Duff
1928-32	Sam Cornett
1932-33	Jesse Cornett
1933-34	Eli Sumner
1934-40	Jesse Cornett
1940	Sam Combs

COUNTY JUDGES*

	Jesse Bolin
1851	Robert S. Brashear
1855	John Hyden, Jr.
	Andy Combs
1866	John C. Duff
1879-80	John Holliday
1880-82	John Walker
1882-86	Josiah H. Combs
1886-88	G. W. Eversole
1890-94	Robert F. Fields
1894-98	Mack Napier
1898-02	H. T. Crawford
1902	Ira Combs, contested out by
1902-06	Cash Eversole
1906-10	H. T. Crawford
1910-14	J. G. Campbell
1914-18	E. C. Duff
1918-22	Dr. A. M. Gross
1922-26	Joshua Smith
1926-30	Dr. K. N. Salyers
1930-34	Joshua Smith
1934-38	Dr. A. M. Gross
1938-42	Billie Baker

(County Judges Con't.)
1942-46 Joshua Smith
1946-50 Taylor Witt
1950 Fred Combs

COUNTY ATTORNEYS
1821 William Mattingly
1831 Henry Harris
1833 A. F. Colwell
1835 John Burns
1849 H. C. Hogg
1860 James B. Fitzpatrick
1866-70 Dr. J. M. Daniel
1886-88 John Morgan
1888-90 Sam Cash
1890-94 Harry Creech
1894-98 Charles Wooten
1898-02 W. C. Eversole
1902-06 Farmer Eversole
1906-10 J. Matt Dixon
1910-14 C. W. Napier
1914-22 Sam Ward
1922-26 Charles Wooten
1926-30 John E. Campbell
1930-34 Henry Johnson
1934-42 Dennis B. Wooten
1942-50 Elbert Strong
1950 Tolbert Combs

COUNTY COURT CLERKS**
1821-74 Jesse Combs
1874-91 Ira Davidson
1894 Arch Cornett
1894-98 G. R. Cornett
1898-1910 Joe E. Johnson
1910 S. B. Johnson
1910-14 J. D. Davis
1914-22 B. P. Combs
1922-26 J. C. Whittaker
1926-34 Ella Hopkins
1934-38 Seba Stamper
1938-42 Nancy Ann Eversole
1942-46 Raymond Lykins
1946 Prentiss Baker

SHERIFFS
1821-25 Henry Duff
1825-26 Robert S. Brashear
1827 Daniel Duff
1829 William Stamper
1831 Benjamen Webb
1835 Jeremiah Combs
1836-37 Elijah Combs, Sr.
1843 John Campbell
1844 Elijah Bolin
1846 Hiram Campbell
1849 Jackson Combs
1850 William Smith
1851 John Campbell
1854 Nicholas Combs

1855 Cyrus Crook
1858-60 Hezekiah Combs
1860 Austin Godsey
1867 John B. Campbell
1868-69 James Turner
1872 McCager Napier
1880 W. W. Baker
1881 Spencer Combs
1886-87 J. W. Combs
1887 William Grigsby
1888 Elisha Holliday
1888-90 B. T. Fields
1890 D. Y. Combs
1891-94 Henry Combs
1894-98 R. C. Napier
1898-02 Eli Cornett, resigned
1902-06 John B. Eversole appointed
1906-10 M. C. Eversole
1910-14 Frank Horn
1914-18 A. B. Combs
1918-22 Richmond Combs
1922-26 Tolbert Holliday
1926-30 William Cornett
1930-34 Dr. A. M. Gross
1934-38 Fillmore McIntosh
1938-42 Justus Begley
1942-46 Charlie Cornett
1946-50 Green Holliday
1950 John Gross

TAX COMMISSIONERS
1827 John Hardin
1892-94 Lute Feltner
 James A. Eversole
1894-98 Tucker Bowling
1898-02 John Watts
1902-06 Buck Campbell
1906-10 Alfred Couch
1910 Van Buren Combs
1910-11 Ed Campbell
1911-14 A. B. Combs
1914-18 Lincoln Eversole
1918-22 Bud Eversole
1922-30 Farmer Johnson
1930-34 Floyd Hall
1934-38 Scott Johnson
1938 Farmer Johnson

SUPT. OF SCHOOLS***
1860-65 John Baker
1866 Elijah Duff
1870 Abner Eversole
1886 John E. Campbell
1890-02 G. P. Combs
1902-06 B. P. Bowling
1906-10 G. P. Combs
1910-17 John McIntosh, resigned
1917-18 John Napier, appointed

(Supt. of Schools Con't.)
1918-51   M. C. Napier
1951   Arthur Eversole

JAILORS
1828   F. Wooten
1832   Elijah Combs
1844-50   Elijah Combs
1854   Isaac Baker
1879   L. D. Baker, resigned
1880   W. O. Davis
1884-86   R. C. Combs
1886-88   Jesse Fields
1889-91   Wiley Couch
1891-94   R. M. Baker
1894-98   Brown Baker
1898-02   S. C. Colwell
1902-06   Mack Eversole
1906   Robert Combs
1906-10   Eli Combs
1910-14   R. C. Baker
1914-18   James Holliday
1918-22   R. C. Baker

1922-26   Van Combs
1926-30   Price Napier
1930-38   Troy P. Combs
1938-42   Grant Campbell
1942-50   Charley Duff
1950   Taylor Porter

CORONERS
1825   Hardin Combs
1835   George Ison
1836   Isaac Brashear
1836   Sampson Brashear
Several Terms   Joe Combs
1906-14   Calvin Stacy
1914-22   Bill Combs
1922-30   Calvin Stacy
1930-34   Bill Combs
1934-38   Dr. Brit Combs
1938-42   Bill Combs
1942-50   Ed Ivey
1950   Hanibal Shockey

* From 1820-1850 Senior Justice in attendance presided over the court as judge. From 1850-1891 the new constitution provided for one presiding judge and two associate judges and two of whom could transact business for the court. After 1891 the county courts had but one judge as presiding judge of the court.

** The offices of Circuit Court Clerk and County Court Clerk were together until the new constitution was adopted in 1891 which required a severance of the offices.

*** Called commissioners before 1860.

POSTMASTERS, 1820-1952

Postmaster   Date of Appointment   Place
Alexander Patrick—May 9, 1821.......Patrick's Salt Work
Robert S. Brashear—Feb. 21, 1829.........Brashearsville
Henry Duff—Sept. 10, 1834..................Grapevine
James C. Brewer—Aug. 21, 1860................Cut Shin
Anderson Cornett—June 8, 1868..............Salt Creek
Joseph Hall—July 24, 1878..........Tunnel Mill (Dwarf)
J. C. Boggs—May 10, 1882................Troublesome
Thomas W. Gibson—July 13, 1883................Dwarf
    Perry Court House (later Hazard)
Elijah Combs, Jr.—Apr. 22, 1824......Perry—later Hazard
Andrew F. Caldwell—Mar. 15, 1834....Perry—later Hazard
William Mattingly—Apr. 1, 1837......Perry—later Hazard
David Butler—Dec. 11, 1837..........Perry—later Hazard
Jackson G. Combs—Mar. 12, 1840.....Perry—later Hazard

Robert H. Godsey—Dec. 16, 1843......Perry—later Hazard
Josiah H. Combs—Dec. 30, 1845......Perry—later Hazard
John G. Lacy—Sept. 5, 1851.........Perry—later Hazard
John G. Lacy—June 20, 1854..........Changed to Hazard
Cyrus E. Crooks—May 17, 1855..................Hazard
H. G. Crooks—Sept. 4, 1855.....................Hazard
Jesse Combs—Dec. 15, 1855.....................Hazard
William H. Combs—Jan. 29, 1858................Hazard
Henry C. Hogg—July 10, 1860...................Hazard
Jesse Combs—Oct. 28, 1862.....................Hazard
Hezekiah Combs—Mar. 6, 1866...................Hazard
Jesse Combs—Feb. 25, 1868.....................Hazard
John M. Morgan—Nov. 12, 1868..................Hazard
Zach Morgan—Jan. 24, 1870.....................Hazard
Ira J. Davidson—Dec. 12, 1871.................Hazard
Joseph Eversole—July 10, 1872.................Hazard
William J. Combs—May 10, 1872.................Hazard
Ira J. Davidson—Jan. 31, 1877.................Hazard
Robin M. Baker—July 20, 1885..................Hazard
German Holliday—Oct. 18, 1890.................Hazard
German D. Holliday—May 19, 1892...............Hazard
William H. Cornett—June 23, 1893..............Hazard
Kendrick C. Combs—April 13, 1895..............Hazard
Martha Johnson—Oct. 21, 1897..................Hazard
Martha Stacy—Aug. 12, 1898....................Hazard
Felix Begley—Jan. 23, 1903....................Hazard
John Baker—June 6, 1913.......................Hazard
B. W. Baker—Dec. 23, 1915.....................Hazard
James B. Fitzpatrick—Mar. 24, 1916............Hazard
Rebel Martin (acting)—Sept. 19, 1917..........Hazard
Barney Baker (acting)—Oct. 16, 1917...........Hazard
Robin M. Baker—Oct. 29, 1917..................Hazard
Luke P. Grigsby—Oct. 4, 1919..................Hazard
Rebel Martin—Apr. 1, 1920.....................Hazard
Dewey Daniel—Sept. 1, 1921....................Hazard
Anna M. Moore—Apr. 1, 1936........Still serving, Hazard

There is no record of mail routes in Perry (later Hazard) before 1830 but a few of them including Perry in the 1830's were:

No. 1775, from Cumberland Ford, Knox County, to Perry Court House, Perry County, let for the period 1830-34 to Elisha Green of Harlan Court House, Kentucky, 90 miles, once in two weeks.

No. 1757, from Manchester, Clay County, to Irvine, Estill County, let for the period 1830-34 to Elijah Combs of Manchester, Kentucky, 127 miles, once a week at $400 per annum.

No. 1820, from Prestonsburg, Floyd County, to Perry Court House, Perry County, let for the period 1830-34, to Thomas Ward of Greenup Court House, Kentucky, 50 miles once a week at $200 per annum.

No. 1829, from Lebanon, Russel County, to Perry Court House, Perry County, let for the period 1830-34, to Andrew Craig of Whiteley Court House, Kentucky.

No. 3221, from Mount Sterling, Montgomery County, to Perry Court House, Perry County, let on October 18, 1837, to Samuel Hall of Irvine, 116¼ miles and back once a week, $444 per annum.

No. 3264, Perry Court House, Perry County, to Manchester, Clay County, let on October 30, 1837 to E. Smith and J. A. Moore of Mount Vernon, Kentucky, 40 miles and back once a week, $286 per annum.

No. 3265, Perry Court House, Perry County, to Estillville, Virginia, let on April 11, 1839 to Ezekiel Brashear of Perry Court House, Perry County, Kentucky, 75 miles and back once a week, at $76 per annum.—(The National Archives, Washington, D. C.)

Tunnel Mill (later Dwarf)

Joseph Hall—July 24, 1878.................Tunnel Mill
Newton Smith—Aug. 9, 1880...............Tunnel Mill
Thomas Gibson—July 13, 1883..........Changed to Dwarf
William G. Cornett—Mar. 6, 1888................Dwarf
Martha Cornett—July 10, 1895..................Dwarf
William G. Cornett—Mar. 6, 1898................Dwarf
Elbert B. Owens—May 16, 1908..................Dwarf
Isabel Ritchie—Feb. 21, 1920....................Dwarf
David Ritchie—Apr. 21, 1921....................Dwarf

Ida Oliver—Nov. 26, 1922.........................Dwarf
Felton F. Combs—Feb. 14, 1923..Dwarf
George Cornett—Oct. 26, 1925....................Dwarf
J. B. Campbell—1930, still serving

FIRST TAX BOOK — PERRY COUNTY 1821-1822
(Kentucky Historical Society)

Amis, Thomas
Allin, John
Adams, Benjamin
Anberry, Robert
Allin, Joshua
Adams, Benjamin Cin. (Sr.)
Adams, Spencer Cin. (Sr.)
Adams, Stephen
Adams, John
Adams, Stephen Cin. (Sr.)
Adams, Simpson
Adams, Soloman
Adams, Spencer, Jr.
Adams, Daniel
Adams, Benjamin, Jr.
Allin, William
Adams, George
Adams, Jessee, Jr.
Adams, Jesse, Cinar (Sr.)

Bolin, John, Cinar (Sr.)
Begley, William, Cinar (Sr.)
Begley, William, Jr.
Baker, John
Baker, Jesse
Butery, William
Bannett, Isom
Barker, George
Brient, John
Bargen, John
Bennet, Joshua
Bush, Dewey
Bayer, Abraham
Bolin, Jesse Cin. (Sr.)
Bolin, Jessee
Bolin, Jesse
Bolin, Justice
Bolin, Elijah
Bolin, John
Bolin, Jesse
Bronson, Hezekiah
Bentley, Daniel
Bentley, Benjamin
Bentley, Soloman
Bentley, Lewis
Bentley, John
Brown, John
Brown, Stephen
Brown, Lijah

Brown, Daniel
Brown, John, Jr.
Brown, William
Brown, Elijah
Burchfield, Adams
Baker, John
Brown, Jesse
Banks, William
Bernard, John
Bates, William
Brashear, Robert

Carnagy, James
Cockerl, John
Cope, Wiley
Cope, James, Sr.
Cope, James
Childress, Elisha
Cockerl, Jeremiah
Clemmons, Frances
Clemmons, Elizabeth
Cuning, Euriah
Campbell, Lewis
Combs, Matthew
Clemmons, Wm.
Campbell, John
Campbell, Caleb
Combs, John
Combs, John, Sr.
Combs, Benjamin
Campbell, William
Campbell, John, Sr.
Campbell, James
Campbell, John
Cauch, James
Cauch, James
Combs, Nicholas, Jr.
Combs, Nicholas, Sr.
Combs, Nicholas
Combs, Samuel
Carnitt, Robert
Combs, Jesse
Combs, Jeremiah
Combs, Elijah
Combs, George
Combs, Henry, Sr.
Combs, Henry
Combs, Washington
Combs, Jeremiah

Chapin, Nancy
Carpenter, Fields
Callahoun, David
Callahoun, Thomas
Cockrel, Joseph
Combs, Mason
Craft, Archelaus
Craft, John
Combs, William, Sr.
Cornett, Samuel
Combs, Jeremiah
Combs, Brown
Combs, Mason
Cornett, John
Callahan, Robert
Cornett, William
Cornett, Hiram
Caudle, Henry
Caudle, Benjamin
Caudle, Mathew
Collins, James
Caudle, Abner
Caudle, Thomas
Caudle, Stephen
Craft, James
Caudle, Samuel
Coudah, John
Collins, Valentine
Combs, Shadwick
Cornett, Nathaniel
Cornett, Jesse
Cornett, William
Creece, Peters
Combs, William
Combs, Harden
Church, Pall
Childers, Abraham
Cornett, William
Cornett, Archabal

Dent, Walter
Davis, Henry
Dickerson, Griffity
Deaton, John
Deaton, Lewis
Davison, White
Davison, Silus
Davison, Daniel
Deaton, Brantley
Davison, Samuel
Denieer, Lewis
Denieer, Peter
Discan, John
Discan, Thomas
Duff, Henry
Davis, Gary
Davis, Nancy
Davis, Erin
Davis, James
Davis, Robert

Duff, Daniel
Davis, John

Eversole, Joseph
Eversole, Walery
Eversole, Abraham
Eversole, John
Ely, Charey
Everidge, Joseph

Felchner, Henry
Fugit, Gahathore
Fugit, Ely
Fugit, Charles
Fugit, Martin
Frances, James
Fugit, Henley
Frier, Daniel
Fields, John
Fields, Stephen
Fulenton, David
Furgeson, William
Fleetwood, Adam
Fleetwood, Thomas
Fleetwood, Isaac
Fleetwood, Isaac
Fleetwood, John
Fleetwood, Jonathan

Graham, William
G'nye, Henry
Gibs, Nathaniel H.
Grigsby, John
Grigsby, Thomas
Gibson, Jachrah
Gibson, Nathan
Gibson, Ezekiel
Gibson, Enich
Graves, Hady
Gibson, Archabald
Gibson, William
Gibson, Martain
Gibson, James
Gibson, John
Gullet, William

Hays, William
Hurst, William
Hurst, Henry
Hurst, Samuel
Hurst, Elisha
Hagins, Thomas
Haddon, John
Haddon, Henley
Haddon, Nancy
Hail, Zachariah
Hays, John
Harry, Andrew
Hurst, Harmon
Haddon, Cvalba
Haddon, William
Huff, William

Heaton, Frederick
Hendrickson, William
Hall, John
Hall, Jesse
Hinkle, Randle
Hagins, William
Hagins, John
Hagins, Gilbert
Hix, James
Hale, Anthany
Hampton, Turner
Hicks, Robert
Haris, John
Herley, Samuel
Hagg, James
Hampton, Lenestan
Hensley, Isaac
Hagard, Richard
Hamman, Benjamin
Hensley, George
Hamman, William
Hale, William
Halbraks, Randal
Haldbrooks, John
Hogg, Hirum (or Hagg)
Hogg, Stephen (or Hagg)
Hammans, Joseph

Isaacs, Samuel C.
Isaacs, Samuel
Isaacs, Godfrey
Ingle, Henry
Isam, George
Ingram, John

Johnstan, James
Jacabs, George
Jett, Stephen
James, John
Joseph, William
James, William
John, Apsalem
John, James
John, Thomas
John, Patrick

Kelly, Johnson
Kelly, John Jun
Kelly, John C.

Lewis, John
Lewis, Thad
Lewis, Nathan
Lewis, James
Lewis, Samuel
Lewis, Joseph
Lewis, Apsalem
Lucky, Jesse
Little, Edward

Lewis, James
Lunceford, Majer
Lewis, Charles
Lusk, Samuel

Mackintush, Raderick
Mays, William
Mays, Abraham
McQuin, Alexander Singleton
McQuin, Charles
McQuin, Braxton
McDanil, Thomas
McDanill, George
Murfrey, Zepha
Miller, Stephen Fugit
Marram, Jesse
Miller, Martein
Miller, Pally (Polly)
Miller, Samuel
Miller, Andrew
Miller, William
Miller, Benjamin
Marram, John
Mackintush, Samuel
Mackintush, Peter
Mackintush, Nimrod
Moor, Allin
Martain, William
Minyard, Israel
Maddnan, Elezabeth
McDaniel, Thomas
Maselly, John
McDaniel, William
Mullins, John
Mullins, Joshua
Maden, George
Mallet, Thomas
Mallet, Thomas G
McDanill, John

Neace, Austin
Neace, Jacob
Noble, Enoch
Noble, Nathan
Nance, Clem Jesse C.
Neutan, William

Olliver, Joshua Jesse

Pennington, Abel
Pennington, William
Praeter, Thomas
Patrick, Alexander
Pennington, Abel
Pace, John
Prappit, Joseph
Prappit,
Polly, Edward
Polly, Henry
Proffitt, Jeremiah

Polly, James
Prapitt, Silvester
Purkins, Lewis
Pramey, Isaacs
Price, Danill

Riley, John
Rilley, Joseph
Roger, George Singleton
Riley, James
Rose, John G.
Rogers, Jesse
Rogers, Adenstan
Rose, Barrin
Rose, John C.
Ritchy, Crockit Fugit
Roberts, John
Rusel, Barna
Reppy, James
Ratliff, Harper
Rippy, Joshua
Roark, James
Roberts, James
Rogers, Henry
Rogers, William

Sweeten, Absolem
Sanders, Samuel
Sanders, John
Singleton, Richard
Smith, Hardin
Salyers, John
Salyers, William
Stephen, Barnit
Shipley, Isaac
Sperlock, Jesse
Stamper, Joel (?)
Smith, Richard
Smith, Thomas
Sanders, James
Scot, Alexander
Smith, Charel
Spencer, James
Spencer, John Cincox (?)
Strang, Edward
Spencer, Elijah
Standerferd, Samuel
Spencer, John
Sizemore, William
Stacy, Benjamin.
Stacy, Jesse
Smith, George
Stacy, Simon
Sumner, John
Stacy, George
Stamper, James
Stamper, William
Stamper, John
Stuward, Isaac

Stuard, Thomas
Smith, William
Sparkman, William
Sewell, James
Smith, William
Stacy, James
Smoote, Edward
Selvege, James
Sewel, Joseph
Smith, Rubin

Turner, John
Turner, Roger
Turner, Thomas
Turner, David
Turner, Rogers
Turner, Rogers Jun.
Templeton, James
Templeton, Sary
Todd, William
Tomas, Owen
Tolson, Peter
Tomkins, Jersham
Tolson, Thomas
Tolsam, Warren
Tomkins, James

Wilson, Andrew
Walters, George
William, William
William, Riley
Wooten, William
Wooten, Gary
Williams, Majer
Walters, William
Williams, Hardin
Williams, Robert
Williams, John
Willhite, John
Webb, Pally
Watson, Pearson
Wadkins, Benjamin
Williams, Coalman
Wats, George
Whitaker, John
Whitaker, Isaac
Webb, Benjamin
Webb, James

Young, John
Yates, William
Young, Samuel
Young, Thomas
Young, Hiram
Young, Apsalem
Yanks, William

Spellings copied exactly as on tax list.

HAZARD CHAPTER OF THE
DAUGHTERS OF THE AMERICAN REVOLUTION

1952

Mrs. D. C. Amick
Mrs. John E. Campbell
Mrs. John O. Cannon
Mrs. M. D. Chrisovergis
Mrs. E. C. Combs
Mrs. Eli L. Combs
Mrs. Peggy F. Cornett
Mrs. Dewey Daniel
Mrs. W. H. Douglas
Mrs. Elmer E. Gabbard
Mrs. H. M. Gallaher
Mrs. John Fitzhugh Gilbert
Mrs. Roy Goldsmith
Mrs. Dudley H. Goodlette
Mrs. Perry F. Gorman
Mrs. A. M. Gross

Mrs. Lamar Harris *
Mrs. T. H. Hines
Mrs. Howard Johnson
Mrs. Rice J. Kirby **
Mrs. Denver Minniard
Mrs. William D. Nave
Mrs. Edna McIntosh Newman
Miss Bertha Pendleton
Mrs. A. N. Peters ***
Mrs. John W. Scholtens
Mrs. Lou O. Sizemore
Mrs. A. Karl Tatum
Mrs. L. T. Tayloe
Mrs. O. S. Warren
Mrs. C. C. Wells
Mrs. Charles N. Whitehead

* Assisted with typing.
** Assisted with proof-reading and typing.
*** Assisted with research.

INDEX

Abernathy, A. R., 141
Acts of the General Assembly, 1, 3, 4, 44, 105, 106, 180
Adams, Rev. Bennett, 125, 127
Adams, Hattie, 131
Adams, John, 13, 120-121
Adams, Rachel, 120
Adams, Sally Ann, 128
Adams, Rev. Spencer, 13, 120, 121
Adkins, J. I., 155
Agriculture, 14,15
  Farm Program, 15
Airport, 185, 186
Alexander, J. T., 203
Allen, J. B., 147
Allen, John, 133
Allen, Sam, 211
Allen, Samuel, 227
Alloway, Joe, 133
Alloway, Mrs. Joe, 133
Amburgey, Ambrose, 225
Amburgey, Humphrey, 225
Amis, Ed., 125
Amis, O. J., 125
Amis, Wm., 125
Anderson, Mrs. Joe
Anderson, Rev. O. C., 147
"Angelus" Buckhorn, 77
Anniversary Celebration, One Hundredth, 28
Arnett, Mrs. Duff, 53, 157
Asher, Armelda, 135
Asher, Mrs. Grant, 149
Asher, Susan, 135
Ashley, Rev. Jordan, 122, 225

Babbitt, Carlisle, 128
Badgett, Rev. Frank, 142
Baker, Barney, 143
Baker, Bett, 144
Baker, Betsy, 207
Baker, Betty Johnston (Mrs. Roderick), 207
Baker, Bill, 207
Baker, Mrs. Bill, 207
Baker, Rev. Bill, 207
Baker, C. A., 144
Baker, Cloe McIntosh (Mrs. John), 207
Baker, Dave, 207
Baker, Eliza, 129
Baker, Elizabeth, 140
Baker, Elizabeth Griffith (Mrs. Isaac), 207
Baker, Emaline Combs (Mrs. Dave), 207
Baker, E. N., 123

Baker family, 207
Baker, Fanny, 144
Baker, Frances, 30
Baker, Henry, 207
Baker, Isaac, 129, 207
Baker, Jack, 207
Baker, James, 144
Baker, John, 207
Baker, Katherine Jameson (Mrs. John), 207
Baker, Louanna, 207
Baker, Margaret, 129, 207
Baker, Minerva, 207
Baker, Nan Vermillion (Mrs. Bill), 207
Baker, Nancy Ann, 140
Baker, Poppy, 144
Baker, Rachel, 207
Baker, Rebecca, 207
Baker, Robin, 129, 207
Baker, Dr. Roderick, 125, 140
Baker, Sally, 207
Baker, Sally Combs (Mrs. Wilson), 207
Baker, Sarah Hill, 132
Baker, Sarilda Johnson (Mrs. Henry), 207
Baker, Susan Johnson, 207
Baker, Tom, 142
Baker, Rev. W. M., 125
Baker, Wilson, 207
Ball, R. H., 155
Bandy, T. H., 131
Bank, First, 85
Barger, Abram, 209
Barnes, Rev. George O., 129
Barr, Rev. Winn T., 142
Bartlett, A. G., 154
Bartlett, Tilman, 146
Bates, Rev. T. G., 125
Bawer, Earl E., 151
Beal, R. A., 145
Beams, Susan C., 144
Beck, Frank, 148
Begley, Judge A. L., 114
Beley, Anne York (Mrs. Pleasant), 208
Begley, Betty Lusk (Mrs. Edward), 208
Begley, Chester, 138
Begley, Cynthia Allan (Mrs. Hiram), 208
Begley, Edward, 208
Begley, Elijah R., 214
Begley family, 208
Begley, Fanny Martin (Mrs. Felix T.) 208
Begley, Felix G., 136

INDEX—Continued

Begley, Felix T., 208
Begley, Hiram, 108, 208
Begley, Mahala, 208
Begley, Margaret Boggs, 136
Begley, Pleasant, 208
Begley, Rebecca, 208
Begley, Russel, 208
Begley, Sally Baker (Mrs. William, Jr.), 207
Begley, William, Sr., 208
Begley, William, Jr., 207, 208
Begley, Winnie Sizemore (Mrs. William, Sr.), 208
Bellow, Paul, 138
Benton, G. C., 155
Black, Rev. T. W., 155
Boats, coal, 51
Bobby Davis Memorial Library, 90, 91
Boggs, A. D., 136
Boggs, Clyde, 131
Boggs, Dr. J. P., 132
Boggs, Polly Anne, 126
Bohan, Rev. C. L., 130
Boleyn, Rev. Charles W., 131
Bolin, Sarah, 219
Bolin, A., 219
Boling, family, 209
Boling, Jesse, 19, 158, 209
Boling, John, 13, 209
Boling, John E., 209
Boling, Polly (see Combs), 209
Boling, Polly Green (Mrs. Jesse), 209
Boling, Susan Sizemore (Mrs. John E.), 209
Boothe, W. W., 122, 123
Bowling, Cynthia, 147
Bowling, Deborah Duff (Mrs. William), 209
Bowling, Elijah, 209
Bowling, Elizabeth (Betty), 209
Bowling family, 209
Bowling, George, 209
Bowling, Hannah, 209
Bowling, Hanna Reed (Mrs. Justice), 209
Bowling, Rev. Jesse, Sr., 12, 80, 106, 209
Bowling, Jesse, Jr., 209
Bowling, John, 209
Bowling, John D., 147
Bowling, Major John, 209
Bowling, Justice, 209
Bowling, Mary Pennington (Mrs. Jesse), 209

Bowling, Nancy, 209
Bowling, Patsy, 209
Bowling, Polly Lewis (Mrs. John), 209
Bowling, Polly, 209
Bowling, Rachel, 209
Bowling, Col. Robert, 209
Bowling, Robert, 125
Bowman, Charlie, 130
Bowman, Elvira, 130
Bowman, Lowry, 136
Boyd, Joseph, 145
Boyd, Robert, 123
Brashear, Benois, 210
Brashear, Cordia, 144
Brashear, Eli, 143
Brashear, Elizabeth, 143, 210
Brashear, Elizabeth Young (Mrs. James), 103, 210
Brashear, Ezekial, 80, 210
Brashear family, 210
Brashear, Isaac, 210
Brashear, James, 103, 210
Brashear, John, 210
Brashear, L. B., 125, 155
Brashear, Margaret, 210
Brashear, Margaret Bright (Mrs. Sampson), 210
Brashear, Rev. M. C., 148
Brashear, Mrs. M. C., 148
Brashear, Margaret Eakin (Mrs. Samuel), 210
Brashear, Marion, 144
Brashear, Mary Ann, 125
Brashear, Minerva Combs (Mrs. Ezekial), 210
Brashear, Peggy, 210
Brashear, Phoebe, 210
Brashear, Polly, 125
Brashear, Polly Everage (Mrs. Robert S.), 128, 210
Brashear, Preston, 144
Brashear, Rachel Owens, 142
Brashear, Robert S., 17, 80, 99, 125, 158, 210
Brashear, Sally, 125
Brashear, Sampson, 210
Brashear, Samuel, 126, 210
Brashear, Troy, 148
Brashear, Mrs. Troy, 148
Brashear, Dr. Walter, 210
Brashear, W. M., 126
Bratcher, L. M., 147
Breckenridge, Supt. R. J., 107
Breeding, Carlice, 224
Bridges, 176-183, 193-199
Bridges, early, 176
Bridge, Hazard, first, 183

INDEX—Continued

Bridges, railroad, 193, 194, 199
Brizendine, Rev. Wm., 134
Brock, Aaron, 144
Brock, Orlena, 144
Brooks, Rev. A. C., 134-148
Brown, Arzo, 131
Brown, John, 123
Brown, Mrs. Morton, 148
Brown, Rev. William C., 136
Buckhorn, Community of, 68-77
Bullard, C. E., 133
Bullard, Mrs. C. E., 133
Bullard, Fred, 92, 185
Bullock, John, 150
Bunyard, John, 120, 122
Burgy, Robert, 123
Burlingham, William
Burns, Rev. Alvin, 154
Burns, Andrew, 18
Burton, Bob, 69
Burton, Robert, 125
Bush, Bobby, 150
Bush, Mrs. Bill, 150
Bush, Doris, 150
Bush, Drury, 18

Callahan, Athlene, 148
Callahan, Eli, 125
Callahan, Stella, 148
Calvert, Cleon K., 114
Campbell, Adam, 207
Campbell, Andy, 211
Campbell, Bill, 211
Campbell, Caleb, 211
Campbell, Callie, 143-144
Campbell, Dan, 211
Campbell, Elijah, 211
Campbell, Elizabeth, 143
Campbell, Ellen, 135
Campbell family, 210, 211
Campbell, Frank, 211
Campbell, George, 122
Campbell, Hiram, 211
Campbell, Jack, 211, 229
Campbell, James, 143, 211
Campbell, J., 123
Campbell, John, 211
Campbell, John C., 144
Campbell, John D., 211
Campbell, Judge J. G., 111, 160
Campbell, Lewis, 211
Campbell, Mary, 211
Campbell, McKinley, 135
Campbell, Mollie, 143, 144
Campbell, Nancy Ann, 135
Campbell, Peggy, 143-144
Campbell, Polly Allen (Mrs. William), 211
Campbell, Polly Couch, (Mrs. John), 211
Campbell, Rebecca (Mrs. Dan), 211
Campbell, Rachel Allen (Mrs. Lewis), 211
Campbell, Sallie Holliday (Mrs. John D.), 211
Campbell, Scott, 121
Campbell, Stephen, 211
Campbell, William, 125
Campbell, W. M., 144
Campbell, Zack, 211
Cannigan, Rev. Matt, 125
Carter, Ben, 145
Carter, Mary, 145
Casinelli, Tony, 89
Caudill, Benjamin, 119
Caudill, Cindy, 125
Caudill, Elizabeth, 125
Caudill, G. M., 126
Caudill, Isom, 125
Caudill, James, 18, 119
Caudill, John A., 125, 215
Caudill, Mary, 119
Caudill, Nancy, 125
Caudill, Sarah, 120
Caudill, Stephen, 18, 120, 121
Cecil, Geneva, 150
Cecil, Millard, 150
Cecil, Odessa, 150
Cemetery, oldest (Hazard), 93
Chase, Rev. Herbert, 134
Christain, Angeline, 142
Churches, 118-156
  Baptists—
    Balls Fork, 125
    Berean, 148-149
    Bethana, 149-150
    Big Leatherwood, 125-126
    Browns Fork, 142
    Carrs Fork, 122
    Clear Creek, 127
    Dwarf, 142-143
    First Baptist, 139-142
    Grapevine and Campbells Bend, 120-121
    Huff Island, 127
    Indian Bottom, 120
    Ira Combs Memorial, 127, 128
    Jeff, 150-151
    Johnson United Baptists, 125
    Liberty, 122
    Lone Pine, 148

INDEX—Continued

Lotts Creek, 122
Lothair, 147-148
Mt. Olive, 145-146
Mt. Olivet, 143-144
Mt. Zion, 145
Petrey Memorial, 146-147
Sandlick, 121
Stony Fork, 143
Typo, 150
Yerkes, 144-145
Catholic—
  Mother of Good Counsel, 151-154
Christian—
  Campbell Creek, 135
  Hazard Christian, 133-134
Church of God—
  Hazard, 154
  Pentecostal, 154, 155
Episcopal—
  St. Marks, 155-157
Methodist—
  Bowman Memorial, 128-131
  Lothair, 131
  Phillips Temple, 131, 132
Presbyterian—
  Buckhorn, 139
  Harveyton, 138
  Hazard, 135, 137
  Walter H. Hull Memorial, 137
  Vicco, 138-139
Circuit Riders, 168-171
Cisco, F. L., 33, 185
Civil War, 18, 81, 208, 226, 229
Coal, 51-67
Coal boats, 51
Coal, discovery, 50
Coal sales, 54, 55, 59
Coal Statistics, 63, 66
Cockerel, Joseph, 13
Codell, J. C., 150
Coleman, Maggie Hall, 131
Collins, Arch, 157
Collins, Mrs. Arch, 157
Collins, Jack, 137
Collins, James, 13
Collins, Dr. R. L., 29, 88, 118
Colwell, Cassie, 144
Colwell, G. C., 144
Colwell, Hobert, 144
Colwell, J. C., 144
Colwell, Margaret, 144
Colwell, Nancy, 144
Colwell, Vina, 144
Combs, A. B., 194
Combs, Alicia (See Smith), 214

Combs, Alexander, 122
Combs, Alfred, 122
Combs, Andrew J., 214
Combs, A. M., 148
Combs, Mrs. A. M., 148
Combs, Amos, 148
Combs, Bill, 142
Combs, Biram, 211, 212
Combs, Boneparte, 212
Combs, Carl, 29
Combs, C. B., 133
Combs, Chester, 128
Combs, Claiborne, 212
Combs, Clinton, 207, 212
Combs, Curtis, 135
Combs, Cynthia, 126
Combs, Daniel Garret, 214
Combs, Dewey, 30
Combs, D. Y., 12, 50
Combs, Edmond, 114
Combs, Elijah, Sr., 3, 6, 11, 16, 42, 80, 93, 107, 158, 165, 173, 176, 211
Combs, Elijah, Jr., 22, 211
Combs, Elijah C., 226
Combs, Eliza Combs (Mrs. Nicholas, Jr.), 214
Combs, Eliza Godsey (Mrs. Robert C.), 214
Combs, Eliza Lacey, 110
Combs, Elizabeth, 212
Combs, Elizabeth (Mrs. Andrew J.), 214
Combs, Elizabeth Jane (Mrs. Wiley), 214
Combs, Elizabeth Ison, 128
Combs, Elvira, 140
Combs, Elzira, 128
Combs, Estill, 132
Combs family, 211, 214
Combs, Felix, 140
Combs, G. P., 111
Combs, Garrett, 133
Combs, George, 12, 211
Combs, Harriet, 133
Combs, Rev. Henry C., 140, 141, 142
Combs, Henry Harrison, 12, 52, 211, 212
Combs, Herman, 150
Combs, Rev. Ira, 126-127
Combs, Jack, 166
Combs, Jackson, 165, 176
Combs, James O., 135
Combs, Jenny, 133
Combs, Jenny Richardson (Mrs. Mason), 211
Combs, Jeremiah, 12, 50, 80,

INDEX—Continued

158, 174
Combs, Jeremiah C., 214
Combs, Jesse, Jr., 165, 212
Combs, Jesse, Sr., 7, 164, 165, 209, 212
Combs, Dr. Jesse, 107, 109
Combs, John, Jr., 211, 213
Combs, John, Sr., 211
Combs, John, 166, 211
Combs, John D., 164
Combs, John G., 110
Combs, John S., 140
Combs, Josiah H., 8, 16, 81, 109, 135, 165
Combs, Dr. Josiah, 52
Combs, Lizzie, 136
Combs, Louanna, 125
Combs, Louisa (See Cornett), 212, 215
Combs, Lucinda (See Duff), 212
Combs, Lucy, 214
Combs, Lydia Herald (Mrs. George), 174, 212
Combs, Marshall, 135
Combs, Mart, 212
Combs, Martha, 150
Combs, Mary, 128
Combs, Mary, 14, 54, 214
Combs, Mary, 150
Combs, Mason, 12, 158, 211
Combs, Mary H. Burke (Mrs. William), 214
Combs, Matilda, 212
Combs, Millie (See Smith), 213
Combs, Minerva, 210
Combs, Nancy, 212, 214
Combs, Nancy, 147
Combs, Nancy (Mrs. John), 211
Combs, Nancy Cornett (Mrs. Samuel), 214
Combs, Nicholas, Jr., 212
Combs, Nicholas, Sr., 12, 80, 158, 166, 213, 214
Combs, Pearl, 114, 140
Combs, Polly Ann, 81, 135
Combs, Preston, 212
Combs, Rachel, 214
Combs, Rachel Turner (Mrs. Daniel Garrett), 214
Combs, Rebecca, 140, 214
Combs, Robert, 129
Combs, Sally Grigsby (Mrs. Jeremiah C.), 214
Combs, Rev. Sam, 127, 128
Combs, Sam, 150

Combs, Samuel, 125, 214
Combs, Sara, 140
Combs, Sarah Roark (Mrs. Elijah), 6, 11
Combs, Sarah Jane, 135
Combs, Shadrack, 213
Combs, Susan, 110
Combs, Tabitha, 212
Combs, Talton, 128
Combs, Tarleton, 212
Combs, Vina, 132
Combs, W. C., 115
Combs, Washington, 212
Combs, Watson, 128
Combs, Wiley, 214
Combs, Mrs. William, 157
Combs, William, 211, 212, 214
Combs, Willie, 212
Conn, W. B., 131
Conrad, Bernice, 149
Cook, Norman, 136
Cook, Will, 133
Cope, Betty Hammond (Mrs. James D.), 214
Cope family, 214
Cope, James D., 214
Cope, Thomas T., 215
Cope, Wiley, 215
Cope, William Jackson, 123, 215
Cornett, Alex, 145
Cornett, Anderson, 125
Cornett, Arch, 215
Cornett, Archibald, 125
Cornett, B., 126
Cornett, Mrs. Blaine, 149
Cornett, Carrie, 143
Cornett, Celia (Mrs. Elijah), 22
Cornett, Charles L., 126
Cornett, Dan, 143
Cornett, Dora, 143
Cornett, Eli, 126
Cornett, Elijah, 22, 49, 55, 162
Cornett, Elizabeth, 126, 215
Cornett, French, 143
Cornett, Jane, 126
Cornett, Jasper, 128
Cornett, John, 215
Cornett, John B., 78
Cornett, John B., 126
Cornett, Joseph, 128
Cornett, Joseph E., 216
Cornett, Judy McDaniel (Mrs. Arch), 215
Cornett, Mrs. K. W., 144
Cornett, K. W., 144
Cornett, Lester, 142
Cornett, Louise Combs (Mrs.

INDEX—Continued

Robert Bustard), 215
Cornett, Lucy (See Eversole), 215
Cornett, Lydia Caudill (Mrs. Nathaniel Woolery), 216
Cornett, Margaret, 128
Cornett, Martha, 140
Cornett, Mary Everage (Mrs. William), 215
Cornett, Morgan, 128
Cornett, N. W., 122
Cornett, Nancy, 215
Cornett, Nannie, 142
Cornett, Nathaniel Woolery, 216
Cornett, Polly Ann, 124
Cornett, Polly Adams (Mrs. Samuel), 215
Cornett, Polly Lewis (Mrs. Roger), 215
Cornett, Rachel, 215
Cornett, Rachel Smith (Mrs. John), 215
Cornett, Robert Bustard, 215
Cornett, Robert, 160
Cornett, Robert G., 7
Cornett, Roger, 126, 215
Cornett, Sally Brown (Mrs. Joseph E.), 216
Cornett, Stella, 149
Cornett, Susanah, 125
Cornett, Vernice, 149
Cornett, William, 215
Cornettsville, 77
Couch, Balis, 140
Couch, Cynthia, 146
Couch, Eli, 140
Couch, Lucinda, 135
Couch, Polly, 140
Couch, S. C., 150
Craft, Achilles, 18
Craft, Archelous, 120
Crank, Rev. S. F., 155
Crates, Rev. J. M., 130
Crawford, Bertha, 150
Crawford, Polly Ann, 126
Creech, Mrs. Henry, 150
Cropper, Rev. Walter V., 130
Crutcher, Mr., 148
Crutcher, Mrs., 148

Daniel, Dewey, 33, 195
Daniel, Lee, 22, 57, 111, 129, 171, 177
Daniel, Dr. John Marcus, 88, 207
Daniel, Marcus, 110

Davenport, John, 138
Davis, Celia, 129
Davis, Inez, 131
Davis, Lawrence, 30, 90, 92
Davis, Louie, 131
Davis, R. O., 49
Davis, W. O., 42, 50, 87, 113, 114, 175
Davis, W. Y., 146
Davidson, Arminia, 217
Davidson, Bob, 217
Davidson, Daniel, 216
Davidson, Dock, 117
Davidson, Dulcie, 217
Davidson, Elijah Combs, 217
Davidson family, 216, 217
Davidson, Goodloe, 149
Davidson, Henry, 217
Davidson, Ira, 80
Davidson, John A., 217
Davidson, Lettie Duff (Mrs. Dock), 217
Davidson, Mahala, 217
Davidson, Mary Ann Combs (Mrs. John A.), 217
Davidson, Mary Spencer (Mrs. Elijah Combs), 217
Davidson, Nancy, 217
Davidson, Nancy Anne, 121
Davidson, Sallie, 83, 128
Davidson, Sarah Duff (Mrs. Daniel), 217
Davidson, Shade, 121
Davidson, Shadrock, 217
Davidson, Silas, 12
Dawhare, Willie, 157
Dawhare, Mrs. Willie, 157
Day, Grover, 121
Deaton, Allen, 140
Deaton, Charles, 155
Deaton, Sarah, 140
Deed, first, 164, 165
Deeds, 6, 164, 165
Denny, M. C., 148
Diary, Guerrant, 82
Dickson, Robert, 67
Discovery of Coal, 50
Dixon, Angeline, 136
Dixon, Rev. James, 125
Dixon, John, 120
Doctors, early, 85
Donnelly, Rev. George, 153
Duff, Alexander, 217
Duff, Catherine Noble (Mrs. Alexander), 217
Duff, Colson, 217
Duff, Colson, 89
Duff, Rev. Daniel, 120, 121,

INDEX—Continued

217, 218
Duff, Deborah (See Bowling), 217
Duff, Drucilla, 217
Duff, Elijah C., 110
Duff, Elizabeth Gilbert (Mrs. Colson), 217
Duff, family, 217
Duff, Henry, 16
Duff, Dr. H. P., 121
Duff, Joe, 144
Duff, John A., 7, 79, 217
Duff, Lucinda Combs (Mrs. Shadrack), 217
Duff, Margaret, 217
Duff, Martha, 217
Duff, Mary, 217
Duff, Matilda, 217
Duff, Nancy Ann Allison (Mrs. Daniel), 217
Duff, Polly Combs (Mrs. J. A.), 217
Duff, Rachel, 217
Duff, Shadrack, 218
Dunson, William, 142
Dwarf, Community of, 78

Edwards, Jack, 214
Edwards, Sarah Ellen, 135
Elam, Proctor S., 131
Electricity, first, 87
Ellis, Charles, 18
Engle, James, 140
Engle, Zada, 150
Estep, Carrie, 148
Estep, M. M., 148
Evans, Louisa Morgan, 147
Everage, Mary, (See Cornett), 215
Everage, Polly, (See Brashear), 126, 215
Everage, Solomon, 229
Eversole, Abraham, 219
Eversole, Absalon, 219
Eversole, Annie Phipps, 219
Eversole, Ap, 159
Eversole, Billy, 219
Eversole, Elihu, 219
Eversole, Elijah, 219
Eversole, Elmer, 31
Eversole, Elizabeth, 219
Eversole family, 218, 219
Eversole, Farmer, 135
Eversole, Hence, 219
Eversole, Hiram, 219
Eversole, Irvin, 121
Eversole, Rev. Jacob, 118, 119, 218, 219

Eversole, James, 219
Eversole, John B., 56, 59, 118, 135
Eversole, J. C., 30
Eversole, John C., 113
Eversole, Joseph, 16, 109, 218, 219
Eversole, Lewis, 219
Eversole, Louise Couch (Mrs. Joe), 219
Eversole, John (Mrs. Orphus), 219
Eversole, Lucy Cornett (Mrs. Woolery), 219
Eversole, Mary Kessler (Mrs. Jacob), 218
Eversole, Mary Hubbard (Mrs. John), 219
Eversole, Orphus, 219
Eversole, Peter, 219
Eversole, Roland, 219
Eversole, Roy G., 33, 117, 119
Eversole, Sally, 219
Eversole, Susan, 135
Eversole, William, 219
Eversole, W. C., 115
Eversole, Woolery, 219

Fairchild, Stephen, 127
Farnsworth, Charles, 136
Farrell, Rev. Malachy, 154
Faulkner, Alma, 133
Faulkner, Mrs. H. C., 133
Faulkner, Ernest, 133
Faulkner, Rev., 145
Faulkner, Mildred, 133
Faust, Miss, 148
Feltner, Alfred, 135
Feltner, Brack, 121
Feltner, Curt, 29
Feltner, Joe, 30
Feltner, Luke, 221
Ferry, first, 11
Fields, Alta C., 150
Fields, Eliza Jane, 150
Fields, Hiram, 126
Fields, John, 12
Fields, Mary, 126
Fields, Susan, 146
Fields, Walter, 150
Finsley, P. K., 146
First Court, 158
First Land Grants, 11, 12
First Mine, 59, 60
First Post Office, 21, 41
First Train, 196

INDEX—Continued

Fischer, Rev. Carl, 153
Fitz, George, 67
Fitzpatrick, Capt. Jacob, 19
Fitzpatrick, John, 19
Flannery, John, 120
Flannery, Lydia, 150
Floods, 17
Foeman, Rev., 142
Folk Lore, 35-40
Foreman, Ellen Bane Hull (Mrs. F. G., Jr), 137
Foreman, Frank G., Jr., 155
Foreman, Rose Osborne, 154
Francis, Anne, 220
Francis, Cassie B. Smith (Mrs. Simeon), 220
Francis, Elizabeth, 220
Francis, family, 219, 220
Francis, Jane Hammonds (Mrs. Thomas), 219
Francis, Leodicia Hogg (Mrs. Samuel), 220
Francis, Lourania (See Smith), 220
Francis, Lourania Hagan (Mrs. Thomas), 220
Francis, Ora Lee, 149
Francis, Rebecca, 220
Francis, Sarah (See Johnson), 220
Francis, Samuel, 220
Francis, Simeon, 220
Francis, Thomas, 122, 174, 219, 229
Franklin, Rev. W. L., 150
Fritts, Effie Hohn, 131
Fryman, Rev. W. P., 130
Fugate, Dan, 220
Fugate, Elizabeth Smith Mrs. Martin), 220
Fugate family, 220
Fugate, Hannah (See Ritchie), 220
Fugate, Jonathan, 220
Fugate, L. D., 220
Fugate, Martin (Fugit), 158, 220
Fugate, Martin, Jr., 220
Fugate, Martha, 220
Fugate, Mary, 220
Fugate, Minerva, 220
Fugate, Polly Smith (Mrs. Zachariah), 220
Fugate, Prewitt, 220
Fugate, Phoebe, 122
Fugate, Zack, 121-123
Fugate, Zacharias, 220

Gabbard, Edd, 125
Gabbard, Elmer E., 31, 75, 139
Gabbard, I. H., 125
Gabbard, O. B., 148
Gabriel, Sister Mary, 154
Gallahar, Pat, 151
Garnet, Mrs. James, 131
Garriot, Walter B., 130
Gay, Nelse (Guy), 71, 209
Gayheart, Chester, 143
Gayheart, Richard, 142
Gaw, Warren, 137
Geer, Edward F., 77, 139
Geer, Mrs. Edward F., 77
Gilbert, John F., 185
Gist, Christopher, 9, 50
Glasure, Rev. Alton B., 136
Gockel, Rev. William, 153
Goodlette, Mrs. D. H., 133
Goodlette, Richard, 92
Gorman, John P., 67
Gorman, Perry, 61, 136
Grace, Estelle, 133
Green, Walter N., 44
Greenleaf, Rev. John, 149
Greer, H. E., Sr., 30
Greer, William, 140
Greisinger, Rev. Aloysius, 153
Griffith, Edward, 126
Griffith, Elizabeth, 126
Griffy, E. L., 130
Grigsby, Ben, 122
Grigsby, Bill, 221
Grigsby, Cynthia (See Cornett), 221
Grigsby, Eliza Jane (Mrs. Samuel),
Grigsby, family, 221
Grigsby, Jim, 217
Grigsby, John, 122, 221
Grigsby, Lourania Jones (Mrs. Thomas), 221
Grigsby, Luke, 221
Grigsby, Martha, 221
Grigsby, Martha Campbell, 221
Grigsby, Nancy (See Combs), 221
Gribsby, Sally, 221
Grigsby, Samuel, 221
Grigsby, Thomas, 122, 221
Gross, Judge A. M. (Doctor), 33, 85, 88, 180
Gross, Archie, 154
Gross, Bill, 221
Gross, Dorcas Becknell (Mrs. Simon), 221
Gross, Dorcas Smith (Mrs. Peter), 221

INDEX—Continued

Gross, Ella Riley (Mrs. John), 68, 71, 77, 221
Gross family, 221
Gross, Henry, 221
Gross, Jack, 221
Gross, Jennie, 221
Gross, John, 71, 77, 221
Gross, Lucinda, 221
Gross, Mary, 221
Gross, Nance, 221
Gross, Ned, 221
Gross, Peg Ingram (Mrs. Jack), 221
Gross, Peter, 221
Gross, Polly, 221
Gross, Richard, 221
Gross, Sally McIntosh (Mrs. Tod), 221
Gross, Simon, 221
Gross, Tod, 221
Guerrant Letters, Grace, 23-28, 74
Guerrant, Dr. E. O., 135
Guerrant, W. O., 139
Gum, C. Prewitt, 67
Gunn, Jimmy, 125

Haddix, John, 16
Hagan, William, 18
Hagedorn, Henry, 152
Hahn, Effie, 131
Hale, Leonard, 155
Hall, Abigal, 126
Hall, Anthony, 18
Hall, B., 122
Hall, Elizabeth, 126
Hall, Elizabeth Branson (Mrs. P. W.), 222
Hall, Elizabeth Whisman (Mrs. John, Jr.), 222
Hall, Ezekial, 222
Hall family, 222
Hall, Floyd, 150
Hall, Rev. James, 114
Hall, Rev. J. M., 126
Hall, John, Jr., 222
Hall, John, Sr., 222
Hall, John H., 126
Hall, Maxine, 150
Hall, P. H., 143
Hall, Mrs. P. H., 143
Hall, P. W., 102, 222
Hall, Wm. Walter, 157
Hall, Will, 143
Hall, Mrs. Will, 143
Hamblin, Isaac, 127
Hamblin, Taylor, 121
Hammon, Peter, 18
Hammons, Joseph, 174

Hampton, M. M., 147
Handy, Thomas, 123
Hancy, W. P., 154
Harding, Will, 131
Harris, I. H., 132
Harris, James, 120
Harwell, Andrew, 18
Hatcher, Clarice, 149
Hatter, H. G. M., 142
Hayden, Gwyn, 31
Haywood, Rev. James, 145
Hazard Baptist Institute, 114
Hazard Coal Operators Association, 67
Hazard, 79-93
  Developments, 80-90
  Early days, 82
  Named for, 79
  Town plat, 8
Health Department Perry County, 29
Helton, Earl, 149
Helton, Mrs. Earl, 149
Helton, Ragan, 142
Henry, Herbert, 131
Hibbard, Nancy, 143
Hicks, Rev. Basil V., 136
Hicks, Robert, 158
Highways, 172, 185
Hill, Carley, 150
Hill, Sarah Baker, 132
Hines, J. V., Jr., 157
Hines, Mrs. J. V., Jr., 157
Hines, T. H., 200
Hogg, Elizabeth Kelly (Mrs. James), 231
Hogg, Hiram, 13
Hogg, James, 231
Hogg, Will, 145
Hogg, Stephen, 106
Holcomb, Judy, 150
Holcomb, Mary, 125
Holcomb, Millard, 144
Holcomb, Wm., 125
Holbrook, Sallie, 143
Holliday, Allie Justice (Mrs. John H.), 222
Holliday, Amy Smith (See Smith), 223
Holliday, Bill, 223
Holliday, E. C., 114
Holliday, Elisha, 223
Holliday, family, 222, 223
Holliday, Green, 223
Holliday, Harriet Godsey (Mrs. Elisha), 223
Holliday, John H., 222

INDEX—Continued

Holliday, Rachel Napier (Mrs. Tolbert), 223
Holliday, Sally, 223
Holliday, T., 123
Holliday, Rev. Tolbert, 223
Holliday, Walter, 223
Hollon, I. R., 130
Homeplace, 94
Hopper, Louis, 67
Horn, C. M., 113
Horn, Frank, 115
Horn, Montgomery, 89
Hoskins, Dr. John, 133
Hoskins, W. R., 132
Hospitals, first, 88
Hospitals
  Brainard Memorial, 71
  Homeplace, 97
  Hurst-Snyder, 88
  Mount Mary, 88
Holt, Mable, 145
Holt, William, 157
Holt, Mrs. William, 157
House, first, 11
Houses, oldest, 10
Howard, Francis W., 150
Howard, James, 18
Howard, M. C., 135
Howard, Thomas, 18
Howard, Turner, 150
Howell, J. E., 147
Hubbard, Nancy, 143
Hudson, A. C., 147
Huff, Floyd, 126
Huff, William, 125
Hughes, M., 125
Hull, Kate, 137
Hull, Walter A., 137
Hurst, Henry, 18
Hyden, John, 108

Ingram, Price, 221
Ison, Annie Ingram (Mrs. George), 224
Ison, Bill, 126
Ison, Bertha, 143
Ison, Cintha, 224
Ison, Mrs. Denver, 149
Ison, Dixie, 126
Ison, Elizabeth, 224
Ison family, 223
Ison, George Gideon, 215, 223
Ison, Gideon, I, 223
Ison, Gideon, II, 223
Ison, John, Jr., 224
Ison, Jonah, 126, 224
Ison, Judy, 126
Ison, Lizzie, 133

Ison, Marion, 143
Ison, Matilda (Mrs. Jonah), 126, 224
Ison, Moses, 13
Ison, Polly, 224

Jackson, Joe, 143
Jackson, M. L., 146
James, Henderson, 145
Jail, first, 158
Jent, Jno., 126
Johnson, Adelphia Carter (Mrs. Thomas), 174, 224
Johnson, Adelphia (See Combs), 225
Johnson, Anna, 140
Johnson, Artie (See Smith), 225
Johnson, Asbury, 70
Johnson, Charlie, 31
Johnson, Cam, 125
Johnson, Dick, 123
Johnson family, 225
Johnson, Fanny, 125, 225
Johnson, Fielding, 225
Johnson, George, 125, 225
Johnson, George Washington, 220, 225
Johnson, Howard, 30, 61
Johnson, I. D., 125
Johnson, J. E., Sr., 61, 62, 114, 136
Johnson, J. L., 49, 61, 83, 114, 140
Johnson, Kate (Mrs. J. L.), 140
Johnson, Leslie, 225
Johnson, Logan, 147
Johnson, Luther, 125
Johnson, Lucy Eversole (Mrs. Thomas), 225
Johnson, Martha, 140
Johnson, Patrick, 225
Johnson, Polly T., 125
Johnson, Sarah, 225
Johnson, Sarah Francis (Mrs. George Washington), 225
Johnson, Susan (See Eversole), 225
Johnson, Simeon, 225
Johnson, Thomas, 25, 224, 225
Johnson, Thomas, II, 225
Johnson, William, 225
Jones, Allen, 136
Jones, Anna Johnson, 114, 140
Jones, Elizabeth, 68
Jones, Farris, 217
Jones, Sherman, 146

INDEX—Continued

Jones, S. A. D., 60-86
Jones, W. M., 60
Jordon, R .F., 130
Justices, Early County Court, 13
Justices, first, 158
Justice, Simeon, 18, 119-121

Keathley, Thomas, 122
Keen, Paul, 15, 45
Keith, Louis, 147
Kelly, Amy, 120
Kelly, G. W.
Kelly, John, 18
Kelly, Mathias, 120
Kentucky River Mining Institute, 66
Kesheimer, Myrtle, 152
King, Rev. Frank, 131
Kingler, Rev. David, 131
Kraff, Rev. Anthony, 154

Land Companies, 56-58
Land Grants, 11, 12
Land Sales, Coal, 56, 57
Land values, 57
Landrum, R. W., 128
Laws, mining, 66
Lawson, Bill, 138
Leases, Coal, 56, 57
Leatherwood, Community of, 98-100
Lee, Rev. A. L., 145
Lee, Charles, 145
Legislators, early, 16, 17
Lenning, Rev. J. L., 155
Library, Bobby Davis Memorial, 90, 91
Little, Belle, 143
Log College, 74
Logan, Dalton, 143
Logan, Powell, 140
Lovern, E. B., 33
Lumber, 43-49, 100
Lusk, Betty (See Begley), 226
Lusk, family, 226
Lusk, John W., 226
Lusk, Louise Brashear (Mrs. John W.), 226
Lusk, Polly Davis (Mrs. Samuel), 226
Lusk, Sally, 226
Lusk, Samuel, 226
Lusk, William, 226
Luttrell, Anice Turner, 146
Lyttle, Bertha, 134
Lyttle, Lewis, 125, 143
Lyttle, Roscoe, 135

Madison, R. J., 145
Maggard, Sam, 125
Magoni, Rev. Anthony, 154
Manna, J. J., 132
Marriage License, first, 163
Marsee, W. R., 62
Martin, Eugene, 157
Martin, Mrs. Eugene, 157
Martin, Rev. Lewis, 141-148
Massa, Rev. James, 151
McCain, Mildred, 137
McCrystal, Rev. John W., 153
McDaniel, George, 18
McDaniel, Sally Everage (Mrs. Thomas), 215
McDaniel, Thomas, 215
McGee, H. G., 132
McGee, S. L., 132
McIntosh, Asberry, 135
McIntosh, Bangor Bill, 221
McIntosh, J. C., 142
McIntosh, Jeremiah, 135
McIntosh, John, 111, 116, 133
McIntosh, Mrs. John, 133
McIntosh, Levi, 221
McIntosh, Peter, 221
McIntosh, Roderick, 12, 221
McIntosh, W. M., 125
McIntyre, Dianah, 125
McIntyre, Estill, 30
McIntyre, William, 124
McMillan, N. M., 145
Meadows, Joe, 132
Medaris, F. M., 67
Medlock, Bobby, 150
Medlock, Christine, 150
Memorial Gymnasium, 91, 92
Merrick, Rev. J. E., 156
Messer, Nancy, 146
Messer, Reuben, 125
Metcalf, Charles, 92
Miller, C. D., 145
Miller, J. Ross, 133
Miller, W. W., 147
Mine Operators, 62
Mineral Rights, 57, 58
Mines, Primitive, 52, 53
Mines, railroad, 61, 62
Mines, truck, 63
Mines, wagon, 58
Mining Methods, primitive, 52
Minniard, A. L., 143, 149
Minniard, Mrs. A. L., 149
Minniard, Denver, 149
Minniard, George, 143
Minniard, Mrs. George, 143
Minniard, Irene (Mrs.

INDEX—Continued

Denver), 149
Minor, Clarence, 149
Minor, Milford, 149
Minor, Mrs. Milford, 149
Mirse, Rev. Ralph P., 131
Mitchell, J. T., 136
Moody, William R., 156
Mooney, C. R., 149
Mooney, Mrs. C. R., 149
Moore, Anna Mae, (Mrs. Tom), 90
Moore, Elias, 123
Moore, G. W., 125
Moore, James W., 123- 125
Moore, J. T., 159
Moore, T. E., Jr., 46, 49, 182
Morgan, Bud, 8, 226
Morgan, Charles, 89, 135
Morgan, Elijah C., 56
Morgan, Ella, 129
Morgan, Emily, 129
Morgan family, 226
Morgan, Jesse, 56, 131, 148, 180, 226
Morgan, Kate, 135
Morgan, Louisa Combs (Mrs. Zachariah), 129, 226
Morgan, Zachariah, 16, 129, 226
Morris, Elias, 125
Morris, Wiley, 125
Morrison, Jim, 59
Mullins, Elias, 121
Mullins, Joseph, 122
Mullins, Joshua, 18
Mullins, Lika, 131
Mulloy, Rt. Rev. William T., 150
Muncy, Cynthia Morgan, 147
Murdock, Harvey S., 71, 139
Murdock, Louise Saunders, 72

Napier, Edward, 227
Napier, Eliza Jane (See Grigsby), 227
Napier, family, 227
Napier, Jerome, 120
Napier, James, 121-123
Napier, Jim, 227
Napier, John, 227
Napier, Leana Lewis (Mrs. McCager), 227
Napier, Mack, 227
Napier, Mat, 217
Napier, M. C., 111
Napier, McCager, 227
Napier, Paddy, 227
Napier, Polly Campbell (Mrs. Edward), 227
Napier (Napper), P. P., 122
Napier, Sam, 135
Napier, Stephen, 227
Napier, William, 227
Napier, Sir William Francis Patrick, 227
Neace, Austin, 227
Neace, Malinda Allen (Mrs. Austin), 227
Neblett, P. H., 116
Newspaper, early, 88
Nicholas, Monroe, 133
Nicholas, Mrs. Monroe, 133
Nicholson, G. W., 148
Nickerson, J. C., 203
Noble, Deliah Fugate (Mrs. James), 227
Noble, Ethan, 227
Noble family, 227, 228
Noble, Henry, 227
Noble, Isobel Aikman (Mrs. Henry), 227
Noble, Jack, 227
Noble, James, 227
Noble, James B., 121
Noble, Lawson, 227
Noble, Nathan, Sr., 227
Noble, Nathan, Jr., 227
Noble, Virginia Neace (Mrs. Nathan), 227
Noble, W. G., 123
Noble, William, 227
Nofsinger, B. F., 151
Num, Clarence, 131

Oaks, James, 122
Ockerman, Rev. L. F., 131
O'Hara, M. J., 132
Olinger, Dan, 117, 133, 142
Olinger, George, 142
Oliver, James, 132
Oliver, Joshua, 217
Operators, Mine, 59
Organizations, mine, 66, 67
Orchards, 14
Orphanages
  Buckhorn, 28, 29, 71
  Open-door, 28, 29
Osborne, Kathleen, 151
Osgood, Russell, 134
Owens, Elbert, 142
Owens, Flora, 142
Owens, J. M., 142
Owens, Nita, 142

Parker, J. R., 131

INDEX—Continued

Patrick, Alexander, 13, 17, 21, 41, 158
Patterson, Alexander, 156
Patterson, Leslie, 138
Payne, Rev. Duke, 134, 183
Payne, Mrs. Minor, 157
Payne, Dr. Minor, 157
Pegram, R. M., 136
Pennington, Abel, 13, 120, 161, 209
Pennington, Levi, 214
Perkins, A. R., 131
Perry County (Collins early sketch), 16, 17
Petrey, Rev. A. S., 84, 114, 139 140, 146
Petrey, M. A., 124
Petrey, Sarah, 140
Petrie, Rev. John C., 156
Peyton, W. K., 31
Phillips, C. H., 131
Pierce, Rev. A. B., 142
Pigman, Leonard, 18
Pike, E. K., 130
Pilow, C. P., 131
Piper, John, 157
Pittman, W. M., 148
Polly, Edward, 18
Porter, J. W., 141
Post Offices
  County, 21
  First, 21
Powell, Clarence, 155
Powell, Mrs. H. C., 32
Pratt, Eli, 126
Pratt, Hiram, 126
Pratt, James, 126
Pratt, J. W., 126
Pratt, Rhoda, 124
Prentiss, G. D., 131
Priest, Rev. Edmund, 153
Prichard, John, 131
Prichard, Rev. Thomas A., 139
Puryear, Susie, 117

Radio Station, WKIC, 33, 93
Railroads, 190-206
  Branch lines, 198, 203, 204, 205
  Construction of, 191, 196
Rainey, G. M., 131
Razor, Julia, 131
Red Cross Chapter, Perry County, 32
Rembrant, Rev. W. R., 155
Reimondo, Rev. Richard, 154

Revolutionary Soldiers, 18, 161
Richardson, Jesse, 131
Richmond, Rev. R. W., 146
Riddle, Granville, 126
Riddle, L. C., 126
Riley, Murdock, 138
Riley, Squire M., 125
Rison, Rev. W. M., 154
Ritchie, Alex, 229
Ritchie, Arry, 229
Ritchie, Austin, 228
Ritchie, Betty, 229
Ritchie, Crockett, 228
Ritchie family, 228
Ritchie, Gabe, 229
Ritchie, Hannah Fugate (Mrs. James), 229
Ritchie, Hiram, 229
Ritchie, Isom, 229
Ritchie, James, 220, 228
Ritchie, John, 229
Ritchie, Kizzie Smith (Mrs. Thomas), 229
Ritchie, Mary Fugate (Mrs. Alex), 229
Ritchie, Nicholas, 229
Ritchie, Nancy Campbell (Mrs. Gabe), 229
Ritchie, Nancy, 229
Ritchie, Nannie, 142
Ritchie, Omah, 229
Ritchie, Polly, 229
Ritchie, Rachel Everage (Mrs. Austin), 228
Ritchie, Susan Grigsby (Mrs. Crockett), 228
Ritchie, Silas, 142
Ritchie, Mrs. Silas, 142
Ritchie, S. M., 142
Ritchie, Thomas, 228
Roads, 172-185
  Asphalt, 179, 182
  Concrete, 184
  Dirt, 173, 176
  Gravel, 180, 185
Roan, James A., 151
Roberts, Jerry, 221
Roberts, Meb, 149
Roberts, Mrs. Meb, 149
Roberts, R., 131
Roberts, Riley, 123
Robin, Levi, 125
Robinson, Charles, 149
Robinson, Clifford, 150
Robinson, J. H., 123
Robinson, Mrs. Tom, 150
Rodgers, Leslie M., 131

INDEX—Continued

Rodgers, V. L., 203
Rolfe, Jayne (See Bowling), 209
Rolfe, John, 209
Rolfe, Thomas, 209
Rowdy, Community of, 100

Sales, Coal, 54, 55, 59
Sales, Coal land, 56, 57
Salisbury, William, 118, 119, 120, 121
Salt, 41, 43, 99, 187
Sandlin, Bill, 221
Saunders, Dr. Miles, 72, 137
Sawyer, Matt R., 135
Schools, Baptist, 84, 114, 117
Schools:
  County, 111, 112, 117
  Districts, 108, 110
  Early, 107, 110
  New, 112
Schools City:
  Allais, (graded), 115
  Hazard High, 115, 117
  Liberty St., (Col.) 116, 117
  Lothair (Grade), 116
  Lower Broadway (Grade), 112
  Upper Broadway (Jr. High), 117
  Vocational, 112
Scouting, 29
Seams of Coal, 50, 64
Selby, Rev. R. A., 130
Seminary land, County, 105, 106
Senter, J. H., 122
Settlers, early, 10
Sexton, John, 135
Sexton, Lula, 135
Sexton, Nancy, 135
Shepherd, Andy, 143
Shepherd, Mrs. Andy, 143
Shepherd, Clent, 125
Shepherd, Susan, 143
Shepherd, Usley, 149
Shockley, Rev. James B., 129
Simms, S. L., 146
Sizemore, Elmer, 147
Sizemore, H. G., 148
Slemp, Community of, 101
Slone, Robert, 143
Slone, Seba, 143
Smallwood, H. D., 148
Smith, A. E., 131
Smith, Aggie, 230
Smith, Albert, 131

Smith, Alex, 229
Smith, Alicia Combs (Mrs. Richard), 229
Smith, Amy Holliday, (Mrs. Joshua), 230
Smith, Arminda, 230
Smith, Artie Johnson (Mrs. Nicholas), 230
Smith, Bill, 230
Smith, Boaz A., 139
Smith, Cynthia Stacy (Mrs. Isaac), 230
Smith, Cynthia, 230
Smith, Dan, 230
Smith, Edgar, 152
Smith, Elizabeth, (See Fugate), 230
Smith, Elizabeth Stacy (Mrs. Jeremiah), 230
Smith, Elkany, 230
Smith, Emaline, 230
Smith, Eva, 125
Smith family, 229, 230
Smith, I., 123
Smith, Ike, 230
Smith, Isaac, 230
Smith, James, 123, 230
Smith, J. J., 145
Smith, Jeremiah, 230
Smith, Jerry, 69
Smith, John, 122, 230
Smith, Joshua, 230
Smith, Judge Joshua A, 178, 179
Smith, Kathleen, 157
Smith, Kizzie (See Ritchie), 230
Smith, Laura, 143
Smith, Lorenzo Dow, 230
Smith, Louise, 230
Smith, Lourania Francis (Mrs. Thomas), 229
Smith, Lucy, 152
Smith, Lute, 230
Smith, Mary Ashley (Mrs. Alex), 229
Smith, Martha Ashley, (Mrs. William), 230
Smith, Matilda, 230
Smith, Millie Combs (Mrs. Wm.), 229
Smith, Nancy, 137
Smith, Nicholas, 230
Smith, Odis, 127
Smith, Patsy, 230
Smith, Polly (See Fugate), 230

INDEX—Continued

Smith, Polly Kelly, (Mrs. Richard), 229
Smith, Rebecca, 230
Smith, Rhoda Owens (Mrs. James), 230
Smith, Richard, 119, 229, 230
Smith, Sam, 121
Smith, Samuel, 112, 230
Smith, Samuel Jr., 230
Smith, Samuel, 123
Smith, Sarah, 230
Smith, Sceatti, 230
Smith, Tom, 135
Smith, Mrs. Tom, 135
Smith, Thomas, 229, 230
Smith, W. M., 145
Smith, William, 229, 230
Smith, William B., 220
Smith, Willie Combs (Mrs. John), 230
Snyder, Dr. Dana, 88
Society of Soul Winners, 72, 73
Spain, Rev. Paul, 153
Spalding, Henry, 185
Spanish American War, 20
Sparks, E. T., 87
Speaks, E. G., 56, 60
Spencer, Franklin, 122
Spencer, J. D., 122, 123
Spencer, Joseph, 122, 123
Spencer, W. T., 122
Spoonamore, A. G., 203
Spurlock, Jesse, 13
Squabble Creek, 69
Stacy, Eileen, 157
Stacy, Rev. E. T., 155
Stacy, John, 230
Stacy, Nancy Ann, 135
Stacy, Troy, 147
Stallard, W. S., 12, 147
Stamper, Elizabeth, 231
Stamper, Emily Polly, 231
Stamper, Emily Polly (Mrs. Wm.), 231
Stamper family, 231
Stamper, Hiram H., 231
Stamper, Hiram, 220
Stamper, Isaac D., 231
Stamper, Isom, 13
Stamper, James, 220
Stamper, James, B., 231
Stamper, John Whit, 231
Stamper, Martha, 231
Stamper, Matilda Hogg (Mrs. Hiram H.), 231
Stamper, Nancy, 231
Stamper, Polly, 231

Stamper, Polly Adams (Mrs. Isaac)
Stamper, Rachel, 231
Stamper, Sarah, 231
Stamper, William, 55, 56, 231
Stamper, William Buckner, 231
Stamper, William R., 231, 125
Stanafer Sam, 132
State Highway, 181
Statistics, coal, 63, 66
Stephens, Rev. C. D., 141
Stephens, L. B., 115
Stephens, James, 126
Stewart, Fred, 157
Stewart, Mrs. Fred, 157
Stewart, James, 125
Stewart, Ruben H., 134
Stidham, Allen, 155
Stidham, Henry, 137
Stidham, Samuel, 18
Stiles, L. H., 134
Stiles, Mrs. L. H., 134
Stone, Rev. Albert, 131
Stout, Emmett, 135
Stout, Josephine, 135
Stout, Polly, 135
Stout, William, 135
Stout, Mrs. William, 135
Stray Pen, 159
Streets, early, 182
Strong, John, 154
Sturgill, William, 33, 67
Sumner, Finley, 135
Surveys
 State, 55-56
 U. S. Geological 56, 58
Sweat Mary, 145
Sydnor, Rev. Charles, 138

Tatum, Dr. A. K., 156
Tatum, Mrs. A. K., 156
Taulbee, Isaac, 120
Taulbee, W. M., 123
Taverns, early prices, 167
Taverns, first, 80
Tayloe, Ward, 31
Taylor, Claude, 145
Taylor, J. A., 146
Theatre, first, 89
Thompson, Electious, 119, 120, 121
Timber, 43-50
 early prices, 45, 46, 48
Tinsley, Rev. Ben, 156
Town lots, sale of, 80, 81
Townes, H. T., 145
Transportation

INDEX—Continued

aviation, 186
highways, 72, 185
railroads, 192-206
river, 186-190
Turner, A. H., 146
Turner, Eli, 125
Turner, James, 13
Turner, Roger, 18
Tyree, Susan, 128

Underwood, Grace Brainard, 74
Underwood, John T., 74

Verlin, Polly, 149
Viper, community of, 101-104

Wages, miners, 54
Wagon, first, 177
Wagon, mines, 58, 59
Walker, Allie, 146
Walker, Ann, 146
Walker, John W., 140
Walker, Lona, 146
Walker, Polly, 146
Wallins, Rev., J. H., 136
Walls, Chas., 131
Walls, Mrs. Chas., 131
Walters, Thomas D., 131
Ward, Araminta, 129
Ward, I. J., 81, 84
Ward, John, 113, 115, 128
Ward, Malta, 128
Ward, Mary, 129
Warr, Rev., 131
Water-works, first, 87
Watkins, Thomas, 18
Watts, A. C., 129
Watts, D. E., 151
Watts, Mrs. D. E., 151
Watts, John, 100, 104
Webb, Benjamin, 120
Webb, Col. N. M., 233
Webb family, 232
Webb, James, 120
Webb, Jennie Adams (Mrs. Benjamin), 232
Weiss, Mrs. Carl, 157
Wells, William, 120, 121
Westberry, L. T., 148

Whitaker, G. C., 148
Whitaker, Mrs. G. C., 148
Whitaker, Isaac, 120
Whitaker, Marnie, 143
Whittinghill, R. T., 115
White, Rev., 145
White, Sally, 145
Wills, early, 165-166
William, John, 214
Williams, Albert, 113
Williams, E., 117
Williams, E. L., 155
Williams, Lucinda, 145
Williamson, Rev. Lamarr, 137
Wilson, Allen, 134
Wilson, Grover, 137
Wilson, John, 115
Wilson, W. T., 135
Wireman, John, 122
Wise, W. B., 131
Witherspoon, Rev. John, 136
Witt, A. J., 132
Witt, Taylor, 135
WKIC, radio station, 33, 93
Wood, Ralph J., 131
Woods, Cindy, 126
Woods, D. T., 145
Woods, Theopolis, 126
Woodward, George, 133
Woodward, Rev. Leonard, 136
Wootton, Bailey P., 59, 84, 87, 114, 152
Wootton, Clara, 152
World War I, 20, 21
World War II, 21
Wright, Arman, 149
Wrightson, Arthur, 29

Yancey, Henry, 155
Yancey, O. L., 155
Yates, Rev., 142
York, John, 121
York, John W., 221
Young, Reece, 229

Zahn, R. A., 132
Zoellars, Mrs. Bess, 134
Zoellars, Tony, 89

www.ingramcontent.com/pod-product-compliance
Lightning Source LLC
Chambersburg PA
CBHW020643300426
44112CB00007B/216